Sabine Fischer, Heiko Pleines (eds.)

Civil Society in Central and Eastern Europe

CHANGING EUROPE

Edited by Dr. Sabine Fischer, Dr. Heiko Pleines and
Prof. Dr. Hans-Henning Schröder

ISSN 1863-8716

1   Sabine Fischer, Heiko Pleines, Hans-Henning Schröder (eds.)
    Movements, Migrants, Marginalisation
    Challenges of societal and political participation in Eastern Europe and the enlarged EU
    ISBN 978-3-89821-733-0

2   David Lane, György Lengyel, Jochen Tholen (eds.)
    Restructuring of the Economic Elites after State Socialism
    Recruitment, Institutions and Attitudes
    ISBN 978-3-89821-754-5

3   Daniela Obradovic, Heiko Pleines (eds.)
    The Capacity of Central and East European Interest Groups to Participate in EU Governance
    ISBN 978-3-89821-750-7

4   Sabine Fischer, Heiko Pleines (eds.)
    Crises and Conflicts in Post-Socialist Societies
    The Role of Ethnic, Political and Social Identities
    ISBN 978-3-89821-855-9

5   Julia Kusznir, Heiko Pleines (eds.)
    Trade Unions from Post-Socialist Member States in EU Governance
    ISBN 978-3-89821-857-3

6   Sabine Fischer, Heiko Pleines (eds.)
    The EU and Central & Eastern Europe
    Successes and Failures of Europeanization in Politics and Society
    ISBN 978-3-89821-948-8

7   Sabine Fischer, Heiko Pleines (eds.)
    Civil Society in Central and Eastern Europe
    ISBN 978-3-8382-0041-5

Sabine Fischer, Heiko Pleines (eds.)

CIVIL SOCIETY IN CENTRAL AND EASTERN EUROPE

ibidem-Verlag
Stuttgart

Bibliografische Information der Deutschen Nationalbibliothek
Die Deutsche Nationalbibliothek verzeichnet diese Publikation in der Deutschen Nationalbibliografie; detaillierte bibliografische Daten sind im Internet über http://dnb.d-nb.de abrufbar.

Bibliographic information published by the Deutsche Nationalbibliothek
Die Deutsche Nationalbibliothek lists this publication in the Deutsche Nationalbibliografie; detailed bibliographic data are available in the Internet at http://dnb.d-nb.de.

∞

Gedruckt auf alterungsbeständigem, säurefreien Papier
Printed on acid-free paper

ISSN: 1863-8716

ISBN-10: 3-8382-0041-1
ISBN-13: 978-3-8382-0041-5

© *ibidem*-Verlag
Stuttgart 2010

Alle Rechte vorbehalten

Das Werk einschließlich aller seiner Teile ist urheberrechtlich geschützt. Jede Verwertung außerhalb der engen Grenzen des Urheberrechtsgesetzes ist ohne Zustimmung des Verlages unzulässig und strafbar. Dies gilt insbesondere für Vervielfältigungen, Übersetzungen, Mikroverfilmungen und elektronische Speicherformen sowie die Einspeicherung und Verarbeitung in elektronischen Systemen.

All rights reserved. No part of this publication may be reproduced, stored in or introduced into a retrieval system, or transmitted, in any form, or by any means (electronical, mechanical, photocopying, recording or otherwise) without the prior written permission of the publisher. Any person who does any unauthorized act in relation to this publication may be liable to criminal prosecution and civil claims for damages.

Printed in Germany

Contents

Foreword 7

PART I. DISSENT UNDER SOCIALISM

Kacper Szulecki
1. Smashing Concrete with Words.
   The Central European 'Dissidents', Their Representations and Discourses 11

Patryk Wasiak
2. The Second Life of the Polish Art World in the Eighties 25

PART II. CIVIL SOCIETY AND ETHNIC DIVISIONS. THE CASE OF THE WESTERN BALKANS

Tonči Valentić
3. History and Memory. Media Discourse and
   the Construction of National Identities 37

Bojan Bilić
4. Mapping the Ephemeral.
   Yugoslav Civic Activism and the 1990s Conflicts 47

Franziska Blomberg
5. External Democracy Promotion of Civil Society
   in Ethnically Fragmented Post-Socialist Countries 59

PART III. FINDING ONE'S PLACE IN CIVIL SOCIETY. EXAMPLES FROM RUSSIA

Christian Fröhlich
6. Walking the Tightrope. Russian Disability NGOs' Struggle
   with International and Domestic Demands 77

Ulla Pape
7. Striving for Social Change. NGOs in the Field of HIV/AIDS, Drug Policy
   and Human Rights in the Russian Federation 89

Part IV. Civil Society after EU Accession

Julia Langbein
8. Differential Empowerment for Institutional Change.
 The EU's Impact on State and Non-State Actors in Eastern Europe ... 103

Senka Neuman Stanivuković
9. The Introduction of Regional Self-Governance in the Czech Republic
 and Slovakia. EU Conditionality vis-à-vis Domestic Societal Pressures ... 117

Lars Breuer
10. German and Polish 'Memory from Below' ... 129

Part V. Political Participation and Lobbying

David Cadier
11. Can Civil Society Play a Role in Foreign Policy?
 Societal Groups in the Czech Republic ... 141

Olena Fimyar
12. The (Un)Importance of Public Opinion in Educational Policy-Making
 in Post-Communist Ukraine. Education Policy 'Elites' on the Role of
 Civil Society in Policy Formation ... 155

About the Authors ... 173

Foreword

The roles of civil society in Central and Eastern Europe are manifold. Before the end of socialism, civil society in this region was associated with dissident movements, human rights activists and, above all, the Polish Solidarity movement. However, nationalist movements, which are sometimes referred to as the dark side of civil society, were also present under socialism. Once socialism had come to an end, civil society organizations in most Central and East European countries grew in number and quality. They have gained new opportunities to influence the development of their countries, but also face challenges ranging from European integration in Central Eastern Europe to authoritarian pressures in some CIS and Balkan countries.

In examining the role of civil society in these societal developments away from socialism, care should be taken to avoid placing the focus exclusively on non-governmental organizations (NGOs), as formalized NGOs are only one part of societal mobilization and self-organization. It is also important to look not only at the level of organization and activities, but also at the underlying individual motivations and perceptions as part of specific political cultures.

Utilizing a wide range of empirical cases, the contributions in this edited volume highlight these different aspects of the role, development and societal background of civil society in Central and Eastern Europe. The first part of the book deals with dissent under socialism in order to illustrate the limited room for manoeuvre as well as the self-perception of civil society activists in the socialist regimes of Central Eastern Europe in the 1970s and 1980s. The second part of the book looks at the role of civil society in the Western Balkans in the context of the breakup of the former Yugoslavia and the related ethnic conflicts. The third part goes on to examine the role of civil society in the post-Soviet region, which is marked by authoritarian tendencies. The fourth part returns to Central Eastern Europe with an analysis of the impact of EU accession on the role of civil society and considers the underlying aspects of a 'common European memory'. The final section of the book looks at two cases – one from Central Eastern Europe, one from the CIS region – of political participation and lobbying by civil society organizations.

This book presents a selection of the papers discussed at the Changing Europe Summer School on 'Civil Society in Central and Eastern Europe' held at the National University of 'Kyiv-Mohyla Academy' (NAUKMA), Ukraine in July 2009. Organised since 2006 by the Research Centre for East European Studies (Forschungsstelle Osteuropa) at the University of Bremen, the Changing Europe Summer School has every year invited twenty to thirty young academics from different disciplines (political science, sociology, history, anthropology, economics, law, geography) to share their research on Central and Eastern Europe. Our main goal is to give them a chance to present and discuss their research projects as well as to help them become more integrated into the academic community. Participants are selected by means of an anonymous review process that is kindly supported by the members of our international review panel (for more information on the Changing Europe Summer Schools, see www.changing-europe.de). The results of each Summer School are published in this book series.

It goes without saying that this book would not have been possible without ample support. First of all, our thanks go to our partners from NAUKMA, namely Larysa Chovnyuk and Tamara Martsenyuk, and to the participants themselves, whose enthusiasm and knowledge made the Summer School a truly worthwhile event. We would also like to thank all the referees who aided us in the selection process for appropriate participants. We are additionally grateful to all those who helped to organize the Summer School and the book production, namely Hilary Abuhove (language editing), Stefan Forstmeier (Summer School organization), Judith Janiszewski (style editing), Julia Kusznir (organizational support) and Matthias Neumann (layout).

Last but certainly not least, we want to express our gratitude to the Volkswagen Foundation for its generous support of the Changing Europe Summer Schools.

Bremen and Paris, February 2010
The Editors

Part I. Dissent under Socialism

Kacper Szulecki

1. Smashing Concrete with Words. The Central European 'Dissidents', Their Representations and Discourses

1.1. Introduction

What do a Burmese monk, a Chilean writer, a Russian chess champion and an Iranian feminist have in common? Not much, it seems. And yet they are all crammed into one (supposedly descriptive) category – they are 'dissidents'. As a Czech playwright known more for his political activities once wrote:

> From time to time I have a chance to speak with Western intellectuals who visit our country and decide to include a visit to a dissident in their itinerary – some out of genuine interest, or a willingness to understand and to express solidarity, others simply out of curiosity. Beside the Gothic and Baroque monuments, dissidents are apparently the only thing of interest to a tourist in this uniformly dreary environment.[1]

'Dissidents' have always been the object of Western attention, and there are many reasons (not only aesthetic and voyeuristic as the quote could suggest) for why that is the case. Who are the 'dissidents', how do they come to be, and what sort of impact do they have? This contribution proposes to look back at the democratic opposition movements in Central Europe in order to define the 'dissident' as an analytical rather than simply descriptive concept. Putting aside the debate about the actual role of domestic and societal forces in bringing down Communism in Central and Eastern Europe, we can easily agree that there is something fascinating about the phenomenon of dissidentism in general. While 1989 is a caesura of groundbreaking importance for Central Europeans, on the global scale it meant that prisoners of conscience from this part of the world would nearly disappear from the pages of Amnesty International bulletins. Opposition to authoritarianism and dictatorial power continues world-wide, and so does dissidentism. The latter is not only an act of civil courage characterized by the Greek term *parrhesia*, meaning the conscious act of speaking the truth to power at the risk of grave consequences.[2] It is, perhaps more importantly, an instance of transnational recognition in which an oppositionist from one country is recognized for something larger and wider than he or she is, becomes a symbol of certain values and is taken for an example of a predefined social and political setup. To put it simply, 'dissident' is not a mere label, and empowerment does not boil down to the

---

1 Havel, Vaclav: Open Letters. Selected prose, 1965–1990, London: Faber and Faber, 1991, p. 261.
2 *Parrhesia* is extensively discussed in: Foucault, Michel: Fearless Speech, Los Angeles: Semiotext(e), 2001.

dollars transferred by human rights foundations in the West. The term has performative qualities of its own.

The dissertation project presented here is based on the assumption that the 'dissidents' constitute a socio-political phenomenon that is different from democratic opposition movements. The 'dissident' is thus seen as a rhetorical and political *figure* which is empowered through international recognition; however, it is the translation of the figure of the 'dissident' into local contexts that enables it to function internationally. The project therefore seeks to investigate the historical roots as well as the changing meanings of the concept of 'dissident' in the context of Central Europe, and look into the ways the concept itself was employed by those who were labelled as such. The example of human rights (HR) and pacifist discourse is provided as an example of how the specific position the 'dissidents' were in and their role as metaphorical 'bridges' between 'East' and 'West' were used to translate or *localize* values usually considered universal.

1.2. Literature on Dissent in Central Europe. A Critical Review

Two decades after 1989, scholars in the humanities and social scientists are still struggling to understand and explain what really 'brought the Iron Curtain down'.[3] International relations theorists and prominent historians generally focus on the macro-scale power politics leading to the 'end of the Cold War' and on the emergence of a new world order from the debris of the old system.[4] The emphasis on international processes and great power politics seems to have had an impact on the general Western discourse, which emphasizes the symbolic 'fall of the Berlin Wall' rather than the 'democratic revolutions' of Central Europe (CE) or the 'Autumn of Peoples'. These studies explain the events of the late 1980s either through material[5] or ideational factors,[6] putting more emphasis on either on Western or Soviet policies; what they share is a general tendency to dismiss the importance of societal actors such as democratic opposition

---

[3] I purposefully call up the different metaphors and expressions used to describe the events of the late 1980s and early 1990s in Central and Eastern Europe to show how varied scholarly and political perspectives are. For an overview of most recent scholarship on '1989' see: Ash, Timothy Garton: 1989!, in: New York Review of Books, 2009 (Vol. 56), No. 17.

[4] E.g. Wohlforth, William C.: Realism and the End of the Cold War, in: International Security, 1994–5 (Vol. 19), No. 3, pp. 91–129; Brooks, Stephen G. / Wohlforth, William C.: Power, Globalization and the End of the Cold War. Reevaluating a Landmark Case for Ideas, in: International Security, 2000–1 (Vol. 25), No. 3, pp. 5–53; Hyde-Price, Adrian: Normative Power Europe. A Realist Critique, in: Journal of European Public Policy, 2006 (Vol. 13), No. 2, pp. 217–234.

[5] Kotkin, Stephen / Gross, Jan T.: Uncivil Society. 1989 and the Implosion of the Communist Establishment, New York: Random House, 2009.

[6] For ideational explanations of Soviet non-intervention policy see: Checkel, Jeffrey: Ideas and International Political Change. Soviet/Russian Behavior and the End of the Cold War, New Haven/CT: Yale University Press, 1997; English, Robert: Russia and the Idea of the West. Gorbachev, Intellectuals, and the End of the Cold War, New York: Columbia University Press, 2000.

movements. In a recent, and otherwise impressive, history of post-war Europe, Tony Judt is clear about that:

> Illusions and reborn hopes (…) that is all [societal actions] were. They were not in themselves a harbinger of the downfall of Communist power. […] Communism was about power. [The mass dissent and the events in Poland] were a stirring prologue to the narrative of Communism's collapse, but they remained a sideshow. The real story was elsewhere.

He also dismisses intellectual oppositionists as 'a tiny minority of the population [who] represented only themselves […]'. In his view, '[T]he intellectual opposition in Central Europe had little immediate impact.'[7]

Other strands of political science (e.g. comparative politics) are interested mostly in the institutional outcomes of the 'regime shift' and thus rarely ask about its causes and history.[8] They employ Western categories of liberal democracy as an ideal type, creating such concepts as 'transition economies' and 'post-Communist nascent democracies' to explain the discrepancy between what is actually observed in CE and the ideal typical expectation. They fail, however, to problematize the notion of democracy as a general idea that is reformulated in various local (national) contexts.

Many important sociological and historical works challenge the writings mentioned above, arguing that change was often ideational and to a great extent came from below – i.e. from the domestic level of Central European societies. John L. Gaddis notices the 'shift in power from the supposedly powerful to the seemingly powerless', and clearly acknowledges the role of East and Central European societal movements:

> They were ordinary people with simple priorities who saw, seized, and sometimes stumbled into opportunities. In doing so they caused a collapse no one could stop. Their 'leaders' had little choice but to follow.[9]

This sentiment, however, still depicts the societal actors as having been driven by some exogenous opportunities. Padraic Kenney suggests that younger opposition movements in Central Europe were especially able to create opportunities for themselves, thus finding a niche for action.[10] Studies counterbalancing the materialist and intergovernmental views of 1989 often work with the concept of the civil society,[11]

---

7   Judt, Tony: Postwar. A History of Europe since 1945, London: Verso, 2007, pp. 589–590, 576.
8   E.g. Miklaszewska, Justyna (ed.): Democracy in Central Europe 1989–99. Comparative and Historical Perspectives, Kraków: Meritum, 1999; Krouwel, Andre: Measuring Presidentialism and Parliamentarism. An Application to Central and East European Countries, in: Acta Politica, 2003 (Vol. 38), No. 4, pp. 333–364; Wydra, Harald: Communism and the Emergence of Democracy, Cambridge: Cambridge University Press, 2007.
9   Gaddis, John Lewis: The Cold War, London: Penguin, 2007, p. 238.
10   Kenney, Padraic: Framing, Political Opportunities, and Civic Mobilization in the Eastern European Revolutions. A Case Study of Poland's Freedom and Peace Movement, in: Mobilization. An International Journal, 2001 (Vol. 6), No. 2, pp. 193–210.
11   Cohen, John L. / Arato, Andrew: Civil Society and Political Theory, Cambridge: MIT Press, 1994, and earlier: Keane, John: Democracy and Civil Society, London: Verso, 1988. Compare: Wnuk-

emphasizing the role of dissident intellectuals[12] and the impact of ideational factors;[13] however, they often focus solely on the events of 1989 (under the label of 'transition studies')[14] and not their roots.

The historical trajectories of oppositional sentiments and early examples of social movements have been explored already in a plethora of studies dating back to the late 1970s,[15] with special emphasis on movements such as those spearheaded by the Polish 'Solidarity' and the *Workers' Defence Committee* (KOR), or by the Czechoslovak *Charta 77*.[16] Recently, a younger generation of Central European historians, making use of the new sources available, has recently been attempting to re-tell the story of the demise of Communism,[17] and the key actors of these events are also sharing their reflections.[18] The most striking dissonance is, however, that many of the written histories – factual accounts – of the democratic opposition movements as well as studies attempting to grasp the processes behind the democratic revolutions of 1989 fail to put forth any hypotheses about the mechanisms through which Communism was dismantled. Very interesting research seeking to fill this gap was conducted from the perspective of 'inside-outsiders', i.e. Western scholars pointing out processes and patterns less visible for academics enmeshed in their national contexts, discussing such

---

Lipiński, Edmund: Vicissitudes of Ethical Civil Society in Central and Eastern Europe, in: Studies in Christian Ethics, 2007 (Vol. 20), No. 1, pp. 30–43.

12 Bozóki, András (ed.): Intellectuals and Politics in Central Europe, Budapest: CEU Press, 1998; Friszke, Andrzej: Przystosowanie i Opór. Studia z Dziejów PRL, Warsaw: Więź, 2006.

13 As HR norms in: Thomas, Daniel C.: The Helsinki Effect. International Norms, Human Rights, and the Demise of Communism, Princeton/NJ: Princeton University Press, 2001; Evangelista, Matthew: Unarmed Forces. The Transnational Movement to End the Cold War, Ithaca/NY: Cornell University Press, 1999.

14 E.g. Ekiert, Grzegorz / Kubik, Jan: Rebellious Civil Society. Popular Protest and Democratic Consolidation in Poland, 1989–1993, Ann Arbor/MI: University of Michigan Press, 1999.

15 Poland from Inside, special issue of Survey – a Journal of East and West Studies, 1979 (Vol. 24), No. 4; Leftwich Curry, Jane (ed.): Dissent in Eastern Europe, New York: Praeger, 1983; Ash, Timothy Garton: The Polish Revolution. Solidarity 1980–82, London: Jonathan Cape, 1983; Havel, Vaclav et al.: Power of the Powerless. Citizens against the State in Central-Eastern Europe, New York: Palach Press, 1985.

16 Prečan, Vilem: Charta 77. 1977–1989. Od Morální k Demokratické Revoluci, Bratislava: Archa, 1990; Branach, Zbigniew: Mit Ojców Założycieli. Agonia Komunizmu Rozpoczęła się w Gdańsku, Bydgoszcz: Cetera, 2005; KARTA. Słownik Dysydentów. Czołowe Postacie Ruchów Opozycyjnych w Krajach Komunistycznych w Latach 1956–1989, Tom I, Warsaw: Karta, 2007; Friszke, Andrzej / Paczkowski, Andrzej: NiepoKORni. Rozmowy o Komitecie Obrony Robotników, Kraków: Znak, 2008.

17 Codogni, Paulina: Okrągły Stół, czyli Polski Rubikon, Warsaw: Collegium Civitas, 2009. From a more contestatory perspective: Musiał, Filip / Szarek, Jarosław: Precz z Komuna. Z Archiwum Bezpieki – Nieznane Karty PRL, Kraków: IPN, 2006.

18 Geremek, Bronisław / Żakowski, Jacek: Rok 1989, Warsaw: Agora, 2008; Wałęsa, Lech: Moja III RP. Straciłem cierpliwość!, Warsaw: Świat Książki, 2007; Michnik, Adam: Wyznania nawróconego dysydenta, Warsaw: Zeszyty Literackie, 2003; Havel, Vaclav: Tylko krótko, proszę. Rozmowa z Karelem Hvížďalą, zapiski, dokumenty, Kraków: SIW Znak, 2007. Also, biographies were made available, e.g.: Kurski, Jarosław: Wódz. Mój przyczynek do biografii, Warsaw: BGW, 2008; Bouyeure, Cyril: Adam Michnik, biografia. Wymyślić to, co polityczne, Kraków: Wydawnictwo Literackie, 2009.

notions as anti-politics or the blurred relationship of (counter)culture and power.[19] Especially the latter project, developed by Kenney, constituted a very important and interesting attempt to bridge the factual and the process-oriented approaches with the idea of a 'carnival of revolution', while at the same time providing an alternative narrative of the history of Central European opposition in the late 1980s (which was, prior to this work, an under-researched lacuna).[20] In the field of international relations, Central European human rights movements were analysed using the transnational models of normative change developed in earlier studies.[21] These models unfortunately downplay the role of domestic traditions and ideational contexts, and hence overlook the complexity of the 'grafting' and 'localizing' of norms.

Even though all these studies should be praised for adopting a bottom-up perspective and for their sensitivity to the role of societal actors (such as domestic opposition movements), little or no meta-reflection on the way we perceive Central European dissidents has appeared, and the idiomatic character of the concept of 'dissidents' has not yet been investigated.[22] The notion of *civil society* in Eastern European contexts is mostly used to underline the conflict between the authoritarian state and the society. I argue that the figure of the 'dissident' and the mechanism of its construction can tell us more about the features of (and preconditions for) civil society in totalitarian/authoritarian states. This focus highlights the importance of transnational recognition and the complex interplay between the West and its Eastern neighbourhood in the development of civil society structures in Central Europe, while also emphasizing the socially constructed aspects of this process.

1.3. Research Strategy and Theory. Identities, Discourses and Dissidents

This is where the project sets off. Theoretically, it rests on the post-structuralist theories of discourse and the role of language as an ontologically significant, constraining and

---

19 Ost, David: The Defeat of Solidarity, New York: Cornell University Press, 2005; Kenney, Padraic: A Carnival of Revolution. Central Europe 1989, Princeton/NJ: Princeton University Press, 2002.
20 Compare: Skórzyński, Jan: Rewolucja Okrągłego Stołu, Warsaw: SIW Znak, 2009.
21 Thomas, Daniel C.: The Helsinki Accords and Political Change in Eastern Europe (Chapter 7), in: Risse, Thomas / Ropp, Stephen C. / Sikkink, Kathryn (eds): The Power of Human Rights. International Norms and Domestic Change, Cambridge: Cambridge University Press, 1999, pp. 205–233; Chilton, Patricia: Mechanics of Change. Social Movements, Transnational Coalitions, and the Transformation Processes in Eastern Europe, in: Risse-Kappen, Thomas (ed.): Bringing Transnational Relations back in. Non-state Actors, Domestic Structures and International Institutions, Cambridge: Cambridge University Press, 2003, pp. 189–226.
22 Langenohl, Andreas: Zweimal Reflexivität in der gegenwärtigen Sozialwissenschaft. Anmerkungen zu einer nicht geführten Debatte, in: Forum. Qualitative Social Research, 2009 (Vol. 10), No. 2, http://nbn-resolving.de/urn:nbn:de:0114-fqs090297

constitutive structure of all political action.[23] The 'dissident' is a concept developed in Western discourses on Eastern Europe and, more generally, on non-Western Others.[24] It is *performative* in the sense that the 'dissidents' are 'created' – i.e. constructed and empowered through transnational recognition.[25] It is *idiomatic* in the sense that it presupposes a certain implicit assumption about both the relationship between the West and Eastern Europe as well as the role 'dissidents' play in relation to their own societies (with respect to representing their societies; we can therefore treat the 'dissidents' as a part taken for the whole – a *synecdoche*)[26] and their rulers.

The first step is therefore a critical historical analysis tracing the formation and evolution of the concept of the 'dissident' based on the public discourse understandings and the historical uses of the term. The resulting definition of 'dissidents' sees them as a position in a web of power and meaning rather than specific individuals. 'Dissidents' are created through transnational recognition and are also empowered by it. It is therefore necessary to trace the evolution of the figure of the 'dissident' by analysing all levels on which it has operated: the domestic (official and underground), international (public and official), and exilic.

However, looking only at the formation of the 'dissident' concept would not help us understand the role it, and the people subsumed under it, played. It is therefore important to see the 'dissidents' in the context of larger processes of identity creation, in which Western Europe forged its notion of Self in relation to a certain Eastern European Other.[27] The material reality of the Iron Curtain reinforced the imagined division between the two, leading Westerners to construct the identity of the Eastern Other mostly in spatial terms.[28] The figure of the 'dissident', also symbolizing the society,

---

23 Cf. Foucault, Michel: The Order of Things. An Archeology of the Human Sciences, New York: Vintage, 1994. Also: Foucault, Michel: Porządek Dyskursu, Warsaw: Słowo/Obraz/Terytoria, 2002; for a more empirical application: Hansen, Lene: Security as Practice. Discourse Analysis and the Bosnian War, New York: Routledge, 2006.
24 The West itself is understood here in the political sense of the Cold War context, meaning the capitalist and more often than not democratic (however blurred the concept is) states of non-Communist Europe as well as the US and Canada.
25 Searle, John: The Construction of Social Reality, New York: Free Press, 1995.
26 This logic is explained in: Szulecki, Kacper: The Other Europe. How the West Created the Dissidents, presented at the conference: Intellectuals, Empire and Civilizations in 19th and 20th centuries, Warsaw University, 22 June 2007.
27 For the historical foundations of this thesis see: Wolff, Larry: Inventing Eastern Europe. The Map of Civilization on the Mind of the Enlightenment, Stanford/CA: Stanford University Press, 1994; as well as Neumann, Iver B.: Uses of the Other. 'The East' in European Identity Formation, Minneapolis: University of Minnesota Press, 1999; also Hansen, Lene: Security as Practice. Discourse Analysis and the Bosnian War, New York: Routledge, 2006.
28 As Lene Hansen notes, identities can be created on spatial, temporal and moral grounds. In the case of the Western discourse on the Eastern European Other, I argue that that space was used in the process of differentiation (West vs. East), while the identities of East European 'dissidents' included an element of moral and ideational similarity. The demise of Communism in East-Central Europe and the fall of the imaginary spatial division involved a reformulation of

suggested a split within the Other – prompting Westerners to construe the 'dissidents' as (at least potentially) sharing the values of the West and (supposedly) representing their own societies, while opposing the state socialist apparatus – a 'fifth column of Western establishments east of the Yalta line' as Vaclav Havel jokingly remarked.[29] This view impacted Western official policies and public opinions about the situation of Eastern European societies. It contained, however, some obvious simplifications that were difficult for Central-Eastern European oppositionist intellectuals to accept and often caused grave misunderstandings and fierce conflicts.[30]

Discursive structures are difficult to transform, but they can be resisted and even destabilized. The discourse of 'Central Europe' constituted such an attempt to question and destabilize Western Europe's perspectives on its Eastern neighbours. Because the identity of the Eastern European Other was constructed spatially, 'Central Europe' was a means to separate the inhabitants of Soviet satellite states (and of some western Soviet republics) from the Russian East also in geographical terms. The 'dissidents'' own intellectual activity influenced the social imaginaries[31] of Central European societies (in fact, the very notion of 'Central European societies' is an effect of the circulation and diffusion of formerly elite ideas).[32] The next step in this project is therefore to probe official and samizdat publications for traces of these discourses. Additionally, the project embarks from these assumptions on a comparative analysis of the discourses of Polish, Czech and Slovak dissidents. What role did the idea of Central Europe play in joining the 'dissidents' from the countries in this region?[33] Are the 'dissident' ideas homogeneous in content, or is it the 'structural' similarity of power relations that makes 'dissidents' comparable? These questions are explored through a discourse analysis of 'dissident' writings and a historical analysis based on secondary sources.

Bearing in mind the specific role the 'dissidents' had to play – being suspended between the West and the domestic 'Eastern' settings, taken as a symbol of the 'Western Self' within the 'Eastern Other', the project takes a closer look at the practices of localization of wider (European and universal) ideas and discourses. The 'dissidents' attempted

---

the Eastern European Other in temporal terms – as 'underdeveloped' and 'on the path to stable democracy'. Compare: Fabian, Johannes: Time and the Other. How Anthropology Makes Its Object, New York: Columbia University Press, 1983.

29 Havel, Vaclav: Open Letters. Selected prose, 1965–1990, London: Faber and Faber, 1991, p. 292.
30 Some examples of such misunderstandings between intellectuals operating in two separate worlds are given in: Płynie się zawsze do źródeł, pod prąd, z prądem płyną śmiecie, A. Michnik's interview with Z. Herbert, in: Herbert nieznany. Rozmowy, Warsaw: Zeszyty Literackie, 2008; and famously: Miłosz, Czesław: Zachód, in: Idem. Zniewolony umysł, Kraków: Wydawnictwo Literackie, 1999.
31 Taylor, Charles: Modern Social Imaginaries, in: Public Culture, 2002 (Vol. 14), No. 1, pp. 91–124; Lee, Benjamin / LiPuma, Edward: Cultures of Circulation. The Imaginations of Modernity, in: Public Culture, 2002 (Vol. 14), No. 1, pp. 191–213.
32 Kundera, Milan: The Tragedy of Central Europe, in: New York Review of Books, 26 April 1984.
33 Contacts between Central European dissidents were established by the 1970s: Biuletyn informacyjny uczestników ROPCiO, 6 October 1978 [samizdat], Archiwum KARTA.

to gradually enlarge and reinforce the public sphere of their societies, understood as the space for open debate on issues of society-wide importance.[34] The 'dissident' intellectuals of Central Europe faced very difficult ideational challenges. Feeling a part of both their 'native realms'[35] and the wider homeland of Europe, they were torn between perspectives on crucial values. To give an example of this logic: democracy is seen as one of the key European values. How did the 'dissidents' reconcile the divergent understanding of democracy coming from Western Europe and 'translate' it, using pre-existing domestic traditions (such as the revived myth of a long-lasting though rather specific democratic experience of the Polish-Lithuanian Commonwealth or the Czech memories of the First Republic),[36] into the context of state-socialist societies? By the same token, I would like to look at the way core European values were carved to resonate with the local traditions and discourses. This form of 'being European, but in our own way' – i.e. feeling like a part of Europe, but bearing some distinct 'Eastern' traces (thus countering the alleged inferiority of the Eastern European Other with a spatial counter-narrative of the 'Centre', the cultural claims to Europe and the traces of regional pride and claims to moral superiority), is also an important part of the intellectual project of 'Central Europe'.

The project seeks to analyse the discursive practices of democratic oppositionist circles in Poland at several points in time while looking for the localizing practices vis-à-vis such European values as *democracy*, *freedom*, *peace* and *environmental protection*.[37] The hypothesis is that even though these concepts were used in the 'East-West' dialogue, the meanings involved were often divergent. The strategies of HR adaptation and localization were creatively used throughout the 1980s by such opposition movements as the Polish *Wolność i Pokój* (WiP) or the Czechoslovak *Hnutí za Občanskou Svobodu* (HOS), and thus paved the way for the revolutions of 1989 and the democratic regimes that followed. The 'dissidents' (making use of the position they gained through the performative function of the 'dissident' as a concept) were attempting to bridge this semantic gap all along, from the establishment of wider intellectual

---

34 Habermas, Jürgen: The Structural Transformation of the Public Sphere. An Inquiry into a Category of Bourgeois Society, Cambridge: MIT Press, 1989.
35 The expression is borrowed from Czesław Miłosz and illustrates very well the problem of being an integral part of Europe, yet simultaneously struggling with one's own peripheral position. Cf. Miłosz, Czesław: Native Realm. A Search for Self-Definition, New York: Farrar, Straus and Giroux, 2002.
36 An example of a possible secondary source is: Holy, Ladislav: The Little Czech and the Great Czech Nation. National Identity and the Post-communist Social Transformation, Cambridge: Cambridge University Press, 1996.
37 Environmental issues are not traditionally perceived as an important element of 'dissident' thought. That is wrong. Even in the writings of the older generation oppositionists one can encounter traces of environmentalist ideas. See: Havel, Vaclav: Krize Identity, in: Idem. O lidskou identitu. Úvahy, fejetony, protesty, polemiky, prohlásení a rozhovory z let 1969–1979, 1990 [1984], London, Praha: Rozmluvy, p. 349, noticing the ecological catastrophe of the Czech Silesia, becoming 'something between the Moon and a garbage dump' (*mezi Měsícem a smetištěm*).

dissent in the mid-1970s (often associated with the Helsinki Accords, and therefore the need to find a way for human rights norms to resonate domestically), through 1989 and beyond, to the proclamation of the Copenhagen Criteria, when an 'operationalization' of European values took place. Through an analysis of 'dissident' texts (declarations, statements, essays but also memoirs), I intend to uncover what strategies were used and what stories were told to localize the HR discourse and norms. In other words, I want to find out what made the discourse resonate with the local populace; did it strike a chord with their values and traditions (or at least – what was *presented* as traditions in order to resonate with human rights)? The answers to these questions can shed new light on the debate about European as well as Central European identity, and the political manifestations of socio-cultural structures in a uniting Europe.

1.4. An Example of Dissident Action. Localizing Human Rights Discourses

The previous sections have discussed a different, figurative approach to the phenomenon of dissidentism. The remainder of this article is an attempt to build on this theoretical framework and to analyse the strategies and practices of localization used by Polish and Czechoslovak oppositionists in the 1980s. The figure of the 'dissident' was creatively used in the exchange between 'East' and 'West', and human rights issues were one of the areas of dialogue.

Localization is understood as a discursive practice through which a seemingly universal discourse (related to a certain idea, norm or value) is rephrased and reconstructed in such a way so as to fit the landscape of the local setting and make these discourses meaningful and legitimate to the given culture. These 'translated' discourses can then feed back outside and add to the universality of the general discourse, which is only possible as long as it also functions locally. In this project I intend to look at the localization of discourses such as human rights, pacifism, disarmament and environmentalism. The transnational dimension here is crucial. In the localization process, we would expect to see instances in which some internationally functioning discourse is picked up and consciously grafted on to existing domestic discourses. All this should be associated with continuous communication between the Eastern actors and their Western counterparts, in which the 'dissidents' play a metaphorical two-level game.[38]

In order to analyse the way a discourse was localized (i.e. 'translated' to fit the local ideational and discursive landscape), we need to consider several levels. Take the issue of human rights. First of all, what is meant by human rights? Secondly, what

---

38 I borrow the two-level game metaphor from Robert Putnam, even though the original formulation dealt with intergovernmental negotiations. Compare: Putnam, Robert: Diplomacy and Domestic Politics. The Logic of Two-Level Games, in: International Organization, 1988 (Vol. 42), Summer, pp. 427–460.

is the relationship between human rights and domestic 'traditions' in Central Europe, and how did human rights fit into the dominant Communist ideology? Once these questions have been answered, we can discuss the practices of localization and the way previously existing ideational structures were employed by the 'dissidents'. As the scope of this article does not allow for the development of a full argument, I will only provide a brief sketch of the way localization should be understood.

Some basic ideas of democracy and civic freedom were deeply engraved into the national self-conceptions of Central European nations, at least in the form of positive 'ideals' to which they claimed to aspire. Self-rule, the right and need to hold authorities accountable, freedom to express one's opinion on cultural, social as well as political issues – all of these elements constitute a rather basic portfolio of fundamental rights and norms according to which a society can function. If we understand local 'traditions' of political thought as foundations of political legitimacy, it becomes clear that the cleavage between the imagined 'ideal' and reality had considerable dissident potential.

Halina Bortnowska, a Polish HR activist in the 1980s, differentiates between two basic understandings of human rights. One touches upon human-to-human relations. It is derived from the vision of humanity as an indivisible whole, and from love and respect for the Other. The second understanding, in the spirit of the Helsinki Accords, is concerned with the relation between the individual and power – especially the state apparatus. The national constitution is seen as a foundation of HR protection, and it is largely the daunting responsibility of lawyers and courts to enforce the law and monitor the state's actions with respect to the constitution. As many studies fail to note, in state socialist societies the problem was not that human rights were unknown or a novelty. It was that the constitutional declarations pertaining to human rights were not respected by the authorities.[39] And so, the 'problem of human rights in state socialist societies' was due to state tyranny and the suppression of individual freedom, despite the existing laws that *de jure* should (and as was proven – could) have been used to protect the people.

I argue that the conscious process of HR discourse localization, especially in the case of Poland, was predominantly an attempt to reconcile the two meanings of human rights presented above so that their formulations would reflect both the local traditions and the external understanding of human rights. In Poland the first understanding had to above all resonate with the vision of humanism rooted in the teachings of the Catholic Church. Bortnowska explains 'Solidarity's' strategy of 'translating' human rights into the language of Christian thought:

> Taking part in common action we can chose certain accents, which someone finds especially important. We simply notice how important community is for people. Christianity

---

[39] Compare: Archiwum Komitetu Helsińskiego w Polsce, 1984, No. 1, [samizdat], Archiwum KARTA.

stresses this aspect; that is why this question is raised more often, while in the pan-humanist perspective there is more emphasis on the rights of the individual. But one does not contradict the other, as for a community to exist, the rights of the individual need to be protected.[40]

The Helsinki Accords played an important role in empowering the HR-based opposition in Central Europe in the mid-1970s. They also made the figure of the 'dissident' conceivable. Jiři Hájek, the Charter 77 spokesman, notes that the whole perspective changes

> the moment that a regime which imposes on society and its citizens its narrow and restrictive, even repressive, interpretation of democracy, rights and freedoms, proclaims or indicates elsewhere, and in other circumstances, its readiness to accept, or at least tolerate, other interpretations.[41]

After the passage of the Accords, the democratic opposition in Central Europe was able to transcend the borders of their states and 'their' bloc. The Human Rights accords provided a common platform for dialogue, upon which definitions of what was at stake had to be made compatible. 'Dissidentism', in the figurative sense I propose here, was only possible once such a platform was in place. Prior to that, opposition to Communism in Central Europe was understood on a different transnational 'platform' – Marxist ideology. Those who opposed the Party's political line were then either 'anti-Communists' (remaining outside the ideological sphere of the Party) or 'reformists' (heretical insiders). The original meaning of the term 'dissident' (from the medieval Latin word for heretic or renegade) refers to the latter. The HR discourse defined by the West stripped the term 'dissident' of the remaining traces of that original meaning and widened it to encompass all those who advocate for a 'common' understanding and practice of human rights (later to be transposed to other values recognized by the West).

At that point the 'dissidents' gained their crucial role of mediating between the West and the domestic context. On the one hand, they were able to use the international discourse of human rights to criticize their governments, in the manner Hájek describes:

> The fact that the regime reacts to criticism of its failure to implement laws and international pledges by persecuting or discriminating against its domestic critics, and it refuses to discuss the implementation of these pledges with its co-signatories, proves that it does not have a clear conscience. When this is done by the regime describing itself as socialist it is a disservice, to say the least, to the cause of socialism, its democratic and humanizing mission and, thus, to social progress itself.[42]

40　Potrzebna jest asymetria, E. Zbiegieni's interview with Halina Bortnowska, in: Znak, 2008 (Vol. 643), December, pp. 43–52, here p. 46.
41　Hájek, Jiři: The human rights movement and social progress, in: Havel, Vaclav et al.: Power of the Powerless. Citizens against the State in Central-Eastern Europe, London: Hutchinson, 1985, p. 135.
42　Ibid., p. 140.

They could thus both hold them accountable for their 'pledges', the dead letter of the domestic law and the even more visibly dead ideals of the preached socialism. That is a strategy that was used by most opposition groups from 1975 on and well into the 1980s. The role of the 'dissidents' as mediators was to take an internationally recognized issue, put it on the domestic agenda using both the existing traditions and laws, as well as international obligations, and then to feed the description of their struggles back to the international community in such a way that the trans-boundary saliency of the issue would be immediately recognized. That strategy was mastered by young opposition movements such as the Polish *Wolność i Pokój,* which chose specific issues, for example 'defending the pacifists refusing military service or environmental problems, [which] caused a lot of trouble for the communist regime, because, as a rule, the demands of the protesters were fully in line with the assurances and declarations of the authorities.'[43] The definition of 'peace' and 'pacifism' adopted by WiP makes these issues an extension of the HR discourse as 'the main condition of peace occurring in the political life of states and nations is the effective guaranteeing of personal freedom to all the people.'[44]

As noted, 'dissidents' were attempting to make their struggles understandable and digestible for the West. This did not happen automatically, as Bortnowska recalls:

> In the beginning of the Solidarity movement the most important issue was to find some foundations, the possibility to call upon the laws seen as binding within the international community, to something that would persuade others to take our side.[45]

Human rights, pacifism, environmentalism, women's issues, and even gay and lesbian rights[46] were all used by the oppositionists not only because they mattered. They were a tool for destabilizing the system, and their use was often clearly strategic, or at least motivated by circumstances.[47] A WiP activist, Jan Żurko, admits that pacifism was chosen as an issue not because of actual convictions (although the activists gradually embraced the issue once they began to fight for it), but because 'pacifist ideas have, contrary to the common opinion, a lot of potential. Especially among the youth, but not

---

43 Kenney, Padraic: Wrocławskie zadymy, Wrocław: ATUT, 2007, p. 115.
44 Deklaracja założycielska Ruchu 'Wolność i Pokój' §2., http://www.tezeusz.pl/cms/tz/index.php?id=1856, accessed 29 May 2009.
45 Potrzebna jest asymetria, E. Zbiegieni's interview with Halina Bortnowska, in: Znak, 2008 (Vol. 643), December, pp. 43–52.
46 Feminist and emancipatory ideas are present in: Uhl, Petr et al.: Program společenské samosprávy, Cologne: Index, 1982. For first discussions of LGBT issues see: A-Capella, 1989, No. 16 [samizdat], Archiwum KARTA.
47 Compare: Kenney, Padraic: A Carnival of Revolution. Central Europe 1989, Princeton/NJ: Princeton University Press, 2002, p. 61. Sometimes inspired by the popularity of an issue in the West, as in the case of environmentalism according to Leszek Budrewicz, in: Kenney, Padraic: Wrocławskie zadymy, Wrocław: ATUT, 2007, p. 122.

only the youth. [...] Even though the Polish society is, seemingly, not very pacifistic."[48] The last quote clearly points to the need for reformulations that made the 'universal' become locally acceptable, by both the society and the various centres of authority ('Even the fact that our ideas were accepted by the Church hierarchy we took as a very positive value').[49] The meaning of the discourse at home and its international representation very often diverged,[50] something that comes as no surprise judging by the way this 'translation' of ideas proceeded.

As this brief empirical illustration suggests, there is still much to be discovered about the nature and role of the Central European oppositionists. The main point is not to remain focused only on Solidarity and Charter 77, not only on 1975 and 1989, but to explore the 'spectre' of 'dissidentism' as it was 'haunting Eastern Europe' in the words of the Czech playwright quoted at the beginning.[51] This spectre, although by nature difficult to grasp, is what this project seeks to reveal.

---

48 Interview with Jan Żurko in: Kenney, Padraic: Wrocławskie zadymy, Wrocław: ATUT, 2007, p. 141. On the intrinsic militarism of Polish patriotism: Bota, Adam: Trzeci ruch okrężny, in: A-Capella, 1989, No. 16, p. 12 [samizdat].
49 Interview with Jan Żurko in: Kenney, Padraic: Wrocławskie zadymy, Wrocław: ATUT, 2007, p. 147.
50 Again, peace is a good illustration. Havel's famous letter to the Amsterdam Peace Conference: Havel, Vaclav: Anatomy of Reticence, in: Idem. Open Letters. Selected prose, 1965–1990, London: Faber and Faber, 1991; also Rokita, Jan Maria: Wolność i Pokój, czyli jak zwiększyć szanse pokoju w Europie, in: Czas Przyszły, 1987, December [samizdat], Archiwum KARTA.
51 Havel, Vaclav: Power of the Powerless, in: Havel, Vaclav et al.: Power of the Powerless. Citizens against the State in Central-Eastern Europe, London: Hutchinson, 1985.

Patryk Wasiak

2. The Second Life of the Polish Art World in the Eighties

2.1. Introduction

In Polish academic discourse, the civil society approach is used mainly to describe social change and the shaping of democracy after the year 1989. In this contribution, however, I aim to show how this framework could be used in an analysis of social phenomena in the Eighties without reference to politics. To present this approach I chose the milieu of visual artists. This group is often perceived as actors participating in the creation of an anti-Communist political discourse. I would like to show how using civil society as a descriptive framework could help us to understand complex social interactions and go beyond the narrow field of political activity.

2.2. Analytical Framework

The Eighties in Poland were a time of continuous collapsing of the social order developed by leaders of the Polish United Workers' Party almost forty years earlier. After the imposition of martial law on 13 December 1981 and the mass repression of people involved in the Solidarity movement, the Communist authorities lost their remaining credibility in Polish society, which had somehow fared fairly well during the relatively stable 'Gierek era'. The Eighties were also a time of continuous economic crisis, which led to the emptiness of shelves in shops. The changes in the political sphere that led to the negotiations between the authorities and opposition leaders at the end of the decade are well documented by Polish historians.[1] But the research focused on this political history has long eclipsed the social history of this period. Academics from various fields have also begun conducting research on various phenomena of the late period of the Polish People's Republic and they often use the framework of civil society to analyse these topics.

I will also use this framework in my contribution. I aim to present a few basic theses concerning visual artists as a particular social and professional milieu. This text exclusively focuses on the creation of visual art as a social activity leading to the creation of particular social interactions. These interactions are based on the creation and distribution of works of art and the spread of information. In Howard S. Becker's

---

[1] See: Friszke, Andrzej (ed.): Władza a społeczeństwo w PRL, Warsaw: Instytut Studiów Politycznych PAN, 2003; Friszke, Andrzej: Przystosowanie i opór. Studia z dziejów PRL, Warsaw: Biblioteka 'Więzi', 2007; Kemp-Welch, Anthony: Poland under Communism: A Cold War History, Cambridge, New York: Cambridge University Press, 2008; Paczkowski, Andrzej: Pół wieku dziejów Polski 1939–1989, Warsaw: Wydawnictwo Naukowe PWN, 2005.

classic work, these social milieus are called the 'art world'.² My main emphasis is on the organization of art exhibitions, which I find to be the most interesting phenomenon in the framework of civil society studies. I aim to present how such informal activities can be discussed in the frames of wider research on the rise of civil society in Central Europe conducted by academics from diverse disciplines.

In contrast to the 'art worlds' of cinematography or literature, in the field of visual art the whole process of creating and circulating visual art could be organized entirely without any support from state-controlled institutions like movie studios, publishing houses, cinemas and bookstores. The analysis of visual art milieus could show how particular groups organized grass-roots initiatives in the social space to cope with their particular situation.³

2.3. Civil Society and 'Art Worlds'

Visual arts in the Bloc are often perceived in academic literature as a sphere of political activity against regimes. Even attempts to make a particular kind of art based on neo-avant-garde Western trends (e.g. happenings, performance art, or even just non-figurative art) are interpreted as outcries against Communist rule, which acknowledged only realistic academic art.⁴ In my research I am describing the activity of visual artists in a different way, i.e. as a social milieu in which members were able to develop their informal social structures in order to present their work in the public (in this case semi-public) sphere.

It is not my objective to analyse the artistic meanings of the presented art pieces. Instead I perceive the creation of art as a particular social activity that is not necessarily a professional career for all practitioners. American anthropologist Stuart Plattner conducted research concerning the life and self-perception of visual artists.

> Some producers make work primarily because their identity and self-respect are defined by their work. These people may want to make money, but their involvement with their work derives from identity rather than money. They may be said to be addicted to their work; economists use the term 'psychic income.⁵

---

2   Becker, Howard S.: Art Worlds, Berkeley/CA: University of California Press, 1982; Becker, Howard S.: Art as Collective Action, in: American Sociological Review, 1974 (Vol. 39), No. 6, pp. 767–776. In Poland a similar concept was developed by Aleksander Wallis, who used the term 'universe of culture', see: Wallis, Aleksander: Atlas kultury polskiej 1946–1980, Międzychód: Eco, 1994, p. 37.
3   This article was exclusively written during my research fellowship at the Herder Institut in Marburg, so I was only able to use the materials available there.
4   See: Piotrowski, Piotr: In the Shadow of Yalta. Art and avantgarde in Eastern Europe, 1945–1989, London: Reaktion Books, 2009.
5   Plattner, Stuart: A Most Ingenious Paradox. The Market for Contemporary Fine Art, in: American Anthropologist, 1998 (Vol. 100), No. 2, pp. 482–493, here p. 483, http://www.stuartplattner.com/AA-ART-Paradox.pdf

2. The Second Life of the Polish Art World in the Eighties

I am interested in the development of the informal mechanisms used to publicize these artworks. Under Communism, the most basic mechanism was the use of social bonds to organize a particular event (e.g. an exhibition) and spread the word about it. Due to these small but valuable social networks, artists were able to avoid having to promote exhibitions through 'official' channels.

The phenomenon of so-called 'alternative' or 'unofficial' culture in the field of visual arts is discussed almost exclusively by art historians. Sociological and anthropological angles are scarce in these analyses. Commentary on this topic also tends to be based on the simple dichotomy of official vs. unofficial artists.[6] Another problem is that many authors make passing judgments on the topic; the artistic values of the artworks are given centre stage rather than descriptive analysis. The conceptualization of my Ph.D. project is instead based on academic works that focus on other informal social phenomena in Communist Poland and other Bloc countries. Aside from the field of culture production and presentation, these topics are well described by academics from diverse fields.[7]

The theoretical framework of this chapter utilizes categories proposed by Jan Kubik and Grzegorz Ekiert in their article *Civil Society from Abroad. The Role of Foreign Assistance in the Democratization of Poland*, which focuses on various aspects of the activities of social groups in Poland in the Eighties.[8] The aforementioned authors call this period 'state socialism disintegration'[9] and define civil society as a 'set of organized groups/associations, whose members deliberate to act collectively to accomplish common goals'[10]. In the case of Poland in the Eighties, these groups existed under the particular set of conditions created by the authorities.

> Under each political regime public space is constituted in a specific way and different types of groups are protected or represented by the state. Under state socialist regimes the space was highly restricted and organized [and] had very little autonomy.[11]

The term 'civil society' in this approach is used only in a descriptive sense. As a normative term, it can be used in research on the discourse of political dissidents' groups.

---

6 See for example: Alan, Josef (ed.): Alternativní kultura. Příběh české společnosti 1945–1989, Praha: Nakladatelstvi Lidové noviny, 2001.
7 See: Kenney, Padraic: A Carnival of Revolution. Central Europe 1989, Princeton/NJ: Princeton University Press, 2002; Wedel, Janine (ed.): The Unplanned Society, Poland During and after Communism, New York/NY: Columbia University Press, 1992.
8 Ekiert, Grzegorz / Kubik, Jan: Civil Society from Abroad. The Role of Foreign Assistance in the Democratization of Poland, in: WCFIA Working Paper Series, No. 00-01, February 2000, Harvard University, http://www.wcfia.harvard.edu/sites/default/files/91__2000-01%20Ekiertfinal2.pdf, accessed 15 June 2009,
9 Ibid., p. 3.
10 Ibid., p. 5.
11 Ibid., p. 7.

In these social movements, 'civil society' was one of the few cores of its ideologies.[12] This approach is inadequate for the artists' milieus but also for phenomena other than social movements that were promoting democracy. Some Polish artists were involved in political dissidence, but at the same time they were focused on their professional careers, establishing their position in art world, and selling their art to galleries. The disintegration of institutional structures enabled (or forced) them to conduct such activities on their own. 'Civil society' as an analytical tool proposed by Kubik and Ekiert is widely used within the discourse of sociology. We can quote two such definitions:

> Civil society is a space or arena between household and the state which affords possibilities of concerted action and social self-organisation… Civil society occupies the middle ground between government and the private sector. It is the space we occupy when we are engaged neither in government activities (voting, paying taxes) nor in commerce (working, producing, shopping, consuming)[13].

> Civil society represents a sphere of dynamic and responsive public discourse between the state, the public sphere consisting of voluntary organisations, and the market sphere concerning private firms and unions. This concept of civil society can be applied to all countries if they have private organizations between the state and the family.[14]

This concept of social actors engaging in collective action is used as a bridge between the 'micro' and 'macro' levels. Finding convergence between the two sociological structures is one of key questions in contemporary sociology. These definitions also provide us with a concept of a space where actors are conducting their interactions, which is a suitable tool for research on various social phenomena.

2.4. Polish Culture in the Seventies

The activity of visual artists in the Polish People's Republic was put into the frames developed by state institutions, which were slowly falling apart by the Eighties. Kubik and Ekiert describe the social activity of these milieus as 'uninstitutionalized autonomy'.

---

12 For the definition of a social movement see: Della Porta, Donatella / Diani, Mario (eds.): Social Movements. An Introduction, 2nd edn, Malden/MA & Oxford: Blackwell Publishing, 2006. See also: Falk, Barbara J.: The Dilemmas of Dissidence in East-Central Europe, Budapest, New York/NY: Central European University Press, 2003; Osa, Maryjane: Networks in Opposition: Linking Organizations Through Activists in the Polish People's Republic, in: Diani, Mario / McAdam, Doug (eds.): Social Movements and Networks. Relational Approaches to Collective Action, Oxford: Oxford University Press, 2003; Staniszkis, Jadwiga: Poland's Self-Limiting Revolution, Princeton/NJ: Princeton University Press, 1984; Touraine, Alain et al.: Solidarity: Poland 1980-1981, Cambridge: Cambridge University Press, 1983.

13 Bernard, Amanda / Helmlich, Henny / Lehning, Percy B. (eds.): Civil Society and International Development, Paris: Paris North-South Centre of the Council of Europe OECD, 1998, p. 28. See also: Bron, Agnieszka; Schemmann, Michael (eds): Civil Society, Citizenship and Learning, Münster: LIT Verlag, 2001, pp. 29-137.

14 Janoski, Thomas: Citizenship and Civil Society, Cambridge: Cambridge University Press, 1998, p. 12.

2. The Second Life of the Polish Art World in the Eighties

They propose interesting categories that can be successfully used to analyse this particular case:

> Consequently, three forms of associations can be identified under state socialist regimes: (1) pseudo-autonomous (e.g. official trade unions or professional associations); (2) semi-autonomous (e.g. some churches and religious organizations); and (3) illegally autonomous (e.g. dissident groups or black-market networks).[15]

The milieus of Polish visual artists constitute a very interesting example of developing new kinds of partly grass-roots initiatives determined by political, social and economic factors. During the Seventies the state-run artists' union (ZPAP – Association of Polish Visual Artists) was very active, but it was also a time of new initiatives. So-called 'authors' galleries' were organized under the sponsorship of the Polish student organization (SZSP – Socialist Association of Polish Students) and were independent from the system of state-owned galleries, which were controlled indirectly by the guidelines of the Ministry of Culture. In the discourse of Polish art history, these galleries are perceived as the most influential phenomenon in the Seventies. It is necessary to present a brief definition of these institutions:

> A phenomenon in Polish artistic life in the Seventies (…); non-commercial display spaces where art exhibitions, artists' (but also critics', academics and just friends) meetings were organized. These galleries were mostly avoiding the censorship (…). (Some of the galleries, e.g. Gallery Remont in Warsaw and Gallery Akumulatory 2 in Poznań, were using a sponsorship of official institutions.) Intentional political art was rather scarce in these galleries. It was rather a movement based on presenting and exchanging information about neo-avant-garde art.[16]

These galleries have played a crucial role in promoting the concepts o neo-avant-garde visual art in Poland. Because of numerous private gatherings, such galleries also contributed to the development of common milieus where information was exchanged. Numerous artists and art critics involved in these activities gathered experience that would be used in the next decade.

The most important factor in the growth of these initiatives was the organized system of sponsorship. Aside from SZSP various institutions, such as local cultural centres, provided space for exhibitions. This support led to the growth of numerous local small-scale galleries. On the other hand, the Seventies also witnessed the creation of the art market. According to approximate statistics, there were 300 galleries in Poland in the Seventies.[17] At the time, a simple yet strict distinction was made

---

15 Ekiert, Grzegorz / Kubik, Jan: Civil Society from Abroad. The Role of Foreign Assistance in the Democratization of Poland, in: WCFIA Working Paper Series, No. 00-01, February 2000, p. 8, Harvard University, http://www.wcfia.harvard.edu/sites/default/files/91__2000-01%20 Ekiertfinal2.pdf
16 Giżycki, Marcin: Słownik kierunków, ruchów i kluczowych pojęć sztuki drugiej połowy XX wieku, Gdańsk: Wydawnictwo słowo/obraz/terytoria, 2002, p. 62.
17 Stokłosa, Bożenna: Artystyczno-społeczna problematyka zrzeszeń plastyków w Polsce w latach 1946–1976. Grupy twórcze i tzw. galerie niezależne, Warsaw, 1981, p. 82. Unpublished material,

between so-called union artists and artists involved in the authors' galleries. The first group encompassed mostly full-time artists whose insurance was organized by their union, which was also responsible for obtaining different contracts for them. But the artists involved in the 'authors' galleries' weren't earning any money. According to the Plattner text, these artists only reaped psychological gains. The whole system of authors' galleries was developed in the Seventies and somehow managed to struggle through all of the Eighties. It formed the basis for organizing exhibitions, but also for communication with other members of the outside world. This system was established not to avoid censorship, but rather to avoid the agency of the state-controlled and bureaucratic artists' union and the Bureau for Artistic Exhibitions. The problem was not only of an ideological nature but also concerned the fact that the employees of these institutions lived in the world of academic, figurative art and they established their own informal client-patron networks. In fact, most of the events in the authors' galleries were approved by the censors; the galleries also developed special tactics to gain the censors' permission to put on exhibitions.

2.5. 'Art Worlds' after Martial Law

In the Eighties this system was enriched by many completely informal galleries in private flats, where everything was organized without any state control; these events were called 'suitcase exhibitions'.[18] At the same time, diverse artistic discourses existed. There were many exhibitions of religious art organized in strict collaboration with the Catholic Church and Solidarity. Legal private galleries were selling functional art, portraits and landscapes. Meanwhile, a few groups of new expressionists arose, but the neo-avant-garde artists also continued their activities and kept in contact with similar circles in the West.

I aim to present a few of the different tactics that members of these informal circles used to publicize their artworks in their grass-roots public sphere. In the Eighties this cultural life was even more important than the one organized by state-owned institutions. Most of the artists boycotted these institutions after the imposition of martial law in 1981. The map of Polish visual culture in the Eighties encompasses a lot of small but well-connected islands. People involved in these activities after 1989 developed a new system of cultural life based on state-owned institutions and the commercial art market as well. This sphere of social activity can be compared with similar phenomena in other circles.

The most important turning point in Polish artistic life was the imposition of martial law on 13 December 1981. In the Eighties such initiatives continued, but the

---

Institute of Art, Polish Academy of Sciences.
18 See: Rottenberg, Anda: Przeciąg. Teksty o sztuce polskiej lat 80, Warszawa: Open Art Projects, 2009.

2. The Second Life of the Polish Art World in the Eighties

situation in the field of visual art was far more complicated than in the previous decade. In keeping with Kubik and Ekiert's approach, I can identify three essentially different art worlds with respect to their level of autonomy in Communist Poland. The first level was pseudo-autonomous and concerned the state-run artists' union, ZPAP. Because of its support for Solidarity in 1983, ZPAP was suspended and liquidated.

> The ZPAP is – with its membership estimated at 11,000 – the numerically strongest creative union in Poland. [...] During the stormy Solidarity days ZPAP unequivocally sided with the free labor movement and was among the first creative unions to join the democratic opposition movement. [...] Following the imposition of martial law in December 1981, ZPAP was suspended, along with all other similar unions and put in official limbo for more than four months. Reactivated on 30 April 1982, it has been exposed to all kinds of ideological, administrative and financial pressure ever since. [...] The community's deliberate refusal to accept the regime's attempts to dictate to it appears all the more heroic as the actual state of artists' working and living conditions has been admittedly deteriorating alarmingly over the last few years.[19]

After disbanding ZPAP the authorities created a new union called ZPAMiG, the Association of Polish Painters and Graphic Artists, which was comprised of so-called *party artists* who were actively (or more often passively) supporting the authorities' policy. The authorities also created the Committee of Polish Party Artists under the auspices of the Department of Culture of PUWP. Artists who participated in this committee were perceived as hard-line Communists and were ostentatiously ignored by other milieus. Some of ZPAP's tasks were taken over by 'Sztuka Polska' (Polish Art), the state-owned art management company, which was responsible among other things for selling art pieces.[20]

Starting in the Seventies, there were also private but completely legal galleries in Poland; these would fall into Kubik and Ekiert's semi-autonomous category by virtue of having more distance from the state than the artists' union. Some of them aimed to show new art and were perceived as kinds of authors' galleries, but apart from such places there were also commercial galleries focused mostly on selling art. The most famous private gallery was run by Anna Maria Potocka in Cracow.[21] Her gallery was located in a private flat, but it was legally registered as an exhibition space.

> The Department for Art and Culture of the city of Cracow is supporting the request of Anna Maria Potocka concerning using her flat as a private /non-commercial/ art gallery. [...] The existence of private galleries is in accordance with cultural policy. The existence of such places is sanctioned by the guidelines of the Ministry of Culture and Art.[22]

---

19   The Taming of Intellectual Dissent. The Fine Arts, Radio Free Europe report 19 March 1983, Herder Institut, Marburg, sign. P 720; Sokołowski, Grzegorz: Wymuszona decyzja, in: Trybuna Ludu, 23–24 April 1983.
20   Han, Ewa: Co to jest 'Sztuka Polska'?, in: Słowo Polskie, 28 September 1983.
21   http://www.moma.pl/, accessed 15 June 2009.
22   Official letter from Director of Department of Culture and Art of the city of Cracow to Director of Krowodrza district 28 February 1980, Potocka Gallery archive.

The running of such a gallery in Cracow was also portrayed very positively in the local newspaper.[23] Apart from such non-commercial galleries, in the Eighties some galleries were dedicated to selling art. The most unique was probably a gallery in Warsaw that sold religious art.

> On the last day of the Pope's visit to Poland, the first and only salon of religious art was opened. The trade company Veritas [which belongs to the Catholic Church – PW] has opened this place because of the growing interest from numerous believers and artists in sacral art.[24]

The Eighties also saw the emergence of new actors on the art market.

> The crisis of the Polish economy has serious consequences for the lives of visual artists. […] A new, previously unknown phenomenon is the growth of attractive orders for visual art from private entrepreneurs and Polish companies with foreign capital.[25]

Polish artists also developed a strategy for participating in the Western art market during their travels to West Berlin.

> Artists departing from Poland for their exhibitions abroad […] were probably selling some of their artwork. These works were mostly sold for relatively low prices – especially in Western Germany and West Berlin – however, these transactions are still profitable for artists because there are no brokers and state companies responsible for foreign trade. Artists can avoid paying taxes and they are exchanging money for black market exchange rates. Another important factor is the situation in our country with respect to the availability of paint, paper, tools and chemicals. Such materials are quite often unavailable in Poland and it is only possible to buy such things abroad.[26]

The third tier of the Polish art world in the Eighties was illegal and autonomous and manifested in the growth of completely informal and illegal exhibitions in private flats, ateliers and churches. This phenomenon was described in a few books and articles mostly written by authors who had participated in these exhibitions.[27] The events are described merely as a kind of political activity, i.e. as an act of resistance against the oppressive Communist state. We need to remember that even this kind of activity could be put in the frame of an artist's professional career. Rottenberg described this issue: Those who were continuously making exhibitions in churches, after 1989 have

---

23 Grzegorczyk, Elżbieta: Z prywatnej pasji zjawisko artystyczne, in: Echo Krakowa, 5 February 1974.
24 W Warszawie powstał pierwsza galeria sztuki religijnej, in: Dziennik Polski, 7 July 1983.
25 Czejarek, Karol: Plastycy wobec kryzysu, in: Życie Literackie, 25 March 1984.
26 Sprawozdanie z wyjazdów służbowych i udziału polskich twórców w międzynarodowych imprezach plastycznych, 1983, Archive of Ministry of Culture, sign. 1511/21.1.
27 The most important book about this activity is: Wojciechowski, Aleksander: Czas smutku, czas nadziei, Warsaw: Wydawnictwa Artystyczne i Filmowe, 1992. Such activity was also recognized abroad, see for example: Kowalski, Sara: Kleiner Umsatz, hohe Belastung. Private Kunstgalerien im sozialistischen Polen, in: Frankfurter Allgemeine Zeitung, 25 July 1986; Kowalski, Sara: Export. Wie Polen an der Kunst verdient, in: Frankfurter Allgemeine Zeitung, 16 August 1986.

established a strong lobby based on claims. This group had recognised they have to be rewarded for their struggle.[28]

The various Polish milieus of visual artists in the Eighties are examples of the politically and economically motivated growth of new forms of social life. Similar to other groups of artists but also engaging in a wider array of different social initiatives, the activity of visual artists had previously been programmed by the Communist authorities through the creation of the artists' union (ZPAP), which was developed to provide welfare services but also to exert control over this milieu. Since the end of the Sixties, however, this system had gradually been decreasing its functions, and in the Eighties, it broke down completely. Different strategies used by Polish artists for organizing their professional careers and supporting themselves were determined by the social and economic situation in Poland. After 1989 individuals involved in the art world mostly continued their activity on the art market or became employees of state cultural institutions. When we are conducting research on phenomena described as 'civil society', we have to remember that the social actors participating in it were motivated by various (sometimes selfish) reasons. They were also often focused on achieving short-term goals. A social change – in this case the field of culture – was caused by different and very complex factors. Describing the activity of particular milieus as a dependent variable can lead to misappropriate teleology.

---

28 Rottenberg, Anda: Przeciąg. Teksty o sztuce polskiej lat 80, Warszawa: Open Art Projects, 2009, p. 387.

*Part II. Civil Society and Ethnic Divisions.
The Case of the Western Balkans*

Tonči Valentić

3. History and Memory. Media Discourse and the Construction of National Identities

3.1. Introduction

In recent decades, the traditional notions of historiography and sociology have changed significantly: the influence of various interdisciplinary perspectives such as philosophy as well as the cultural changes in the field of humanities have fostered processes of analysing historical events as narratives and have unveiled elements of narration in official historical documents. These changes have given rise to different perspectives on a specific historical event and have spurred the growth of approaches that deal with the problem of memory and mental images as reliable scholarly sources when analysing historical data. Self-understandings and subjective descriptions of the world became very important in particular among the historians and sociologists studying Eastern Europe after the collapse of communism due to the dramatic changes that followed. In short, people found themselves in a completely new world, but living with a 'new past', a past which has continually been reconstructed and remapped, both by dominant post-socialist ideologies and by the memories of people who lived under socialism. In that sense, scholars not only found themselves in an awkward position as members of disciplines bewildered by the fictional character of their scholarly subject, but they were also faced with new chronologies and the compression of elapsed historical time that took place in Central and Eastern Europe.

South-eastern Europe (or, more accurately, the Western Balkans) has always been a historiographical battlefield: located between imperial and local powers and shaped by a complex configuration of perpetual changes of borders, it has had to continually rearticulate *collective* and *individual* identities. So far, many prominent scholars have analysed the changes that occurred in the recent decade in terms of sociological, anthropological, psychological or even ethical inquiry. Nevertheless, there is a lack of deeper analysis regarding cultural memory and especially the notion of revising 'official' memory, which tends to pose a major interpretational challenge. My Ph.D. research tries to fill that gap. In the period of transitional and globalization processes, which has provoked further rethinking of collective memory/ies with respect to identity models, research on the region's socialist heritage calls for deeper analysis in the field of national culture as well as rethinking existing texts. In short, I intend to reconsider the highly complex relationship between memory, identity and power with the main goal of analysing various discourses of cultural and social memory as well as 'forgetting strategies' in South-eastern Europe. As I mentioned above, memory plays a very important role in the construction of national, regional and local identities and it has often been misused (or abused) by the power structures that took over and narratively 'occupied' the past as a powerful scientific tool for political wars.

In my Ph.D. thesis, I will focus on mental images and the different discourse mechanisms that produce certain imagery and examine the ways in which they have been (and still are) mentally constructed and distributed in the media. In that sense, I will specifically examine traditional representations of the Balkan region, thereby endeavouring to unveil the mental maps, processes of identity creation and various acts of identification that combined to introduce a discomfited perspective and turn this geographic metonym into a non-geographical referent. Since the discourse on *Balkanism* is double-edged, meaning that it has always been predicated on two extreme notions (i.e. the bloody Balkans versus Oriental Romanticism), both European and indigenous narratives on the respective subject have always been ethically biased. The rhetoric of Balkanization as a sociological concept calls for interdisciplinary research: studying the relationship between identity and power in the Balkan region entails historical, sociological, cultural, post-colonial and philosophical perspectives. Therefore, I intend to combine various approaches in order to answer some basic questions: Which strategies have been enacted and used to cast the Balkans as a notorious 'European Other'? How does the representation of the region in the media reflect processes of Balkanization and does it produce a skewed perspective? Has this discourse been challenged and changed, and is it promoted or rather advocated by local intellectuals? What are the points of reference concerning the reluctance to be considered part of Eastern Europe (both geographically as well as ideologically)? Is that discourse internalized or rather imported from 'outside'? In other words, this contribution, in the form of a Ph.D. outline, focuses on the problem of the interplay between two major actors: both the Western and Eastern notions that have given rise to a variety of media discourses on the above-mentioned subject.

3.2. Framing the Concept

To fully address the subject, it is of crucial importance to assess the media's role in shaping Balkanism as a culturally constructed discourse. Therefore, I will closely examine the role of daily and weekly newspapers and political magazines using a case study on Croatia covering the period from 1995 to 2008. The major field of research is therefore the construction of media discourse on the Balkans in the aforementioned period with the underlying hypothesis that *media produce symbolic identities that are recognizable in the form of reinvented and remapped historical narratives*. Those stereotypes not only reflect dominant political views, but also underscore the distance from Balkanism discourse within societies in the Balkan region: the purveyors of official political ideology and historiography in Croatia in the period from 1995 to 2000 hesitated to symbolically place Croatia in the Balkan region, instead promoting its Mediterranean and Central European identity, i.e. inventing imaginary mental geographies. Following the social and political changes arising from the 2000 elections, there were numerous efforts to cognitively map and (dis)locate Croatian identity as both 'European' and 'Balkan': those social transformations are reflected and easily observable in various media reports, news, essays and commentaries, and are clearly visible in headlines, titles, presentation of various social events, etc.

The major focus in this analysis is on printed media precisely because I want to stress the importance of newspapers as powerful tools in the creation of symbolic identity, whereby politically-induced discourse is deployed to remap collective memory (e.g. the occurrence of so-called 'Yugonostalgia' qualified as a 'return to Balkanization' and scepticism towards integration processes regarding accession to the EU). I argue that there is a strong link between notions of nostalgia (memory) and discourse on Balkanism (pseudo-Orientalism): symbolic identity has been (re)constructed as the interplay between different actors in the field, namely newspapers, public opinion and official political ideology.

Since it is impossible to fully analyse the entire period of time (thirteen years), my Ph.D. thesis focuses on media discourse during three major regional events: a) 1995, the year the war ended in Croatia; b) 1999/2000, when the authoritarian political party lost elections; and c) 2007, when the process of integration into the European Union was forcefully initiated. I argue that those periods are the clearest manifestations of the media's transformation of Balkan discourse into a tool for the collective shaping of cultural and symbolic identity as a sort of relationship between scholarly historiography and individual memory (Balkanism has often been portrayed as a dishonourable legacy of socialism, while the signifier 'Europe' has stood for civilization and cultural progress, which were understood as the main features of Croatian society throughout its entire national history).

3.3. The Discourse on Balkanism and Its Ideological Context

Hermann Keyserling once stated: 'If the Balkans did not exist, it would be necessary to invent them.'[1] Popular notions about the region have mostly been shaped by classical colonial/anthropological methods of collecting data: on the basis of various ethnographic travel reports, accounts of adventure journeys, diplomatic statements, Romantic and gothic novels, both inappropriately false and overtly romanticized images of the Balkan region as a 'middle space' between reality and fantasy have been fabricated. The notion of Balkanism has thus emerged as a completely different

---

1 Quoted in Todorova, Maria: Imagining the Balkans, New York: Oxford University Press, 1997, p. 116.

semantic field from Orientalism. In that sense, the 'ontology of the Balkans' (as developed in Todorova[2]) bears predominant responsibility for the construction of the ethnic, national, social and political sense of belonging, and hence the identity of the peoples in South-eastern Europe has always been relational, i.e. dependent on mental images produced in the West. Consequently, a fictional and historically 'invented' Balkan territory was mythologized, thus becoming synonymous with wars, violence, political upheavals and social disorder. The cultural construction of an imagined 'Other' has not produced Balkanism merely as a prosaic type of ethnocentrism, but moreover as the structural element of the expansion of European capitalism in the beginning of the twentieth century. In that sense, patterns of Balkanization are inevitably classified as negative, and the Balkans, as a 'European Other', have served as a reservoir of negative stereotypes contrasting with the ostensibly more 'civilized' European identity.

Reintroducing that stereotype in the early 1990s was possible mainly due to the academic discourse that presented vague media reports and fictional stories as true and undisputable facts, thus turning false representations into firm, seemingly unambiguous data. Once again, the media's role in producing national stereotypes went hand in hand with 'official' scholarly inquiry and its claims of objective knowledge: akin to the novels from the end of the nineteenth century, the Balkans were now presented in terms of primordial violence, inefficient and authoritarian political leadership, and an inability to assimilate into the civilized world either socially or culturally. Keeping that in mind, it is of crucial importance to unveil the theoretical and conceptual apparatuses that produce Balkan imagery in terms of 'opposite attractions': namely, to simultaneously impress and disappoint Western observers (Romanticism versus barbarism).

Obviously, those negative stereotypes are the inevitable results of long-term *semantic sedimentation*; however, they do not operate merely on the level of linguistics, but as performative discursive tools. In order to understand the ideological mechanisms that produce such imagery, one has to become acquainted with their pragmatic function within a wider context (among numerous contributions to the topic, the works of Savić and Bijelić, Kourvetaris, Detrez and Plas, as well as those of Čolović, Bakić-Hayden and Goldsworthy deserve mention[3]). The rhetoric of Balkanization refers precisely to those connotations, and discourse is understood in its classical philosophical notion as a linguistic structure used as one of the representational forms: it is not

---

2   Refers to the same book.
3   Cited as follows: Savić, Obrad / Bijelić, Dušan (eds): Balkan as Metaphor, Cambridge/MA: MIT Press, 2005; Kourvetaris, George (ed.): The new Balkans. Disintegration and reconstruction, Boulder/CO: East European Monographs, 2002; Detrez, Raymond / Plas, Pieter: Developing cultural identity in the Balkans. Convergence vs. divergence, Brussels et al.: Peter Lang, 2005; Čolović, Ivan: Politika simbola. Ogledi o političkoj antropologiji, Belgrade: XX vek, 2000; Goldsworthy, Vesna: Inventing Ruritania. The Imperialism of the Imagination, New Haven/CT, London: Yale University Press, 1998; Bakić-Hayden, Milica: Varijacije na temu 'Balkan', Belgrade: Filip Višnjić, 2006.

only a medium that depicts reality, but one of its prominent features is to distort it, to make its borders vague and obscure. Knowledge transferred in discourse is institutionalized in practices best described as colonial interpretations. On the other hand, one could convincingly argue that just as there is an 'imaginary Balkans', there is also an 'imaginary Europe', perceived as standing for positive social and cultural values. In that sense, Western Europe is often also seen in Eastern Europe as a reservoir of stereotypes, just as the Balkans are frequently perceived abroad as a dark empire of bloodshed, mystery and brutal political upheaval.

3.4. The Media and Symbolic Construction of National Identity

As already stated, many prominent sociologists, anthropologists and historians have so far reaffirmed role of the media in the articulation of collective identities, but there is a significant lack of deeper inquiry regarding certain countries in the region that has been recently (and politically correctly) dubbed the 'Western Balkans'. Memory plays an important role in shaping social identities, but is often abused by those in power to gain legitimacy. One of the tasks of my Ph.D. project is to point out the ways in which newspaper texts in Croatia in the described periods equated socialism with Balkanism: from an epistemological point of view, one may conclude that there is a cognitive value in the discourse of transition from Balkan to European, and that the notion of Balkan in the public discourse is closely related to the concepts of post-socialism and *Yugonostalgia* in general. Consequently, there is a subtle interplay between the media's rhetoric and symbolic identity, which will be emphasized in this work. The pattern is usually the same: the post-socialist transition brought out 'nostalgia' as a semantically repulsive term, understood as backwardness and regression forged into a lament for times past (one of the most valuable approaches is advocated by Boym[4]).

Different approaches are necessary to appropriately assess the issue of Balkanism as a pulsating historical narrative, and especially to address the problem of the media's reconstruction of personal past experience (socialist culture versus post-socialist, bewildering capitalism), which differs from firm data in its authenticity. History is born at the moment when social memory starts to collapse and disintegrate, when it ceases to be socially functional. According to that view, there exists only one historiography, but there are numerous collective memories. The analytical question still waiting to be answered is this one: Is academic revisionism and rethinking of the past epistemologically advanced and superior to the popular, 'everyday' notion of past? In other words, does historiography, as a complex web of ideologically biased discourses, have greater value than the 'everyday, common memory' of members of a certain community? I believe this problem is clearly visible in Croatia after the collapse of communism and

---

[4] Boym, Svetlana: The Future of Nostalgia, New York: Basic Books, 2001.

the epistemological break resulting from the repression of memory and the creation of a completely new cultural and national identity. On the basis of claiming rights to properly interpret the past, the discourse of Balkanization not only ideologically occupies the field of social memory, but also assumes the false role of archiving collective memory, thus making it appear more coherent, reasonable and 'scientific'.

In the context of my research, it is important to analyse strategies of 'forbidden memory' from the socialist period, i.e. the period before 1991 in Croatia. The ideological function of media discourse up until 2000 was to cut all mental links with the Balkans and to place Croatia and Croatians culturally, socially and geopolitically on the map of Central Europe and the Mediterranean. This tendency was especially criticized among those who witnessed on their own identity as multifaceted, those who neither wanted to equate socialism with Balkanism nor to obey the enforced rules of the newly established patterns of cultural identification. However, the discourse changed after year 2000 and one of the tasks in my dissertation is to point out the main reasons for that epistemological shift. The sociological enquiries in the field to date have tried to analyse claims for the creation of an identity that does not subsume itself under the common umbrella of identity politics.

3.5. Ph.D. Hypothesis

On the premise of the previously developed arguments, theoretical background and interdisciplinary studies mentioned in the first part of this contribution, the main hypothesis on the notion of construction of national identities with respect to the ambivalent link between memory and history within the context of media discourse can be most accurately summed up in the following lines:

The discourse on Balkanism has been widely present in Croatia in the last twenty years and has so far hugely influenced the trajectory of social and political events. The discourse itself underwent major changes in three different periods: firstly, in the period up until 1995, when collective memory on the socialist era was repressed and equated with 'nostalgia for Balkanism'; at the same time, media coverage of social events reflected a political attitude that fostered an image of Croatia as a Western and Mediterranean country, constantly emphasizing its rootedness in the Western European cultural and religious context. 'Balkan' came to be a metaphor for the 'dark ages' of socialism while Europe symbolized civilization. Since 2000, media rhetoric has ceased to present Balkan as an unequivocally negative term, and after 2007 (during debates over whether Croatia should join the European Union) it started to gain some positive connotations, though primarily in the field of popular culture. However, I argue that the ideological matrix of 'Balkanism' is present even now and exceedingly influential when it comes to the construction of symbolic identity. Moreover, that problem has not yet been properly addressed in scholarship done on the issue, especially in disciplines such as sociology and historiography. The main purpose of this thesis is to point out that the social and political matrix is still influenced today by media discourse on Balkanism and Europeanism, a discourse that utilizes the same old patterns of identity creation and similar discursive mechanisms. In that sense, power elites eagerly and consciously use and abuse stereotypes invented in the West in the late nineteenth century, thus reproducing and enforcing collective ethnic and cultural identification that can be most accurately described as approval or recognition of pre-established post-colonial patterns leading up to 'metaphorical colonization'. The discourse on the Balkans was not only created in the West but has also been wisely used and selectively (re)mapped and (re)used under similar conditions in the respective region; for example, the notion of the inferiority complex became normative due to media influence.

Inevitably, using only media discourse in the analysis cannot yield a complete and all-encompassing conclusion on the effects of the media on the public sphere and on the creation of various collective identities. Such an approach would require long-term research of all spheres of society with numerous methodological patterns. For that reason, intensive research focused on the interdependence of politics and media as well as their influence on the social fabric exceeds the scope of a single Ph.D. project, and hence my thesis will concentrate on one aspect of this rhetoric: *the analysis of the production and distribution of stereotypes of Balkanization in the given periods as evidenced in selected newspapers and magazines.*

3.6. Main Methods of Research and Its Major Aim

My research consists of equally weighted theoretical and empirical components. In the theoretical part I will extensively analyse mutual links and interconnections between media rhetoric and national identities, discuss previous research in the field and critically evaluate its contribution. The empirical part is based upon the collection and analysis of data on the ways in which Balkanism has been presented as an integral part of the ethnic and cultural identity of Croatians. The data will be collected from content analysis and discourse analysis of various newspapers from 1995 up to now, concentrating on the notions of 'Balkan' and 'European' in the context of terms such as memory, socialism, civility, etc. Selection will be based on the 'rhetoric of Balkanization' in state-owned magazines and journals (e.g. Vjesnik, Večernji list, Hrvatsko slovo, etc.), independent ones (Feral Tribune, Zarez, etc.) and commercial newspapers (24 sata, Nacional, Globus) in the three periods described above. Printed media have been selected for various reasons: firstly, although television is by far the most powerful media and the major conveyor of political propaganda, research based on televised reports and news is more difficult to execute due to the complexity of analysing visual material and its semantics. Secondly, given the fact that printed media are characterized by a plurality of approaches (there were almost no private TV channels at that time, i.e. channels that were not owned by the state), it is possible to take a comparative approach and put emphasis on the differences between them. Thirdly, textual analysis is more suitable and accurate in this case: in semantic and linguistic interpretations of media coverage, the patterns of Balkanization rhetoric are more observable and discernible. I will not take regional differences (i.e. newspapers from different counties or cities) into consideration as this would require a more detailed analysis that goes beyond the major issues raised in my dissertation.

Some of the research questions are: 1) How is the problem of 'Yugonostalgia' and the socialist legacy in the media associated with the discourse on Balkanism and *why*? 2) What kind of discourse are newspapers using in order to form symbolic identity, i.e. how are political and social upheavals reflected in media texts? 3) What are the most dominant forms of this rhetoric and what is the crucial difference between left-oriented and right-oriented magazines and journals? 4) Why do 'semantic turns' occur in media rhetoric in crucial periods of social distortions (e.g. a pluralist notion of identities as both Balkan and European around 2000, or the disappearance of the term 'Southeastern Europe', which has been subsequently replaced by the politically favoured term 'Western Balkans')? 5) Is media research intrinsically related to the deeper analysis of socio-cultural changes in Croatian society in the given periods? 6) Is there a discrepancy between sociological and ethnographic/socio-anthropological scholarship on belonging to Balkan or European civilization and the existing media coverage? 7) Are the so-called independent or non-commercial newspapers also imbued by the rhetoric of Balkanization and do they follow the same colonial patterns? 8) What are the key words and concepts used to describe the Yugoslav and post-Yugoslav experience in relation to the value-burdened distinctions of equating the Balkans with socialism and underdevelopment, and Europe with freedom and development? These are some of the potential questions that I will try to properly address and answer in the thesis, relying both on a theoretical background and the analysis of empirical data as described above.

The emphasis has to be on the qualitative analysis of empirical data, i.e. on reading texts from a narrative and semiotic perspective, since they tend to be equally important. The main criteria in evaluating this qualitative research will consequently be multiple and executed in three phases: choosing and collecting appropriate data, providing a description for the purpose of structuring the material, and ending with a final evaluation. Equal emphasis will be placed on formal content analysis and purely textual analysis due to their importance: in order to study media discourse, it is necessary to focus on language usage and metaphors, which are its relevant components. For that reason, the main aim of my research is to show the extent to which the media's presentation of the Balkans is based on stereotypes and to question the hypothesis of whether there are causal links that could explain the occurrence of this kind of rhetoric

3. History and Memory

in periods of social reformulation of collective identities and memory politics (e.g. during the years 1995, 2000 and 2008). In addition, as a parallel approach I will also examine the differences between the countries in the region that have already become members of the EU (such as Slovenia) and those in which similar patterns of media discourse can be found (such as in Serbia or Bosnia and Herzegovina). Subsequently, the question of national identity will be analysed from a symbolic and political – and not merely cultural – perspective. Since up to now there has been no systematic and academic analysis of the rhetoric of Balkanization in the media in the Western Balkans region, I hope this Ph.D. thesis can help to bridge the gap from a sociological standpoint. Hence, one of its major tasks is to open a dialogue on that issue, not only within the academic community, but also (and no less importantly) in the wider social context. This will entail questioning the basic structures of media influence on national and symbolic identification in general, which might be a good starting point for forthcoming (not inevitably academic) inquiries.

Bojan Bilić

4. Mapping the Ephemeral.
Yugoslav Civic Activism and the 1990s Conflicts

4.1. Introduction

The extremely violent character of the wars of Yugoslav succession continues to inspire sociological research almost fifteen years after the Dayton Agreement brought peace to the region. Many studies on the issue, mostly grounded in essentialist definitions of ethnic identity, advance the thesis that the conflict in the former Yugoslavia erupted as a consequence of a weak civil society that was incapable of subverting the inflammatory politics of nationalism and xenophobia. However, there were in fact brave efforts to tame the tempest, but these attempts have largely been under-researched due to the emphasis on their alleged 'failure' to achieve peace. These unsung anti-war initiatives deserve closer scrutiny: who drove them and why did they fail?

My doctoral project, whose principal theoretical assumptions are outlined in this chapter, will attempt to unearth and map out the diverse range of civic movements that took place in almost all Yugoslav republics. By examining a wide range of anti-war initiatives, including their programmes and protagonists, this research will endeavour to determine which factors led to their rather quick suppression by nationalist authorities and thus to their 'failure' to stem the tide of violence. I presume that most of the pan-Yugoslav pacifist activism was undertaken by a cosmopolitan and urban cultural elite incapable of reaching the wider layers of society, which ultimately embraced the officially promoted rhetoric extolling ethnic homogeneity. Hampered by impaired communication channels between the republics, Yugoslav peace activists, themselves the products of rigid communist patterns of political and social life, were overwhelmed by the complexity of orchestrating the country's peaceful dissolution. Lacking important mobilization skills and the political experience of independent activism, they simply failed to generate a more relevant anti-war movement. Furthermore, many of the activists were probably unaware of the severity of the situation.

The purpose of this chapter is to identify a knowledge gap in what has by now become a rather prolific area of Eastern European scholarship, i.e. the Yugoslav wars of succession. By zeroing in on the thus far largely neglected anti-war initiatives, I hope to give their protagonists and programmes some long overdue credit in post-Yugoslav scholarship. This will be followed by a brief critical review of three academic contributions about the experience of alternative non-ethnonationalistic forms of political behaviour in the context of the Yugoslav conflict. I will finally explain how my research questions and corresponding working hypotheses stem from the identified deficiencies of the existing literature.

4.2. Yugoslavia's Dissolution and the Non-Ethnonationalist Initiatives

Yugoslav anti-war campaigns immediately prior and during the conflict in the 1990s are rarely, if ever, the focal point of sociological studies on the disintegration of the former Yugoslavia. This is in large part due to the ways in which scholars on the region perceive the causes of the destructive nationalism and the country's ultimate dissolution.

One group of authors, led by Sabrina P. Ramet[1], argues that Communist Yugoslavia should be seen in the framework of internal colonialism, in which the Serbs constituted a hegemonic ethnic group that frequently attempted to obstruct the legitimate interests of its culturally and politically more advanced Western compatriots. Croatia's and Slovenia's claims for independence clashed with Serbia's expansionist attitudes. The tension culminated with the 1989 implosion of socialism in Eastern Europe and the gradual exhaustion of the ideology of 'brotherhood and unity' that had been propagated by the Yugoslav Communist regime over the years.

The American historian of Serbian origin, Alex Dragnic[2], offers a diametrically opposite view by arguing that Slovenia and Croatia were in fact able to assert themselves as autonomous political subjects thanks to the Serbian political elite, which incorporated them into the Kingdom of Yugoslavia. However, many Serbs felt disenfranchised by the emergence of Communist Yugoslavia when they found themselves treated as national minorities in those parts of Croatia and Bosnia where they had constituted the autochthonic population for centuries. On the basis of this logic, Dragnic suggests that it was actually the Serbs, rather than Croats or Slovenes, who were entitled to the formation of an ethnically homogeneous nation-state following the breakdown of Communism.

At the same time, another set of authors (for example, Koen Koch[3]) is trying to understand the reasons for ethno-national mobilization and paying particular attention to the ways in which ethnically-oriented elites inflate certain aspects of ethnicity in order to achieve their political goals. These authors presume that the members of a certain ethnic group might not be equally interested in advancing the group's

---

1 Ramet, Sabrina: Balkan Babel: Politics, Culture and Religion in Yugoslavia, Boulder/CO: Westview Press, 1992.
2 Dragnic, Alex: Yugoslavia's Disintegration and the Struggle for Truth, Boulder/CO: East European Monographs, 1995.
3 Koch, Koen: Conflicting Visions of State and Society in Present-Day Yugoslavia, in: van den Heuvel, Martin / Siccama, Jan (eds): The Disintegration of Yugoslavia, Amsterdam: Rodopi, 1992, passim.

4. Mapping the Ephemeral

separatist aspirations, but recognize that the authorities are able to manipulate the population by exploiting nationalist sentiments and shaping the collective memory to suit their interests. In that sense, Koch posits that towards the end of the Yugoslav Communist regime there might have been an appreciable difference in how the elites and ordinary citizens understood ethnicity.

It appears, more generally, that the research outlined above is based on the paradigm that multinational societies are by definition conflictual and characterized by a tendency towards ethnically homogeneous nation-states.[4] Ethnic identity is in these studies perceived as a fixed category that is superimposed over a whole range of other possible identities. It is therefore no wonder that when essentialized nationalist sentiments acquire central status, not much space is left for anti-war or anti-nationalist initiatives regardless of their form or scope. However, the mere fact that these initiatives are undertaken at all debunks the idea that all political mobilization stems from ethnicity and a universal desire to live in separate and ethnically homogeneous states.[5]

Additionally, there are at least two further reasons for the paucity of Yugoslav civil society studies. The first of these is that civic and political contention is intrinsically episodic. The instances of civic challenges to the rapidly degenerating Communist system in Yugoslavia became increasingly weak and brief.[6] Traditional civil society literature tends to gloss over these short-lived attempts, instead focusing on permanent organizations or at least those that managed to better withstand the pressures of the given regime.[7]

Secondly, more extensive research covering the entire territory of the former Yugoslavia became increasingly difficult in the immediate post-war period due to a couple of inter-related factors. For example, contact with former academic colleagues was scarce and the exchange of information was difficult. After the fragmentation of the country, the focus was quickly and sometimes rather purposefully shifted from the federal (Yugoslav) level to the particular concerns of the newborn nation-states. However, the time now seems ripe for a reversal of this trend. As the deafening nationalist clamour has subsided and some of the deepest wounds are slowly healing, it is the task of post-Yugoslav historiography, sociology and political science to offer critical and empirically founded readings of the events surrounding Yugoslavia's demise.[8]

---

4   Devic, Ana: Anti-War Initiatives and the Un-making of Civic Identities in the Former Yugoslav Republics, in: Journal of Historical Sociology, 1997 (Vol. 10), No. 2, pp. 127–156.
5   Although many sources give national identity centre stage, there are also much more nuanced and historically and culturally informed studies. See e.g. Sekelj, Laslo: Yugoslavia. The Process of Disintegration, Boulder/CO: Eastern European Monographs, 1992.
6   Licht, Sonja: Civil society, democracy and the Yugoslav war, in: Spencer, Metta (ed.): The Lessons of Yugoslavia, New York: Elsevier Science, 2000, pp. 111–124, passim.
7   Kaldor, Mary: Global Civil Society, Oxford: Oxford University Press, 2003.
8   See e.g. Jovic, Dejan: Yugoslavia. A State that Withered Away, West Lafayette/IN: Purdue University Press, 2009.

While I recognize the devastating impact that ideologically manipulated nationalist sentiments had on the course of Yugoslavia's disintegration, my proposed research is prompted by a sense of dissatisfaction with the academic trend of ignoring the range of civic initiatives aimed at averting the Yugoslav catastrophe in the 1990s. I believe that these initiatives, although diverse in size and sometimes contradictory in nature, deserve public appreciation as testaments of civic courage and social responsibility. The study of civic action forces the researcher to take a serious look at Yugoslav politics, society and culture, and thereby to give agency back to the citizens of the devastated country. By the same token, I intend to demonstrate how the war, far from being an inevitability produced by ancient hatreds, was simply one option that could have been avoided.

4.3. Yugoslav Civic Activism

Despite the repressive pre-communist historical legacy as well as the authoritarian character of Yugoslav socialism, certain spheres of social life did enjoy a considerable level of autonomy in communist Yugoslavia.[9] This somewhat permissive climate, especially in the last years of the regime, allowed for the emergence of civil society organizations; however, such groups ultimately failed to launch a socially and politically relevant pacifist movement immediately prior to the eruption of hostilities in the 1990s. Due to the reasons outlined above as well as their failure to cohere into a force that could have decisively resisted the subsequent authoritarian regimes, the efforts of Yugoslav civil society[10] have thus largely been ignored in sociological and political science research on the subject. There are three exceptions.

Ana Devic was among the first to document anti-war initiatives that took place on Yugoslav territory prior to the armed conflict.[11] Her contribution is rather exhaustive in that she lists the campaigns in all Yugoslav republics and provinces. However, due to the absence of a broader theoretical framework, the empirical data (whose source is often not completely clear) fail to cohere into a cogent analysis. Devic offers 'helpful hints from theory' and rightly shows that anti-war activism mobilized the most

---

9   Pavlović, Vukasin: Civilno društvo i demokratija, Belgrade: Službeni glasnik, 2006.
10 *Civil society* is a concept whose long historical evolution is inextricably interwoven with the development of Western European social and political thought. It in that sense resists an easy transfer from the cultural sphere in which it was conceived and continues to evolve. I have nevertheless opted to use the term not only because it is becoming increasingly popular beyond the 'borders' of the Western world, but also because the movements and organizations that will be examined here were trying to promote *civility* in the literal sense. I use the terms *civil society* and *civic activism* interchangeably and perceive *civil society* as consisting of *civic activists* engaged in a wide array of activities ranging from petitions to protests.
11 Devic, Ana: Anti-War Initiatives and the Un-making of Civic Identities in the Former Yugoslav Republics, in: Journal of Historical Sociology, 1997 (Vol. 10), No. 2, pp. 127–156.

4. Mapping the Ephemeral 51

urban segments of Yugoslav society, but she does not really demonstrate how these social movement theories can account for the unmaking of Yugoslav civic identities.

Meanwhile, Eric Gordy gives an empirically rich account of Serbia's political life throughout the 1990s.[12] He analyses how the Serbian regime managed to stay in power in spite of the fact that normal parameters of political science would have predicted a much earlier demise. The author's main argument is that the regime successfully managed to obstruct alternatives in practically all spheres of social and political life. However, Gordy focuses only on Serbia and does not deal specifically with anti-war initiatives and organizations, although they are mentioned in passing in his book.

Finally, Stef Jansen's 'Antinacionalizam' represents the most serious academic engagement to date with the efforts to resist destructive nationalism in the former Yugoslavia.[13] Jansen starts out by analysing Yugoslav feminist activism as the first attempt to thwart the propagation of militarist ideology. He then proceeds to problematize national identity as the fundamental discursive element in (post)Yugoslav political life and explores other resistance discourses through which citizens articulated their dissatisfaction with the situation imposed on them. Jansen's study is significant because it goes counter to the above-mentioned paradigms, which emphasize national identity. He convincingly demonstrates that Yugoslav anti-nationalism played an important role for many people in that it remained the only anchor in times of political, moral and economic instability. Nevertheless, Jansen limits his analysis to Croatia and Serbia or, more precisely, to their capitals. The anti-nationalism he describes therefore cannot be considered universally 'Yugoslav' as many Yugoslav republics were not taken into account. More importantly, Jansen (except for the introductory part in which he pays attention to more institutionalized feminist initiatives), as an anthropologist, is more interested in personal articulations of anti-nationalism in everyday life rather than in more formally organized anti-war campaigns, their protagonists and the reasons for their failure. Ultimately, Jansen focuses on the second half of the 1990s and thus does not address the anti-war initiatives prior to the outburst of the armed conflict in greater detail.

---

12 Gordy, Eric: The Culture of Power in Serbia. Nationalism and the Destruction of Alternatives, University Park/PA: The Pennsylvania State University Press, 1999.
13 Jansen, Stef: Antinacionalizam. Etnografija otpora u Beogradu i Zagrebu, Beograd: Biblioteka XX vek, 2005.

4.4. Doctoral Project

4.4.1. Rationale

Taking into account the limitations of the literature reviewed above, my proposed project aspires to document anti-war initiatives in all of the former Yugoslav republics. This will entail analysing how some of the most prominent Yugoslav activists account for the failure of their initiatives to produce a broader pacifist movement that could have ensured a peaceful transition to democracy, political pluralism and a market economy. I initially thought about focusing on Yugoslav civic activism starting with 1988 and finishing with 1995. While the end date coincides with the passage of the Dayton Agreement, which finally brought peace to the region, the start date is the year in which civic activism intensified in response to the obvious imminence of an armed conflict. It would be possible, however, to broaden the perspective and focus on the time span between 1975 (the year the Helsinki Final Act, which lessened Cold War tensions, was signed) and 1995.

The issue of opposition to Communist regimes has never really managed to acquire mainstream status in Eastern European scholarship; it has instead been pushed aside by a torrent of studies on institutional transformations and the ways in which various countries have shaped their political systems to suit European Union legislation. The proposed research is thus primarily a reaction to the longstanding lack of scholarly literature on political opposition in the Eastern European social sciences. This deficit was glaringly evident throughout both the 1980s and the 1990s despite numerous conceptual developments and the surge of publications stimulated by the anti-government protests in Poland.

In attempting to put the neglected efforts of Yugoslav peace activists onto the research agenda, my study will spotlight two particular concerns that could be theoretically fruitful. The first of these is historical continuity. Recognizing the historicity of the events in question, this project sets out to analyse a dynamic set of processes related to the attempt to bring about political change and avert an armed conflict in the former Yugoslavia. The processes that the study aims to address were embedded in the broader context of the profound structural transformations that were then taking place in Eastern Europe and the world. In that vein, I will attempt to oppose the widespread trend in the scholarship on civil society and democracy of detaching these phenomena from their historical context.[14]

---

14 See Clemens, Elisabeth S. / Hughes, Martin D.: Recovering past protest. Historical research on social movements, in: Klandermans, Bert / Staggenborg, Suzanne (eds): Methods of Social Movement Research, Minneapolis: University of Minnesota Press, 2002, pp. 201–230, here p. 220.

4. Mapping the Ephemeral

More generally, this project will strive to bridge the gap between history and political science and show that in spite of the fact that events (past or present) tend to have identifiable causes conducive to academic inquiry, they should never be viewed as the inevitable consequence of unalterable social forces. Paying closer attention to history, in other words, demonstrates that current and future developments, albeit certainly influenced by power relations, systematic processes or mere vicissitudes of the past, are by no means entirely determined by them. This is particularly relevant for a region in which the past is an unavoidable point of contention that, for the sake of the future, needs to be *mastered* by both the academic community and the broader public.

The second principal theoretical concern of my research is the fact that the vast majority of studies on civil society and social movements focus on how civic initiatives are formed as well as on the ways in which they develop and act as challengers of the political system. There is, however, a conspicuous paucity of social science research on the reasons for which social movements fail, or as John Keane[15] says, 'commit civocide'. Even though they require a substantial level of coordination, protest activities are fluid and nebulous undertakings whose outcomes are always uncertain and dependent on popular support.[16]

Competition over a pacifist or bellicose agenda ought not to be reduced solely to the interplay between activists and regime(s), but should take into consideration the multiplicity and nature of the system challengers and the possibility of competition among themselves. More specifically, the question is why Yugoslav civil society activists did not collectively manage to find a channel that would have given them a higher level of legitimacy. My project will attempt to address this issue and pay particular attention to the logic that ultimately destroyed the nascent Yugoslav civil society initiatives. Studying the mechanisms responsible for the success or failure of independent (political) activism is especially relevant for a region in which the spheres of civil society and the state have not yet been clearly demarcated.

4.4.2. Research Questions

The proposed project aims to acknowledge a range of anti-war/civic initiatives in Yugoslavia immediately prior to the armed conflict and examine how the activists themselves account for their failure to secure a peaceful transition to democracy and political pluralism. It will first try to map the ground and identify the movements, groups and organizations that were involved in the anti-war civic initiatives. Empirical knowledge of these civic organizations is not expected to provide a definitive explanation

---

15 Personal communication, April 2009.
16 Tilly, Charles: The Contentious French, Cambridge/MA: Belknap Press, 1986.

of civil society's role in Yugoslavia's dissolution per se, but it is essential for arriving at a more nuanced analysis of the outcomes of the activists' initiatives.

This research is conceptualized as a *qualitative study of an exploratory nature* and it presumes that civil society should generally be able to provide a platform on which diverse political interests can peacefully co-exist. This ability may or may not be an intrinsic (and as presented here, somewhat ahistorical) feature of civil society; the question now is how, twenty years hence, the activists who attempted to thwart the violent conflict among Yugoslavia's constitutive nations account for their failure to do so.

In the qualitative research tradition in which this project is embedded, research questions are not set in stone, but are continually revised in the light of the collected interview material. The study is perceived as a living process that, while revolving around the central topic, appreciates the uniqueness of personal biography and the historical context surrounding it as well as the researcher's co-constructivist role in producing the analysed corpus of information. Thus the questions proposed here should be understood as points of reference. The project will be guided by the following principal concerns:

1. How do the activists account for the violent conflict of Yugoslav succession?
2. How do they make sense of their participation in the civic activities prior to the conflict?
3. What does 'civil society' mean to the informants and how do they explain their failure to connect to the broader public and thereby possibly avert the armed conflict?
4. How do they explain the fact that some civil societies have had more success, i.e. gone on to become a means of modernization, political opposition and even national emancipation (e.g. in Slovenia)?

4.4.3. Case Selection

By taking only one side of the coin into account (and in this case, the weaker side, that of the 'unsuccessful' activists), I am faced with the dilemma of if and how to incorporate the 'successful' side, i.e. that of the aggressors and passive bystanders, into the research design.[17] In other words, I was initially hesitant to devote my full attention to a rather small group of civil society activists while neglecting both the considerably more numerous proponents of destructive nationalism and the segment of the population that remained silent. (With respect to the latter group, it would be worthwhile to investigate the extent to which their inaction favoured or actually was the desired result of the devastating policies put forward by the political elites.) My choice to zero in on the activists is a conscious one and it is backed by at least two reasons.

---

17 Stef Jansen, personal communication, April 2009.

First, there has recently been a flurry of studies focusing on strong centrifugal initiatives, including those devoted to the (ex)Yugoslav intellectuals who – consciously or not – provided the ideological framework for the dissolution of the country (see e.g. Dragovic-Soso[18]). This corpus is sufficiently large at this point, and it is perhaps time to take the spotlight off the advocates of destructive nationalism. The abovementioned works should now be complemented by studies that examine the various countermovements. Although these studies are unlikely to focus on the vast majority of non-participants, they might nevertheless illuminate some of the reasons for their passivity. New studies would also contribute to our understanding not only of the outcome of events, but of the multiple equilibria that preceded what we today know to be historical facts.

Secondly, I have also refrained from broadening the study to include the representatives of the 'successful option' for a simple technical reason: The proposed project in its current form is already rather broad in its geographical and theoretical scope, and enlarging the sample would require much more time.

In accordance with the idea of examining *one* civil society opposed to violence and destruction, the basic units of analysis in this study could logically be the individual interviewees. However, it would be equally plausible to provide an extensive overview of civic activism in Yugoslavia immediately before the dissolution and then focus on one or two major organizations that would themselves provide sufficient empirical material, such as the *Belgrade Circle* or the *Association for the Yugoslav Democratic Initiative*. In that case, a single movement or organization would constitute the unit of analysis. It is possible to design the study so that it will have different units of analysis in different research phases. The final choice depends on how the project proceeds once it has entered the fieldwork stage.

Finally, this is a case study (in the sense of an in-depth empirical investigation of a smaller number of phenomena that aims at developing broader theoretical explanations[19]) that will consist of a series of inter-Yugoslav comparisons. Once a broader overview of civic activism in Yugoslavia has been provided, however, it might be more feasible to concentrate on a binary comparison between a successful case and a failed case. Slovenia could serve as a case of successful civic efforts that managed to thwart armed conflict, whereas Serbia or Bosnia would constitute counter-examples, i.e. failed cases. This approach would simplify the research design and allow for a more thorough examination of particular cases.

---

18 Dragovic-Soso, Jasna: Saviours of the Nation. Serbia's Intellectual Opposition and the Revival of Nationalism, London: Hurst & Company, 2002.
19 Della Porta, Donatella / Keating, Michele: Approaches and Methodologies in the Social Sciences. A Pluralist Perspective, Cambridge: Cambridge University Press, 2008.

4.4.4. Preliminary Hypotheses

Hampered by an underdeveloped political culture and overshadowed by an authoritarian Communist regime, civil society in Yugoslavia had a rather marginal status by the late 1980s. Although the regime periodically granted broader liberties to some segments of society, the Party retained an iron grip on the country's political life. As a result, all emancipation processes were restricted to big urban centres and limited to a narrow sphere of the intellectual, artistic and economic elite. I would therefore preliminarily hypothesize that the civic activism aimed at averting Yugoslav conflict stemmed from a cosmopolitan elite that was incapable of connecting with the wider public, which easily succumbed to the fierce regime propaganda and quickly embraced the logic of destructive nationalism. What is more, the antinationalist activists did not possess adequate political experience or material resources for generating a more relevant peace movement on the federal level.

4.4.5. Empirical Methods – Recovering Past Civic Activism

Reconstructing and theorizing about Yugoslav civic activism is challenging because the protest activities at issue are separated from us by around twenty years and took place in a country that no longer exists. Moreover, the civil society organizations behind them were generally pitted against authoritarian political regimes that were not amenable to their growth and development. This scenario invariably invokes the metaphor comparing social movements to icebergs, whose substance is mostly hidden below the surface.[20] Every new scholar wishing to reconstruct social movements is therefore advised to research the way in which private grievances break through the surface into public protest.

While scholars of social movements might have diverse theoretical leanings, they all address the vitally important questions of when, how and why people resist authority. Two qualitative research methods are especially conducive to recovering past protest activities. Interviews are a useful tool for studying short-lived or thinly documented social movements that cannot be easily examined by means of structured questionnaires.[21] The so-called *life story/oral history interview*, based on an interview guide prepared in advance, will be used in the proposed project. The idea behind this type of interview is to encourage the participants to provide extended accounts of their lives, i.e. to produce narratives that will provide good evidence about their life experiences

---

20 Clemens, Elisabeth S. / Hughes, Martin D.: Recovering past protest. Historical research on social movements, in: Klandermans, Bert / Staggenborg, Suzanne (eds): Methods of Social Movement Research, Minneapolis: University of Minnesota Press, pp. 201–230, here p. 225.
21 Mason, Jennifer: Qualitative Researching, London: Sage, 2002.

and the meanings attached to them.[22] On the other hand, documentary analysis, with its special attention to authenticity, representativeness and interpretation, can provide both the basis for and complement the collected interview material.[23]

4.4.6. Possible Implications of the Current Study

The proposed study is conceptualized as an acknowledgement of the civic efforts to resist identity politics and prevent war in the former Yugoslavia. At the current stage, it is envisioned that the project might have the following implications:

1. It will unearth a range of civil society initiatives that took place in the former Yugoslavia immediately before the outburst of the 1990s wars.
2. The study will particularly attempt to account for the failure of such civic activism to produce a broader movement that might have ensured a peaceful transition to democracy and a market economy.
3. This research could refine our understanding of the dynamics of civil society development (formation and destruction) in the Communist and post-Communist contexts.
4. More specifically, the analysis will pay particular attention to the mechanisms or logic by which civil initiatives can be destroyed, especially in the light of the fact that many existing studies concentrate on how civil societies form but very few describe how they are killed off.
5. At the most general level, the project might offer further insights into the problems that the Yugoslav succession states have been facing in the process of democratization and accession to the European Union.

---

22 Elliott, Jane: Using Narratives in Social Research. Qualitative and Quantitative Approaches, London: Sage, 2005.
23 Platt, Jennifer: Evidence and proof in documentary research. 1: Some specific problems of documentary research, in: Bryman, Alan / Burgess, Robert (eds): Qualitative Research, Vol. 2, 1999, London: Sage, pp. 206–223.

Franziska Blomberg

5. External Democracy Promotion of Civil Society in Ethnically Fragmented Post-Socialist Countries

5.1. Introduction

For twenty years, the former socialist countries have been on the receiving side of external democracy promotion efforts. They have made varying degrees of progress on the path to democratic consolidation;[1] accordingly, they were often classified as either 'autocracies' or 'democracies' in the past.[2] At a closer look, however, many countries fall somewhere in between the two poles of authoritarianism and democracy. New research is suggesting more distinct classifications for these 'hybrid' forms of statehood,[3] in some cases attempting to provide more discrete categories for analysis in this 'grey' zone.

Two of the factors strongly influencing democratization are highlighted in this chapter: civil society and ethnic fragmentation[4]. They are often assumed to positively and negatively affect democratization, respectively. As for civil society, many authors and practitioners stress the importance of a 'vibrant civil society' for sustainable democratic consolidation.[5] Usually, civil society is considered intrinsically 'good', with its 'dark

---

[1] Freedom House: Nations in Transit. Democracy Score Year-To-Year Summaries by Region 2008, 2008, http://www.freedomhouse.org/template.cfm?page=437&year=2008
[2] For a critical overview see Zinecker, Heidrun: Regime-Hybridity and violent civil societies in fragmented societies. Conceptual considerations, Cornell University Peace Studies, Occasional Paper, 2007, http://www.einaudi.cornell.edu/PeaceProgram/publications/occasional_papers/Zinecker-final.pdf
[3] For this article, I follow Zinecker, who illustrates why many 'minimal types' should not be counted as democracies at all, and who includes a democratically functioning civil society as a crucial aspect of her definition of democracy. See Zinecker, Heidrun: Regime-Hybridity and violent civil societies in fragmented societies. Conceptual considerations, Cornell University Peace Studies, Occasional Paper, 2007, http://www.einaudi.cornell.edu/PeaceProgram/publications/occasional_papers/Zinecker-final.pdf
[4] Ethnic fragmentation here is understood as ethnic self-ascription by the persons concerned. A substantive discussion of indices, such as the one presented by Vanhanen, Alesina et al., and others exceeds the scope of this chapter. Vanhanen, Tatu: Ethnic Conflicts Explained by Ethnic Nepotism, Stanford/CT: Jai Press, 1999; Alesina, Alberto / Devleeschauwer, Arnaud / Easterly, William / Kurlat, Sergio / Warcziag, Romain: Fractionalization, in: Journal of Economic Growth, 2003 (Vol. 8), No. 2, pp. 155–194.
[5] Cf. e.g. Merkel, Wolfgang (ed.): Systemwechsel 5. Zivilgesellschaft und Transformation, Opladen: Leske & Budrich, 2000; Parrott, Bruce: Perspectives on Postcommunist Democratization, in: Dawisha, Karen / Parrott, Bruce (eds): Politics, Power and the Struggle for Democracy in South-East Europe, Cambridge: Cambridge University Press, 1997, pp. 1–39.

sides'[6] conveniently overlooked.[7] However, recent years have seen increasing criticism of this sweeping optimism[8] and instances of 'bad', 'corrupt' or 'faked' civil societies' have not been altogether rare. When considering ethnic fragmentation, ethnic heterogeneity is assumed to be a strong hindrance to democratization[9] and should therefore be given due consideration in democracy promotion.[10] Some scholars argue that the effect of ethnic fragmentation depends more on how the competition between rivalling groups is dealt with.[11] Especially during radical socio-political changes, competing groups will tend to 'rent seek'. Thus, dealing with ethnic fragmentation and promoting cooperation across ethnic lines seem to represent crucial measures for the progress of democratic consolidation.[12] This chapter argues that external democracy promotion of civil society, despite good intentions, may actually run the risk of negatively impacting democratization if promoters underestimate the latent dangers of ethnic fragmentation.

The chapter is structured as follows: first, the theoretical framework is presented, including reflections about the particular context of ethnically fragmented states for external democracy promotion. Then the intention of the study and the guiding main question and research hypotheses are introduced. After a presentation of the planned operationalization, I end with a few concluding reflections.

---

6 Paffenholz, Thania / Spurk, Christoph: Civil Society, Civic Engagement, and Peacebuilding, in: Social Development Papers, Conflict Prevention & Reconstruction, 2006 (Vol. 1), No. 36, pp. 1–47.
7 Roth, Roland: Die dunklen Seiten der Zivilgesellschaft. Grenzen einer zivilgesellschaftlichen Fundierung von Demokratie, in: Geißel, Brigitte et al. (eds): Zivilgesellschaft und Sozialkapital. Herausforderungen politischer und sozialer Integration, Wiesbaden: VS, 2004, pp. 41–64, here pp. 60–61.
8 Cf. Lauth, Hans-Joachim: Ambivalenzen der Zivilgesellschaft in Hinsicht auf Demokratie und soziale Inklusion, in: Nord-Süd aktuell, 2003 (Vol. 17), No. 2, pp. 223–232; Paffenholz, Thania / Spurk, Christoph: Civil Society, Civic Engagement, and Peacebuilding, in: Social Development Papers, Conflict Prevention & Reconstruction, 2006 (Vol. 1), No. 36, pp. 1–47.
9 See e.g. Zürcher, Christoph: Post-Soviet Wars. Rebellion, Ethnic Conflict, and Nationhood in the Caucasus; New York: New York University Press, 2007.
10 Beichelt, Timm: Minorities in New European Democracies. A Source of Destabilisation?, in: European Yearbook of Minority Issues, 2002/3 (Vol. 2), pp. 53–71; Silander, Daniel: Democracy from the Outside-In? The Conceptualization and Significance of Democracy Promotion, Vaxjö: Vaxjö University Press, 2005.
11 Putnam, Robert D.: E Pluribus Unum. Diversity and Community in the Twenty-first Century. The 2006 Johan Skytte Prize Lecture, in: Scandinavian Political Studies, 2007 (Vol. 30), No. 2, pp. 137–174; Fish, M. Steven: Democracy Derailed in Russia. The Failure of Open Politics in Russia, Cambridge: Cambridge University Press, 2005.
12 Zürcher, Christoph: Post-Soviet Wars. Rebellion, Ethnic Conflict, and Nationhood in the Caucasus, New York: New York University Press, 2007. For further discussion of 'rent seeking' see Zinecker, Heidrun: Regime-Hybridity and violent civil societies in fragmented societies. Conceptual considerations, Cornell University Peace Studies, Occasional Paper, 2007, http://www.einaudi.cornell.edu/PeaceProgram/publications/occasional_papers/Zinecker-final.pdf

5.2. The Perception of State- and Nation-Building Approaches among Civil Society Promotion Actors – the Intention of this Study

Given the limited space, this research study only humbly intends to come up with a few reflections on the usefulness of certain instruments possibly useful for fine-tuning civil society promotion and by this try to develop existing theories of civil society. Recent years have seen considerable (re-)ethnicization in many countries of the world, still not giving rise to much hope of finding a 'miracle cure' – as history and decades of research do neither. In order to better grasp the myriad related processes, it is helpful to understand nations as categories of action and to see them as both targets and consequences of 'social engineering' by different actors.[13] Seeing ethnicity as a constructed category – as in Anderson's 'imagined communities'[14] – renders it possible to see ethnicity as a constructed process when it becomes an all-important category – which is why I prefer to speak of 'ethnicized' conflicts rather than of 'ethnic' conflicts. This position also allows for the theoretical possibility of an active de-ethnicization of politics. This study follows the assumption that the mechanisms resulting from the close intertwinement of civil society promotion efforts and the appeasement of problematic ethnic fragmentation have thus far been greatly underestimated and under-researched. I assume, that, actors in the field can reveal important thoughts based on tacit knowledge regarding the subject. Furthermore, they probably possess ideas as to possible approaches of dealing with ethnic fragmentation in a more constructive way. The aim of this chapter is to provide new insight into this field in order to develop increasingly adequate categories for assessment and instruments for civil society promotion in ethnically fragmented countries.

5.3. Democracy Promotion, Civil Society, and Ethnic Diversity. A Theoretical Framework

Democracy cannot exist and certainly cannot improve unless the functioning of institutions (structure) is guaranteed by democratic values (the substance). One constituent element of democracy often called upon when democratization seems to falter is the existence of a 'vibrant civil society'[15]. This is based on the assumption that civil

---

13 Cf. Brubaker, Roger: Nationalism Reframed. Nationhood and the National Question in the New Europe, Cambridge: Cambridge University Press, 1996, here pp. 16–18 and Hobsbawm, Eric / Ranger, Terence (eds): The Invention of Tradition, Cambridge: Cambridge University Press, 1983, here pp. 13–14.
14 Anderson, Benedict: Imagined Communities, London: Verso, 1983.
15 Król, Marcin: Where East meets West, in: Journal of Democracy, 1995 (Vol. 1), No. 6, pp. 37–43, here p. 39.

society is the sphere in which democratic values are internalized (in a Tocquevillian sense).[16] If the development of an 'ethnocracy' is to be avoided – or reversed – we have to consider that formally democratically functioning institutions (democracy as 'one man one vote') probably do not meet the above requirements and could actually serve to strengthen ethnicity as an omnipresent marker.[17]

According to Linz/Stepan, democratic consolidation can only be achieved when democracy is seen as 'the only game in town'[18] and the 'will to democracy'[19] and a democratic culture[20] prevail. Civil society is assumedly can reinforce the process.[21] Hence, establishing a civil society is thought to be a precondition for functioning institutions and a gauge of the legitimacy of a democracy.[22] Civil society protects democratic institutions, restricts undemocratic behaviour of elites and helps to construct a safe basis in times of crisis for the democratic polity.[23]

5.3.1. Democracy Promotion and Civil Society – Haste Makes Waste?

As stated above, civil society is considered an important factor for democratization by theorists and practitioners alike. In keeping with O'Donnell et al.[24], Lauth/Merkel defined different stages of democratic transformation: liberalization, democratization, and (democratic) consolidation, stressing the importance of establishing a civil society at the latest stage.[25] In other words, it is difficult – if not impossible – for a state to achieve democratic consolidation without developing its civil society; it is more likely to 'get stuck' somewhere along the way. Dahrendorf argues that democracy in

---

16 See e.g. Diamond, Larry: Rethinking Civil Society toward Democratic Consolidation, in: Journal of Democracy, 1994 (Vol. 5), No. 3, pp. 4–17, here p. 8.
17 Mullerson, Rein: Minorities in Eastern Europe and the Former USSR. Problems, Tendencies and Protection, in: The Modern Law Review, 1993 (Vol. 56), No. 6, pp. 793–811, here p. 811.
18 Linz, Juan J. / Stepan, Alfred C.: Problems of democratic transition and consolidation. Southern Europe, South America, and post-communist Europe, Baltimore/MD: Johns Hopkins University Press, 1996, here p. 5.
19 Held, David: Democracy and the Global Order. From the Modern State to Cosmopolitan Governance, Stanford/CA: Stanford University Press, 1995, here p. 158.
20 Gunther, Richard / Diamandouros, P. Nikiforos / Puhle, Hans-Jürgen: O'Donnell's 'Illusions'. A Rejoinder, in: Journal of Democracy, 1996 (Vol. 7), No. 4, pp. 151–159, here p. 155.
21 Croissant, Aurel / Lauth, Hans-Joachim / Merkel, Wolfgang: Zivilgesellschaft und Transformation. Ein internationaler Vergleich, in: Merkel, Wolfgang (ed.): Systemwechsel 5. Zivilgesellschaft und Transformation, Opladen: Leske & Budrich, 2000, pp. 9–49.
22 Fukuyama, Francis: Trust. The Social Virtues and the Creation of Prosperit, New York: Free Press, 1995, here p. 8.
23 Merkel, Wolfgang (ed.): Systemwechsel 5. Zivilgesellschaft und Transformation, Opladen: Leske & Budrich, 2000, here p. 7.
24 O'Donnell, Guillermo / Schmitter, Philippe / Whitehead, Laurence (eds): Transitions from Authoritarian Rule, Baltimore/MD: Johns Hopkins University Press, 1986, here p. 3.
25 Lauth, Hans-Joachim / Merkel, Wolfgang: Zivilgesellschaft und Transformation. Ein Diskussionsbeitrag in revisionistischer Absicht, in: Forschungsjournal Neue Soziale Bewegungen, 1997 (Vol. 10), No. 1, pp. 12–34.

5. External Democracy Promotion of Civil Society

Eastern Europe cannot be considered secure until at least two generations, or sixty years, have elapsed.[26]
However,

> [D]espite the widespread recognition of its potential importance, scholars have not agreed on how to define [civil society], nor are they sure what the specific nature of its contribution can be.[27]

Most literature begins by deducing the concept of civil society from the times of Aristotle and concludes with yet another working definition. Usually civil society is situated at the intersection of the private sphere and the state, sometimes, however, it is considered as something explicitly separate from them,[28] and sometimes it is thought to partially overlap the two spheres. For Pollack, and also for this study, civil society will be understood as the entire public sphere in which citizens voluntarily – i.e. irrespective of private interests – come together in associations, movements, etc.[29] Civil society is thus separate from the state but not apolitical.

As the appearance of civil society in transformation states is subject to continuous change, it makes sense to approach it as a non-normative[30] analytical category rather than as a distinct historical form. Croissant et al. identify five functions attributed to civil society in the literature: protection, intermediation, communication, socialization and community.[31] Civil society is assumed to facilitate the aggregation of interests and help citizens to influence policy;[32] it is also supposed to create 'intermediary groups'.[33] The quality of civil society is often measured by counting the number of existing NGOs and the share of population active in them. This criterion might provide some – but far from reliable – information about the state of civil society and democracy in a given

---

26 Chandler, David: Bosnia. Faking democracy after Dayton, London, Sterling/VA: Pluto Press, 1999, p. 13.
27 Schmitter, Philippe C.: Some Propositions about Civil Society and the Consolidation of Democracy, in: Institut für Höhere Studien (ed.): Reihe Politikwissenschaft, No. 10, Wien: Institut für Höhere Studien, 1993, pp. 1–14, here p. 1.
28 Cohen, Jean L. / Arato, Andrew: Civil Society and Political Theory, Cambridge/MA: MIT Press, 1992, p. 5; Hann, Chris / Dunn, Elizabeth (eds): Civil Society. Challenging Western Models, London: Routledge, 1996, p. 4. Whether or not political associations are part of CS remains contested in the literature.
29 Pollack, Detlef: Zivilgesellschaft und Staat in der Demokratie, in: Forschungsjournal Neue Soziale Bewegungen, 2003 (Vol. 16), No. 2, pp. 46–75, here pp. 46–48.
30 Pollack, Detlef: Zivilgesellschaft und Staat in der Demokratie, in: Forschungsjournal Neue Soziale Bewegungen, 2003 (Vol. 16), No. 2, pp. 46–75.
31 Croissant, Aurel / Lauth, Hans-Joachim / Merkel, Wolfgang: Zivilgesellschaft und Transformation. Ein internationaler Vergleich, in: Merkel, Wolfgang (ed.): Systemwechsel 5. Zivilgesellschaft und Transformation, Opladen: Leske & Budrich, 2000, pp. 9–49.
32 Kligman, Gail: Reclaiming the Public. A Reflection on Recreating Civil Society in Romania, in: Eastern European Politics and Societies, 1990 (Vol. 4), No. 3, pp. 393–438, here p. 420.
33 Schmitter, Philippe C.: On Civil Society and the Consolidation of Democracy. Ten Propositions, Stanford/CA: Stanford Department of Political Science, 1995, p. 1.

country.[34] There is still a lack of scholarly literature providing systematic categories for the analysis of civil society in different contexts.

All of these models seem to assume civil society to be miraculously immune against the surrounding 'evils' of the society it is embedded in. Thorny issues like corruption, clientelism/nepotism, nationalism, etc. are rarely included in civil society assessment. Some authors criticize this (naïve) view and add further (potential) 'dark sides' of civil society to the list, such as a low degree of legitimacy, frequent entrenchment in politics, the potential to undermine the development of the state (and thus possibly weaken it), 'projectitis'[35] (organizing funded projects in order to secure jobs and follow the annual 'trends' of calls for tenders) etc.

David Chandler critically reflects on the possible positive and negative effects of civil society promotion: external funding runs the risk of fragmenting society rather than creating a pluralistic exchange of political opinions. NGOs relying on outside funding seem to have no need to engage in discussion or forge broader links to society. So 'the financing of private bodies, as representatives of democracy and development, without a clear policy may in fact encourage the fragmentation of societies under political breakdown rather than encourage pluralism.'[36]

In this line, Paffenholz/Spurk call for a better understanding of the conditions and obstacles that affect civil society's ability to play a constructive role in post-conflict situations, including the behaviour of potential or existing 'uncivil' society actors and the role of fragile or authoritarian states.[37]

5.3.2. Democracy Promotion and Ethnic Fragmentation. The Nation – All for One and One for All?

The construction of civil society is a laborious and lengthy process. Ethnic fragmentation seems even more difficult to channel into democratic functioning and can very easily be (re-)mobilized as a catalyst for conflict.[38] Today almost 90% of the world's states are poly-ethnic – and half of them are divided along ethnic lines.[39] Ethnic fragmentation,

---

34 Vejvoda, Ivan / Kaldor, Mary: Democratization in Central and Eastern Europe, London: Continuum Press, 1997, p. 77.
35 Seifija, Ismet: From the 'Civil Sector' to Civil Society? Progress and Prospects, in: Fischer, Martina (ed.): Peacebuilding and Civil Society in Bosnia-Herzegovina. Ten Years after Dayton, Berlin: LIT/Berghof Research Center for Constructive Conflict Management, 2006, pp. 125–140.
36 Chandler, David: Bosnia. Faking democracy after Dayton, London, Sterling/VA: Pluto Press, 1999, p. 35.
37 Paffenholz, Thania / Spurk, Christoph: Civil Society, Civic Engagement, and Peacebuilding, in: Social Development Papers, Conflict Prevention & Reconstruction, 2006 (Vol. 1), No. 36, pp. 1–47, here p. 46.
38 Chandler, David: Bosnia. Faking democracy after Dayton, London, Sterling/VA: Pluto Press, 1999, p. 46.
39 Giddens, Anthony: The Nation-State and Violence, Cambridge: Polity, 1985, here pp. 216–220.

5. External Democracy Promotion of Civil Society

present in many of today's democratizing countries, should thus be treated as a crucial factor when designing external democracy promotion programmes.[40]

Since 1989, the leaders of the former socialist countries have been faced with the highly demanding task of choosing strategies and instruments for state- as well as nation-building. A new institution-architecture had to be implemented, usually referred to as 'state-building'[41]. After gaining independence, they were also confronted with the daunting task of having to define themselves as a 'nation' and address questions regarding group-belonging through a more or less consciously directed and contested process of 'nation-building'[42] (including the creation of a 'national identity' as a 'collective community of will'[43], etc.). Nation-building has proven especially difficult in the post-socialist states, as politics and the economy have been ethnicized by groups competing for their 'piece of the pie' during unsure transitional (political and financial) resource allocation. Also, following the break-up of the Warsaw Pact, politicians often came to power by playing the 'ethnic card'. This 'ethnicization' is still omnipresent.[44] It is quite likely owing to the fact that the Soviet concept of 'nation' was largely based on an ethnic definition of group belonging. Ethnicity was a predominant category in the Soviet region as well as in the former Yugoslavia.[45]

Many renowned scholars of democratization consider state-building the top priority. They regard it as a necessary precondition for further nation-building processes

---

40 E.g. Silander, Daniel: Democracy from the Outside-In? The Conceptualization and Significance of Democracy Promotion, Vaxjö: Vaxjö University Press, 2005.
41 'State-building is a key concept of successful nation-building. It presupposes a number of practical abilities (a financial bases for a functioning state-apparatus, an organized police and judicial system, an administrative system that is effective and accepted in the entire state, loyal personnel, that identifies with the "nation" – and the state must be able to exert its monopoly on the use of force on the whole state territory.' Hippler, Jochen: Nation-Building the Globalisation Process – A contribution to regional stability and global security, Conference Paper SEF-Symposium 2002 (Development and Peace Foundation), University Club Bonn 11–12 December 2002, 2002, p. 19, http://www jochen-hippler de/neu/pdf-Dokumente/NB%20Paper.pdf
42 Dave defines 'nation-building' as 'the measures taken by the state to unify and homogenize its diverse population under a commonly shared civic identity that prevails over ethnic, linguistic, religious or regional markers.' Dave, Bhavna: A Shrinking State? Language Policy and Implementation in Kazakhstan and Kyrgyzstan, in: Jones Luong, Pauline (ed.): The Transformation of Central Asia. States and Societies from Soviet Rule to Independence, Ithaca/NY, London: Cornell University Press, 2004, pp. 120–155, here p. 123.
43 Hopp, Ulrike / Kloke-Lesch, Adolf: Nation-Building versus Nationenbildung. Eine entwicklungspolitische Perspektive, in: Hippler, Jochen (ed.): Nation-Building. Ein Schlüsselkonzept für friedliche Konfliktbearbeitung?, Bonn: Stiftung Entwicklung und Frieden, 2004, pp. 195–213, here p. 197.
44 Hornstein-Tomić, Caroline: Interethnische Beziehungen in Südosteuropa. Ein Bericht zur Lage in Bosnien-Herzegowina, Kosovo, Kroatien, Mazedonien, Montenegro, und Serbien, Konrad-Adenauer-Stiftung, 2008, pp. 2–3, http://www.kas.de/wf/doc/kas_13999-544-1-30.pdf
45 Halbach, Uwe: Das sowjetische Vielvölkerimperium. Nationalitätenpolitik und nationale Frage, Mannheim: BI-Taschenbuch, 1992, pp. 34–36.

as a second step.[46] For others, the priority is clearly the reverse: Hopp/Kloke-Lesch contend that state-building represents only two of three necessary steps on the way to completing the nation-building process. In their view, nation-building consists of three closely related constituent parts: 1) the development of a functioning and by civil-society-accepted state; 2) a physical, social, and media infrastructure shared by the entire civil society. The first two are essential for what is called 'state-building', whereas in order to achieve 'nation-building' one further component is required, which is 3) a socio-cultural process of creation and integration with the aim of creating shared attributes of identity, values and goals. What matters most in this regard is not a possibly existing homogeneity if attitudes within society but the general acceptance of the heterogeneity of answers and the facilitation of inclusion of diverse citizens.[47]

In the context of external democracy promotion, the (often financial) support state-building measures is sometimes reluctantly but more often openly welcome where the (re-) building of state institutions is concerned. With respect to nation-building, interference by external actors into this field is much more emphatically rejected and the right to self-determination is often emphasized by actors in the countries and international organizations alike. Thus, the difficult mission of nation-building, especially crucial in ethnically fragmented countries, is often left to the countries' politicians.

5.4. Proceedings of the Study

With the aim of shedding more light on the field of external democracy promotion in ethnically fragmented countries this chapter examines the following *main research question:*

How does the choice of strategy regarding the promotion of state- vs. nation-building in external democracy promotion influence the degree of democratic functioning of civil society?

The *variables* examined are:
1. Explaining/independent variable: the choice of strategy regarding the promotion of state- vs. nation-building in external democracy promotion;
2. Explained/dependent variable: the degree of democratization in ethnically fragmented societies.

The following *hypothesis* will be tested:

---

46 E.g. Fukuyama, Francis: 'Stateness' First, in: Journal of Democracy, 2005 (Vol. 16), No. 1, pp. 84–88.
47 Hopp, Ulrike / Kloke-Lesch, Adolf: Nation-Building versus Nationenbildung. Eine entwicklungspolitische Perspektive, in: Hippler, Jochen (ed.): Nation-Building. Ein Schlüsselkonzept für friedliche Konfliktbearbeitung?, Bonn: Stiftung Entwicklung und Frieden, 2004, pp. 195–213, here p. 197.

The less external democracy promotion insists on non-ethnically defined nation-building, the less likely resources for the promotion of civil society will be applied to overcome ethnic fragmentation, thus lessening the possible effects of democratization.

5.5. External Democracy Promotion of Civil Society Revisited. Operationalization and Methodological Approach

The method of choice for this study is a qualitative comparative case study. It does not intend to isolate clearly quantifiable causations of something as complex as a political system and its inhabitants' attitudes. As the study does not aim at generating quantifiable data, the number of n (=cases) is small, but should provide in-depth information about the mechanisms of the field under research.[48]

The goal is to investigate, in an explorative manner, how actors involved at different levels of civil society democracy promotion *perceive* the choice of strategies with respect to state- vs. nation-building by international actors. I assume that actors in different positions have different insights into the state-/nation-building strategies that have been/are being applied in their countries. In order to limit my field of investigation, I will concentrate on programmes of the European Union (as the largest democracy promoter by budget and number of programmes), German political funds (which have a special focus on civil society promotion) and the OSCE (an important promoter of bottom-up democracy promotion through civil society development).

5.5.1. Case Selection

The case selection is based on the assumption that several authors (e.g. Steven Fish, Marc Howard, and Alina Mungiu-Pippidi)[49] have supplied sufficient arguments of certain common social determinants of the post-socialist countries, to concentrate my research on the post-socialist countries instead of starting with a global investigation. I wish to select two cases and examine them to determine the current strategies of the EU, German political funds and the OSCE. The criteria for the two cases will be that they both display high levels of ethnic fragmentation but different degrees of success in terms of their democratization; I also want to investigate how actors at different levels

---

48 Schneckener and Wolff also propose qualitative case studies for research on ethnic conflicts and their dynamics, cf. Schneckener, Ulrich / Wolff, Stefan (eds): Managing and Settling Ethnic Conflicts Perspectives on Success and Failure in Europe, Asia, and Africa, London: Hurst, 2004, p. viii.
49 E.g. Fish, M. Steven: Democracy Derailed in Russia. The Failure of Open Politics in Russia, Cambridge: Cambridge University Press, 2005; Howard, Marc Morjé: The Weakness of Civil Society in Post-Communist Europe, Cambridge et al.: Cambridge University Press, 2003; Mungiu-Pippidi, Alina: Democratization without Decommunization in the Balkans, in: ORBIS, 2006 (Vol. 50), No. 4, pp. 641–655.

describe the mechanisms at work regarding external democracy promoters' choice of strategy with respect to its incorporation of ethnic fragmentation as a factor. Owing to a lack of space in this contribution, I exclude the investigation of further intervening factors vis-à-vis the democratization process and leave this for my Ph.D. dissertation.

Ethnic fragmentation is represented by the ratio of the first and second biggest ethnic groups, based on the assumption that the ethnicized nation-building processes in the former socialist states make it more difficult for the ruling elites to establish state-wide alignment when there is a strong second biggest ethnic group competing for resources and power and possibly threatening to defect.[50]

Democratization is measured by showing a country's so-called 'real' degree of progress in the process by subtracting its Freedom House Democracy Score 1999/2000 from its 2008 score, both of which are measured on a scale of 1 (best) to 7 (worst).[51]

Due to a lack of data ratings for Serbia before 2003, the data for Yugoslavia have been substituted, which might provide roughly reliable information about the status of the later independent countries. Data for Montenegro and Kosovo are difficult to find and too minimal to guarantee a reliable basis for correlations, so both countries are excluded from the study. Both were relatively small parts of Yugoslavia, which means that the representativeness of their data is doubtful in any case.

Figure 5-1 illustrates how the post-socialist countries can be classified along a two-dimensional matrix of:

a) Ethnic fragmentation (Percentage of Second Biggest Ethnic Group of Population Total)

b) Democratization score (Freedom House Democracy Scores 1999–2008)

On the right-hand side of the x-axis we can see a group of countries that all have a large second biggest ethnic group, but score differently on democratization: Macedonia, Estonia, Latvia, Kazakhstan, Montenegro and Bosnia-Herzegovina. As said above, there is not enough data available on Montenegro. Regarding my interest in programmes funded by the EU, OSCE and German political funds, the countries of Latvia and Estonia are already members of the EU and thus no longer targets of the majority of programmes examined. But Kazakhstan (KZ), Bosnia-Herzegovina (BA) and Macedonia (MK) are interesting cases. As an additional selection criteria, the Freedom House classification for regime type are compared: Kazakhstan, with a score of 6.39, is rated as a consolidated authoritarian regime according to Freedom House's range of 6.00 to

---

50 This is based on the assumption that a large second ethnic group will consider the chances for their success higher by bringing forward competing claims, resulting in more frequent, more insistent requests. According to Laitin, groups have four options for dealing with their minority status vis-à-vis the majority: loyalty, exit, voice and arms. See Laitin, David D.: Identity in Formation. The Russian Speaking Populations in the Near Abroad, Ithaca/NY: Cornell University Press, 1998, p. 158.

51 See Freedom House: Nations in Transit. Democracy Score Year-To-Year Summaries by Region 2008, 2008, http://www.freedomhouse.org/template.cfm?page=437&year=2008

7.00; Macedonia qualifies as a semi-consolidated democracy with a high score of 3.86 (range: 3.00 to 3.99); and Bosnia-Herzegovina, with a score of 4.11, falls under the category of transitional governments or hybrid regimes (range: 4.00 to 4.99).[52]

Figure 5-1: Democratization and Percentage of 2nd Biggest Ethnic Group of Total Population

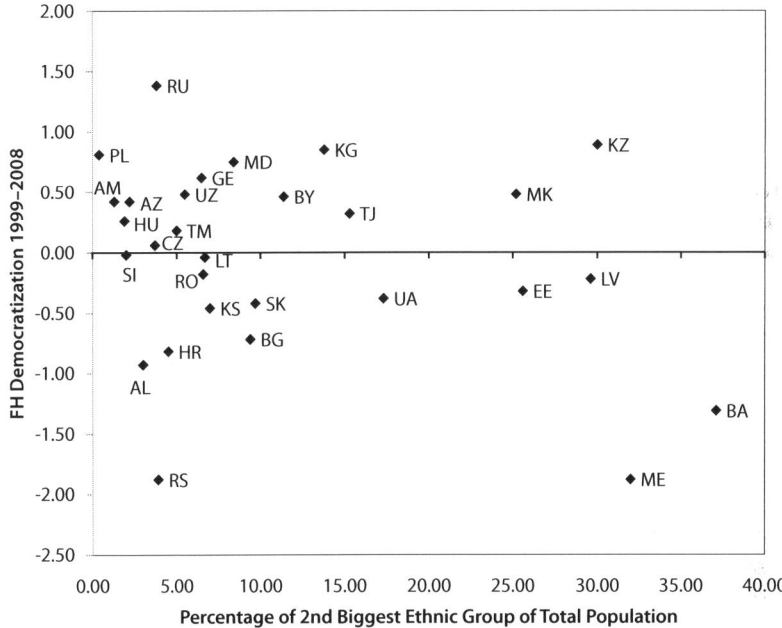

Sources: CIA World Fact Book, https://www.cia.gov/library/publications/the-world-factbook, accessed 2 February 2009; Democracy Score 2008 Rankings by Regime Type, http://www.freedomhouse.org/template.cfm?page=438&year=2008, accessed 3 May 2009.

As noted above, my special interest lies in the question of why some countries seem to advance towards democracy while others seem to 'get stuck' along the way. Kazakhstan, as a consolidated authoritarian regime, is so far from democratization that it might not yield much insight into the process. However, the other two cases, Macedonia and Bosnia-Herzegovina, both ex-Yugoslavian countries with many common context factors, fall between consolidating democracies and hybrid regimes, and thus will very likely provide more information about the dynamics involved for countries that find

---

52 Freedom House: Nations in Transit. Democracy Score 2008 Rankings by Regime Type, 2008, http://www.freedomhouse.org/template.cfm?page=438&year=2008

themselves between the extreme poles of authoritarianism and democracy. This is the final argument for choosing Macedonia and Bosnia-Herzegovina as cases. Macedonia's real democratization for the period 1999–2008 was +0.48 while Bosnia-Herzegovina's was -1.31.[53] The ratio of the first and second biggest ethnic groups is 64.20%/25.20% and 48.00%/37.10%[54], respectively.[55]

5.5.2. Process Tracing – Review of Existing Programmes and Instruments

In order to better prepare and analyse the later interviews regarding the two selected cases, Macedonia and Bosnia-Herzegovina, I will need to collect information. To this end, I will examine the civil society promotion of the European Union, OSCE and German political funds ('Politische Stiftungen'), their goals, programmes, instruments, and if available, evaluations.[56]

5.5.3. Qualitative Interviews – New Insights on Old Questions

Assuming that actors in the field possess particular knowledge, I will ask them to assess how the various international actors' choice of strategy with respect to emphasizing either state- and/or nation-building has influenced (or is expected to influence) the process of democratic consolidation. Depending on their feedback, it might prove interesting to investigate the actors' assessment of the civil society promotion strategies applied in their countries. For example, in Macedonia, the promotion has centred on integrating the large Albanian population, while in Bosnia-Herzegovina the goals of achieving ethnically defined representation and the solution of the de facto non-sovereign status of the country still are pressing issues.

I will conduct sixteen problem-centred and name-generator interviews. They will all be unstructured and guideline-based. My aim is to uncover new perspectives and assessments by giving the interviewees as much freedom to roam as possible.

---

53 Freedom House: Nations in Transit. Democracy Score Year-To-Year Summaries by Region 2008, 2008, http://www.freedomhouse.org/template.cfm?page=437&year=2008
54 The latter number is based on an estimation from the year 2000; new numbers from the EU suggest a more realistic 31%. See Hornstein-Tomić, Caroline: Interethnische Beziehungen in Südosteuropa. Ein Bericht zur Lage in Bosnien-Herzegowina, Kosovo, Kroatien, Mazedonien, Montenegro, und Serbien, 2008, p. 6, http://www.kas.de/wf/doc/kas_13999-544-1-30.pdf
55 CIA: World Fact Book, 2008, https://www.cia.gov/library/publications/the-world-factbook
56 For more on process tracing see Checkel, Jeffrey T.: It's the Process Stupid! Process Tracing in the Study of European and International Politics, 2005, http://www.arena.uio.no/publications/working-papers2005/papers/wp05_26.pdf; and George, Alexander / Bennett, Andrew: Case Studies and Theory Development in the Social Sciences, Cambridge/MA, London: MIT Press, 2004.

	MK	BA
NGO activists	4	4
Personnel from EU/OSCE/GPF	4	4

The selection of the interviewees needs to be representative in a qualitative rather than in a quantitative sense. For now the criteria known to me could roughly provide relevant categories, but I do not yet think I am sufficiently informed about the relevant categories for representativeness in the field. I therefore prefer to follow the methodology used by Kelle and Kluge, i.e. I will determine the final categories once I have conducted more interviews in the field.[57]

5.6. Formal and Informal Rules of the Game? Concluding Reflections

This chapter illustrates the underlying assumptions of a research design and cannot yet rely on enough data to provide reliable results. But what do the findings suggest so far? The intention of this study was to contribute to a better understanding of the influence the choice of strategy between state- vs. nation-building in external democracy promotion has on the degree of democratic functioning of civil society in ethnically fragmented societies. The results of the 'research in progress' (including the first preliminary interviews) suggest that the democracy promotion debate frequently fails to integrate existing knowledge from peace and conflict research about the ethnic fragmentation of societies, including the respective civil society, into theories of democratization.[58] Even though external democracy promoters usually obey the credo of 'do no harm', a meticulous analysis of the societal situation (including ethnic parameters) prior to intervention rarely happens according to numerous authors.[59]

It looks as though the international community has followed largely different strategies, followed by different outcomes, when dealing with the conflicts in Macedonia and Bosnia-Herzegovina. In Macedonia, for example, the EU co-signed the Ohrid Agreement in 2000 (as a basis for restructuring the state) and promised a clear prospect for accession; both efforts seem to have prevented further escalation of the eth-

---
57   Kelle, Udo / Kluge, Susann: Vom Einzelfall zum Typus. Fallvergleich und Fallkontrastierung in der qualitativen Sozialforschung, Opladen: Leske & Budrich, 1999, pp. 99–100.
58   Cf. e.g. Jarstad, Anna K. / Sisk, Timothy D. (eds.): From War to Democracy. Dilemmas of Peacebuilding. Cambridge: Cambridge University Press, 2008.
59   Hippler, Jochen: Nation-states for Export? Nation-building between military intervention, crisis prevention and development policy, in: Hippler, Jochen (ed.): Nation-Building. A Key Concept for Peaceful Conflict Transformation?, London: Pluto Press, 2005, pp. 173–190, also Grävingholt, Jörn / Leininger, Julia / Schlumberger, Oliver: Demokratieförderung. Quo vadis?, in: APuZ, 2009, No. 8, pp. 28–33.

nic conflict there. The Macedonian state acknowledged that all groups not belonging to the ethnic majority group have a constitutive character.[60] In contrast, intervention came very late to Bosnia-Herzegovina, and, of course also based on the high violence of the ethnic conflict, even today ethnicity continues to be the all-determining category for representation and is cemented into the political design. Strategic choices do apparently have consequences.

Alina Mungiu-Pippidi writes that in many cases ethnic clientelistic networks still dominate all sectors of society.[61] Ethnicity continues to be an ever-present topic among civil society activists, as well; negative ethnic categories are frequently reproduced and transmitted.[62] She hints that

> [I]n order to have democracy, one must first have a state, which requires agreement on who makes up the political community and where boundaries should be drawn. For a polity to democratize, *it must first be acknowledged as one by its entire population* and granted the same recognition by the international powers. To meet these two conditions simultaneously has proven exceedingly rare in Southeast Europe. (Emphasis mine – FB)[63]

The most successful states with respect to democratization are either ethnically homogenous (e.g. Poland and Hungary) or have succeeded in establishing equality and peaceful relations among their ethnic groups, including equal representation in the national political community (e.g. Slovenia and Romania). Countries that have failed to achieve parity and mutual understanding among their ethnic groups have been relatively less successful with democratization (e.g. Macedonia).[64]

Regarding the stagnation of democratization at a 'hybrid' level, the future remains uncertain. The impact of the economic crisis in 2008 is strongly visible in all post-socialist states not only but also, in terms of the changing and decreasing investment priorities of Western states. However, the prospect of EU accession may provide impetus for reforms[65] – yet incentives are closer in reach for some, e.g. Macedonia and Croatia, than for others, e.g. Bosnia-Herzegovina and Serbia – not to mention the countries with no prospects for accession. Additionally, unclear politics of the EU regarding pos-

---

60 Hornstein-Tomić, Caroline: Interethnische Beziehungen in Südosteuropa. Ein Bericht zur Lage in Bosnien-Herzegowina, Kosovo, Kroatien, Mazedonien, Montenegro, und Serbien, Konrad-Adenauer-Stiftung, 2008, p. 45, 47, http://www.kas.de/wf/doc/kas_13999-544-1-30.pdf
61 Mungiu-Pippidi, Alina: Democratization without Decommunization in the Balkans, in: ORBIS, 2006 (Vol. 50), No. 4, pp. 641–655.
62 Hornstein-Tomić, Caroline: Interethnische Beziehungen in Südosteuropa. Ein Bericht zur Lage in Bosnien-Herzegowina, Kosovo, Kroatien, Mazedonien, Montenegro, und Serbien, Konrad-Adenauer-Stiftung, 2008, p. 45, http://www.kas.de/wf/doc/kas_13999-544-1-30.pdf
63 Mungiu-Pippidi, Alina: Democratization without Decommunization in the Balkans, in: ORBIS, 2006 (Vol. 50), No. 4, pp. 641–655, here p. 644.
64 Mungiu-Pippidi, Alina: Democratization without Decommunization in the Balkans, in: ORBIS, 2006 (Vol. 50), No. 4, pp. 641–655, here pp. 646–647.
65 Hornstein-Tomić, Caroline: Interethnische Beziehungen in Südosteuropa. Ein Bericht zur Lage in Bosnien-Herzegowina, Kosovo, Kroatien, Mazedonien, Montenegro, und Serbien, Konrad-Adenauer-Stiftung, 2008, pp. 82–83, http://www.kas.de/wf/doc/kas_13999-544-1-30.pdf

sible accession have lead to increasing EU scepticism and a decrease in EU-oriented policies. Maybe as time goes by and future generations grow up, despite the brain drain in some countries, gradual but definite change can happen: young people travel, study/work abroad or see different perspectives in the media (even though they are also immersed in the historical heritage of their own countries).

Although the results of the study might not be statistically robust at this point, they nonetheless strongly indicate that decontextualized democracy promotion and insistence on the installation of the characteristics of Western democracies often only leads to 'democratic façades'.[66] External democracy promotion today has a worldwide annual budget of about 10 billion euros[67] and sometimes is pejoratively referred to as the 'boom-industry' of international cooperation.[68] In fact, the effectiveness of democracy promotion up to date has not been scientifically proven; only the effects of EU accession seem to be clearly detectable.[69] This may be due to various reasons: either changes in value, as said above, take years or decades, or for some reason the strategies do not have the intended effect – or various actors do not mind the *status quo*. Or, in some cases, ethnic fragmentation is not as grave as often stated, but nonetheless competes for external support. Often well-functioning economic cooperation across ethnic divisions might be an indicator for the latter.[70]

Concluding from the literature and first explorative interviews, the two most likely answers to the research question are: 1) State-building is often given priority and necessary nation-building is neglected; and 2) either a) all actors are aware of the ethnic divide, but donors and NGOs need to spend or receive democratization resources, so they ignore the existing ethnicized bias, or b) the ethnic divide is not as threatening as often stated, but different actors exploit the issue so that outsiders will continue to provide resources.

Interviews to be conducted in 2009 and 2010 will provide further insight into this field and contribute to a more detailed categorization of mechanisms at work in the context of external democracy promotion of civil society in ethnically fragmented countries.

---

66   Grävingholt, Jörn / Leininger, Julia / Schlumberger, Oliver: Demokratieförderung. Quo vadis?, in: APuZ, 2009, No. 8, pp. 28–33, here p. 30.
67   Ibid., p. 28.
68   Schraeder, Peter J. (ed.): Exporting Democracy. Rhetoric vs. Reality, London: Lynne Rienner, 2000, cited in Grävingholt, Jörn / Leininger, Julia / Schlumberger, Oliver: Demokratieförderung. Quo vadis?, in: APuZ, 2009, No. 8, pp. 28–33, here p. 28.
69   Grävingholt, Jörn / Leininger, Julia / Schlumberger, Oliver: Demokratieförderung. Quo vadis?, in: APuZ, 2009, No. 8, pp. 28–33, here p. 28; Schimmelfennig, Frank / Scholtz, Hanno: EU Democracy Promotion in the European Neighbourhood. Political Conditionality, Economic Development and Transnational Exchange, in: European Union Politics, 2008 (Vol. 9), No. 2, pp. 187–215.
70   Hornstein-Tomić, Caroline: Interethnische Beziehungen in Südosteuropa. Ein Bericht zur Lage in Bosnien-Herzegowina, Kosovo, Kroatien, Mazedonien, Montenegro, und Serbien, Konrad-Adenauer-Stiftung, 2008, p. 8, http://www.kas.de/wf/doc/kas_13999-544-1-30.pdf

*Part III. Finding One's Place in Civil Society.
Examples from Russia*

Christian Fröhlich

6. Walking the Tightrope. Russian Disability NGOs' Struggle with International and Domestic Demands

6.1. Introduction

Over the course of the social transformations of the 1990s, the Russian social security system faced rapid change due to declining financial and structural resources, and the social situation – especially of handicapped people – became even more precarious. The lack of social welfare distributed by the state, along with the transforming and relatively open political atmosphere, led to an enormous development of nongovernmental organizations (NGO) and grass-roots organizations in the first half of the 1990s to fill the gaps in local health care and social services for people with disabilities.[1]

Although there was little state control, financial support for these organizations was not forthcoming. Searching for funding, the leaders of an emerging Russian nongovernmental sector met with international donors of state agencies or NGOs from mainly Western nations, which were expanding their aid to former states of the Soviet Union as part of globally operating democratization programmes and human rights supporters.

Russian NGOs benefited from these international support measures in some respects, but stable and continuing work by disability NGOs in Russia for the social integration of the disabled is far from being realized. Their constant search for funding and securing their existence cause them to struggle on two fronts. On the one hand, they have to compete for international funding that stipulates specific Western demands on organizational structures and project aims. On the other hand, Russian NGOs have to legitimize their activities within domestic political structures, which often require project activities that are rejected by international donor organizations. This chapter is concerned with the question of how these conflicting international and domestic demands influence the activities of Russian NGOs. The example of disability NGOs is striking because organizational action on the issue of disability is addressed differently by international donors and domestic political authorities. On the basis of preliminary empirical findings from interviews with Russian NGO leaders, representatives of international donor organizations and domestic political actors, which were conducted during a first period of field work in Moscow, St Petersburg and Nishniy Novgorod in February and March 2009, the contribution sheds light on a paradoxical

---

1 Holland, Daniel: Grass Roots Promotion of Community Health and Human Rights for People with Disabilities in Post-communist Central Europe. A profile of the Slovak Republic, in: Disability and Society, 2003 (Vol. 18), No. 2, pp. 133–143, here pp. 136 f.

social field. The following chapter will explore the activities of international donor organizations in Russia. Their relationship to Russian NGOs as well as the risk of cleavage among the Russian NGO community will be discussed. Subsequently, the relationship between Russian NGOs and domestic political structures will be analysed concerning their opposition to international influence, which reinforces the cleavage. Finally, a few remarks will be made about the effectiveness of international funding and the prospects of NGO activities in Russia.

6.2. Russian NGOs and International Donors

Observers of civil society development in Russia are unsure about the extent of international funding for Russian NGOs: some believe that half or more[2] of all Russian civil society organizations have received resources from international donors while others contend that the figure is actually half or fewer.[3] In any case, international funding played a crucial role in the development of civil society in the early 1990s and often constituted the only source of money and knowledge.

The international discussion about the role of civil society in the democratization process hinges mainly on its ability to influence the consolidation of democracy, as for example when advocacy groups support the rights of certain societal segments. In this model of transition, transnational actors of democracy promotion play a crucial role in enabling civil society.[4] These actors are international donor organizations, foundations and (inter-)governmental development agencies. They pursue internationally represented social norms and therefore act not only as 'norm entrepreneurs'[5]

---

2   Henry, Laura Ann: Changing Environments. Green Activism, Civil Society, and Political Transformation in Russia, Berkeley/CA: University of California Press, 2004.
3   Henderson, Sarah L.: Building Democracy in Contemporary Russia, Western Support for Grassroots Organizations, Ithaca/NY: Cornell University Press, 2003, pp. 100; Sperling, Valerie: Woman´s Organizations. Institutionalized Interest Groups or Vulnerable Dissidents?, in: Evans, Alfred B. Jr. / Henry, Laura A. / McIntosh Sundstrom, Lisa (eds): Russian Civil Society. A Critical Assessment, Armonk/NY, London: M.E. Sharp, 2006, pp. 161–177, here pp. 163–164.
4   Carothers, Thomas: Aiding Democracy Abroad, Washington D. C.: Carnegie, 1999; Carothers, Thomas: The End of the Transition Paradigm, in: Journal of Democracy, 2002 (Vol. 13), No. 1, pp. 5–21; Mendelsohn, Sarah E. / Glenn, John K.: The Power and Limits of NGO. A Critical Look at Building Democracy in Eastern Europe and Eurasia, New York: Colombia University Press, 2002.
5   Finnemore, Martha / Sikkink, Kathryn: International Norm Dynamics and Political Change, in: International Organization, 1998 (Vol. 52), No. 4, pp. 887–917; Risse, Thomas / Sikkink, Kathryn: The Socialization of International Human Rights Norms into Domestic Practices. Introduction, in: Risse, Thomas / Roop, Stephen C. / Sikkink, Kathryn (eds): The Power of Human Rights. International Norms and Domestic Change, Cambridge: Cambridge University Press, 1999, pp. 1–38.

on the global scene, but also as 'moral financiers' by providing resources for national campaigns on socio-political topics.[6]

Over the last three decades, the United Nations has adopted a range of norm corpuses addressing the social welfare and social treatment of people with disabilities. These norms can be interpreted as an internationally accepted understanding of what disability is about and how to deal with it on the domestic level.[7] The most recent resolution is the first UN Convention of the new millennium, the 'Convention on the Rights of Persons with Disabilities', which was adopted in December 2006. It took a record time of only four years to ratify, and two-thirds of all member states signed it on the first possible day. Although the principles of equal opportunities, participation, social security and inclusion of people with disabilities experience varying degrees of implementation in domestic policies,[8] this convention and its norms enjoy a high level of acceptance on the level of world society.

Highly accepted and legitimated social objectives and aims are carried and spread by social organizations. Sociological Institutionalism explains this practice with the concept of 'social agency'.[9] These organizations advocate on a collective level for the interests and goals of social groups. On the global level of world society, these agents promote certain kinds of normative principles, such as individualism, universal fairness, and rational and organized actionability.[10] Theorists call this approach the 'world polity', which conceptualizes the world as being oriented on the cultural principles of modern, Western liberalism.[11] This 'world polity' is a highly legitimized norm corpus that defines who is accepted as an actor on the global stage and who is not.

That does not mean that a 'world polity of disability' truly exists. Here it is implied that on a global level international organizations have to conform to these principles and modes of action. In the case of democracy promotion, it means that international

---

6   McIntosh Sundstrom, Lisa: Foreign Assistance, International Norms, and NGO Development. Lessons from the Russian Campaign, in: International Organization, 2005 (Vol. 59), Spring, pp. 419–449, here p. 420.
7   The three main norm corpuses are: the 'World Programme of Action concerning Disabled Persons', adopted in 1982, the 'Standard Rules on the Equalization of Opportunities for Persons with Disabilities', which were adopted in 1993, and the 'Convention on the Rights of Persons with Disabilities', adopted in 2006.
8   Hausotter, Anette: Integration und Inklusion – Europa macht sich auf den Weg. Die Entwicklung integrativer Bildung in den Mitgliedsländern der Europäischen Union, in: Hans, Maren / Ginnold, Antje (eds): Integration von Menschen mit Behinderung – Entwicklungen in Europa, Neuwied: Luchterhand, 2000, pp. 43–83; Maschke, Michael: Behinderung als Feld wohlfahrtsstaatlicher Politik – eine Systematisierung der Behindertenpolitik, in: Berliner Journal für Soziologie, 2004 (Vol. 14), No. 3, pp. 399–420.
9   Meyer, John W. / Jepperson, Ronald L.: The 'Actors' of Modern Society. The Cultural Construction of Social Agency, in: Sociological Theory, 2000 (Vol. 18), No. 1, pp. 100–120.
10   ibid.
11   Meyer, John W. / Boli, John / Thomas, George M. / Ramirez, Francisco O.: World Society and the Nation State, in: American Journal of Sociology, 1997 (Vol. 103), No. 1, pp. 144–181.

organizations tend to cooperate only with actors that can be legitimated on the basis of the 'right' (globally accepted) organizational structures, modes of action and pursued goals. Most international donor organizations therefore have a very precise mode of selecting Russian partner organizations. On the one hand, the requirements for the applicants during grant competitions already show a preference for certain kinds of organizations. Past research on international support for Russian NGOs that are concerned with women's and soldiers' rights demonstrates that international donor organizations often want to support only those projects and NGOs representing liberal Western models of democracy and civil society, such as advocacy for individual and human rights, support for social movements and autonomy from the government.[12]

Likewise, in the process of system transformation, domestic NGOs in Russia refer to international norms in order to obtain guidance or to legitimate their claims and actions. For example, the new foundations in the beginning of the 1990s had no role models within their domestic context from whom they could learn a political agenda for the integration of people with disabilities beyond their personal experiences. But the adoption of international paradigms by domestic organizations is by no means an unquestioned process. Domestic NGOs often have their own understanding of these paradigms and their realization. That is why international norms are often localized in concrete cases as tools to achieve project goals. As many disability activists founded their organizations over the course of the 1990s, the WHO definition of disability from 1990 was still pertinent. Although it 'emphasize(s) the shortcomings in the environment and in many organized activities in society […] which prevent persons with disabilities from participating on equal terms'[13], the focus was still on physical and mental limitations as the causes of disability. This legitimated the organizational project aims of Russian NGOs regarding the provision of social services, which was the most urgent need of disabled people at that time. Many Russian disability NGOs failed to incorporate the change in international paradigms concerning the social integration of disabled people, with a focus on human rights and empowerment during the 1990s, into their agendas. That means that although a wide range of domestic NGOs are orientated on global paradigms, an equivalent adoption of current global norms cannot be assumed. That causes an uneven level of support from international donors, because they prefer to cooperate with NGOs that can demonstrate adoption of the most recent global norms in their project measures and organizational structures.

The observations in this study confirm these arguments: analysis of funding structures shows that international donor organizations prefer to cooperate with NGOs

---

12   Sundstrom, Lisa: Limits to Global Civil Society. Gaps between Western Donors and Russian NGOs, in: Laxer, Gordon / Halperin, Sandra (eds): Global Civil Society and its Limits, Basingstoke: Palgrave McMillan, 2003, pp. 146–165, here p. 150.
13   United Nations: United Nations Standard Rules on the Equalization of Opportunities for Persons with Disabilities. A/RES/48/96. Adopted 20.12.1993, Paragraph 18.

whose leaders have attended at least one international exchange programme and already have a 'funding history', i.e. have already received international funding in the past. These leaders speak the 'language of the West' and know how to articulate their project aims in the framework of human rights, democratization and advocacy. Russian applicants for international funding not only have to master 'application lyrics', but also need to have excellent English language skills, since the applications have to be submitted in English.

The results from the interviews conducted with internationally-funded Russian disability NGO representatives show that this funding often requires many organizational resources. But international donors link their funding measures with advanced training in organizational management, fundraising and accounting. Thus they transfer their modes of action, along with the normative paradigms of a rational organizational structure that are legitimized for rational actors on the global level, to Russian NGOs. In the words of world polity theory, international donor organizations thereby construct their partners as rational actors and fulfil their mission as agents of world polity.

The focus of international donors on already 'Westernized' Russian NGOs and the stringent requirements for application and project realization preclude other Russian NGOs from obtaining funding. The latter group includes disability organizations that are primarily concerned with providing social and medical services on a very local level due to the lack of state provision. The disability NGOs in the sample of this study that received little or no funding from international donors show a much higher level of basic charity and service provision activity than their foreign-funded counterparts Non-internationally-funded organizations have direct contact with their clientele when they e.g. help them with job-seeking or argue with local authorities for accessible buses and depressed kerbs. These NGOs also realize cultural and recreational projects by arranging excursions, sports competitions and collective meals and festivities. Their self-perception and normative framing is not embedded in human rights discourse or opposition to the state authority's status quo; they instead see themselves as partners with the government in solving urgent socio-economic problems.

By excluding these domestic NGOs from their funding, international donor organizations enhance the risk of cleavage in the Russian NGO community and of establishing activist elites rather than supporting horizontal connections between NGOs by focusing too much on the most prominent and powerful organizations and ignoring the smaller players. Very well funded domestic NGOs sometimes have a negative effect on the motivation for application of others. Some organizations refrain from applying for international grants because they do not want to replace their project aims with a human rights agenda or because they anticipate a preference for certain well-established NGOs among international donors.

6.3. Russian NGOs and the Domestic Political Environment

International assistance and funding for NGO development do not occur in a vacuum, but in a political environment in which NGOs are embedded and restrained in their activities. Scholars point out political barriers against democratic reforms which take the form of bureaucratic obstacles and political harassment of activists.[14] Others argue that the political system and governmental structures set specific barriers for NGO activities by delegitimizing certain normative modes of actions.[15]

It is often discussed whether and how the state should be involved in civil society and NGO development and at what point the autonomy of NGOs is compromised by a relationship with state authorities.[16] On the one hand, coherent governance could be fruitful for civil society by implementing laws and setting up legal conditions for NGO activities, as can be seen in Western liberal and democratic states. But on the other hand, government involvement could be dangerous in post-Communist states with authoritarian histories.[17] The tradition of 'gosudarstvennost' ('loyalty to the state') shaped the state-civil society relationship even before the Soviet Union and is being revitalized under the Putin administration.[18] This tendency is often perceived as dangerous for civil society development because it leads to a 'quasi-civil society' comprised of a network of technically nongovernmental organizations that continuously support governmentally-defined issues.[19]

---

14 Mendelssohn, Sarah E.: Democracy Assistance and Political Transition in Russia. Between Success and Failure, in: International Security, 2001 (Vol. 25), No. 4, pp. 68–106.
15 Schmitz, Hans Peter / Sikkink, Kathryn: International Human Rights, in: Carlsnaes, Walter / Risse, Thomas / Simmons, Beth A. (eds): Handbook of International Relations, London: Sage, 2002, pp. 517–537, here p. 523.
16 Hale, Henry E.: Civil Society from Above? Statist and Liberal Models of State-Building in Russia, in: Demokratizatsiia, 2002 (Vol. 10), No. 3, pp. 306–321; McMann, Kelly M.: The Civic Realm of Kyrgyzstan. Soviet Economic Legacies and Activist´s Expectations, in: Jones Luong, Pauline (eds): The Transformation of States and Societies in Central Asia, Ithaca/NY, London: Cornell University Press, 2003, pp. 213–245, here p. 242.
17 Diamond, Larry Jay: Developing Democracy: Toward Consolidation, Baltimore/MD: Johns Hopkins University Press, 1999, here pp. 250–260; Fish, Steven M.: Russia´s Fourth Transition, in: Diamond, Larry Jay / Plattner, Marc F.: The Global Resurgence of Democracy, 1996, pp. 264–275, here pp. 272–273.
18 McIntosh Sundstrom, Lisa / Henry, Laura A.: Russian Civil Society. Tensions and Trajectories, in: Evans, Alfred B. Jr. / Henry, Laura A. / McIntosh Sundstrom, Lisa (eds): Russian Civil Society. A Critical Assessment, Armonk/NY, London: M.E. Sharp, 2006, pp. 305–322, here p. 316.
19 Evans, Alfred B. Jr.: Vladimir Putin´s Design for Civil Society, in: Evans, Alfred B. Jr. / Henry, Laura A. / McIntosh Sundstrom, Lisa (eds): Russian Civil Society. A Critical Assessment, Armonk/NY, London: M.E. Sharp, 2006, pp. 147–158, here p. 152; Hale, Henry E.: Civil Society from Above? Statist and Liberal Models of State-Building in Russia, in: Demokratizatsiia, 2002 (Vol. 10), No. 3, pp. 306–321, here p. 310, 314–319; Squier, John: Civil Society and the Challenge of Russian Gosudarstvennost, in: Demokratizatsiia, 2002 (Vol. 10), No. 2, pp. 166–183. An example of tense state-civil society entanglement is the formation of so-called 'government organized non-governmental organizations' (GONGOs).

6. Walking the Tightrope

In Russia, two characteristics of the political environment for NGOs need to be emphasized. On the one hand, the traditionally strong entanglement of the government and domestic NGOs influences civil society-state relationships by pushing the latter into the direction of social service provision. On the other hand, the government's tendency to interpret NGO human rights-based activities as oppositional and offences against the state are constantly restraining the scope for internationally funded project implementation. Most of the existing Russian disabilities NGOs were set up in the late 1980s or in the first half of the 1990s. Most of the interviewed activists began their engagement back then in informal self-help groups and grass-roots organizations. Those developments were triggered by the state's failure to provide social welfare services during the 1990s, which led to cooperation between the state and NGOs.[20] The tense relations with governmental structures also facilitated the consolidation of NGOs due to state provision of material resources like accommodations and equipment.[21] The norm corpus in social policy toward disability, with its focus on social protection, favours social security measures. Although in 1995 a new legal status for people with disabilities entailing equal political, economic and civil opportunities was introduced, the Federal Law Nr. 181 'On Social Protection of Persons with Disabilities in the Russian Federation'[22] was oriented on the UN Standard Rules on the Equalization of Opportunities for Persons with Disabilities[23] and has still not yet been revised with regard to current changes in the international norm corpus (e.g. the 'International Classification of Functioning, Disability and Health'[24]). Medical categories of impairment still shape disability policy in Russia. Even though Russia signed the UN Convention on the Rights of Persons with Disabilities in September 2008 and President Medvedev officially put support for the disabled on the priority list, patronizing paternalistic norms still play a powerful role in the social security system for people with disabilities. Therefore, domestic NGOs that focus on social and medical services for their clientele face preferential treatment by official authorities. On a formal level, social security for the disabled is assured but regulations to protect them from discrimination are absent.[25] There are almost no forms of administrative action regard-

---

20 Salamon, Lester M. / Anheiner, Helmut K.: Social Origins of Civil Society. Explaining the Nonprofit Sector Cross-Nationally, in: Voluntas, 1998 (Vol. 9), No. 3, pp. 213–148.
21 Thomson, Kate: Disability Organizations in the Regions, in: Evans, Alfred B. Jr. / Henry, Laura A. / McIntosh Sundstrom, Lisa (eds): Russian Civil Society. A Critical Assessment, Armonk/NY, London: M.E. Sharp, 2006, pp. 229–245, here p. 230.
22 Rossiiskaya Federatsiya: Federal'nyi zakon Rossiiskoi Federatsii 'O sotsial'noi zashchite invalidov v Rossiiskoi Federatsii', Glava 1. 24.11.1995. N 181-FZ.
23 United Nations: United Nations Standard Rules on the Equalization of Opportunities for Persons with Disabilities. A/RES/48/96, adopted 20.12.1993.
24 World Health Organization (WHO): International Classification of Functioning, Disability and Health (ICF), Genf, 2001.
25 Zhavoronkov, R.: Russian Federation. International Disability Rights Monitor 2007. Regional Report of Europe, in: International Disability Network, Chicago: Center for International Rehabilitation,

ing state responsibility for rehabilitation, which has caused a lack of regulations on how integration projects should be financed.[26] Likewise, these conditions have a paradoxical effect: On the one hand, a huge bureaucratic apparatus consolidates things, but on the other hand, there are very few controls and rules to keep its actors in line. Therefore, decision making and actions among local officials vary strongly in regard to their professional qualifications, sensitivity about social problems, and capacity for effective work.[27]

Human rights activities and social and political advocacy within certain Russian NGOs developed as reaction to these shortcomings. These NGOs take a human rights approach when promoting anti-discrimination and equality for people with disabilities via public promotion campaigns or by negotiating with local authorities for enforcement of the laws. International donor organizations focus on these organizations because their projects and efforts reflect Western norms and values concerning the rule of law and citizenship. But many other Russian NGOs focus on social and cultural activities, which are also attempts to decrease social exclusion, but they are not promoting a human rights agenda. Conventionally, these disability NGOs are virtually invisible to international donors, because the latter support 'politics of difference', which fight structural inequality by articulating new and positive identities for hidden and stigmatized social groups.[28]

But disability organizations face difficulties in adopting this 'Western' political and analytical approach because the Putin Administration discredits Russian civil society organizations receiving grants and other resources from international donors or private foundations as state-decomposing entities. Internationally-funded organizations or activists who advocate for human rights are often interpreted as questioning the status quo of the government. When they for example push for more self-determination and political and social participation for people with disabilities, they risk being labelled as dissidents and being marginalized and oppressed by state authorities.[29]

These patterns came to light in the conducted interviews. Citing fear of oppression otherwise, a representative of a Russian disability NGO in St Petersburg justified his organization's focus on social and cultural activities. He explicitly reasoned that the NGO could become a target for tax fraud investigation if it were to engage either in

---

2007, pp. 359–397, here p. 369.
26 Maleva, T. M. / Vasin, S. A.: Invalidy v Rossii. Uzel starykh i novykh problem, in: Pro et Contra, 2001, No. 3, pp. 80–104.
27 Romanov, P. V. / Yarskaya-Smirnova, E. R.: Ideologiya sotsial'noi politiki i praktika sotsial'nogo obsluzhivaniya v period liberal'nykh reform, in: Sotsial'naya politika v sovremennoi Rossii. Reformy i povsednevnost', Moskwa: Variant, 2008, pp. 80–105.
28 Young, Iris M.: Inclusion and Democracy, Oxford: Oxford University Press, 2002, pp. 81–120.
29 Evans, Alfred B. Jr.: Vladimir Putin´s Design for Civil Society, in: Evans, Alfred B. Jr. / Henry, Laura A. / McIntosh Sundstrom, Lisa (eds): Russian Civil Society. A Critical Assessment, Armonk/NY, London: M.E. Sharp, 2006, pp. 147–158; here pp. 149f.

criticism of political decisions or in campaigns against discrimination. That is why he would not apply for international grants to run human rights projects. Simultaneously, a member of Russian Parliament (DUMA) voiced his fear in an interview that international organizations could erode Russian society by funding and supporting activities for domestic NGOs, because the supported activities were critical of the states' status quo.

But that does not mean that disability NGOs that are too enmeshed with governmental structures to receive international support necessarily have more influence on state policies and social welfare structures. The degree of impact deeply depends on the level of individual engagement in governmental structures and on the commitment of the organizations' activists.

The example of the largest Russian disability NGO network 'All-Russian Society for the Disabled' (Russ. VOI) illustrates this. On the one hand, the highest level of the organization's hierarchy was directly involved in the elaboration of the 1995 law and they are currently participating in several government committees as consultants. In some cases, NGO representatives hold political offices and thus play a dual role. But these individuals do not necessarily use their positions to lobby for policy change. A typical opinion of NGO representatives with close ties to the state was articulated in an interview with a high-ranking representative of VOI. He expressed scepticism toward NGOs that strive for quick and widespread changes in Russian social policy for disabled people. Instead, he advocated a slow process of implementation and evaluation of existing laws. Analogously, the study also contains feedback from a local branch of VOI in Moscow. Its activists had good contacts to local authorities, but did not use them to influence social policy and struggle for change, but rather to negotiate for the implementation of the pre-existing right to appropriate access to the public sphere. For example, activists work with local decision makers to install sunken kerbs in order to improve wheelchair accessibility.

But on the other hand, there are – albeit very few – Russian NGOs who base their activities on a human rights approach and can therefore be seen as 'oppositional' to the state's approach to disability issues; they are, however, also successful in engaging with local authorities and politicians. In the study, a Moscow-based, internationally well funded NGO was found to regularly involve a DUMA deputy in their anti-discrimination campaigns and to have evolved cooperation with local authorities in order to establish an inclusive school for children with and without disabilities. Activists of this NGO constantly try to widen the scope of possibilities and introduce Western forms of integration measures. In Moscow they converge with a relatively open-minded and contemporary atmosphere among authorities in comparison with the situation in other Russian regions.

In any case, the examples show that cooperation with state authorities is crucial for implementing rights for the disabled and introducing new integration measures. The state's prejudices against international donor influence on Russian civil society can be overcome by the activists' individual commitment and engagement with state officials. In the absence of a formal, general framework of NGO-state relationships, improving the lives of disabled persons in Russia requires one act of individual negotiation and personal struggle after another.

6.4. Conclusion

It cannot be denied that the activities of international donor organizations have had very positive effects on the development of nongovernmental support and advocacy for the problems and needs of people with disabilities. Due to their funding and knowledge transfer, Russian NGOs are able to address the various concerns of the disabled in Russia and develop a wide range of supporting activities. The adoption of 'Western' human rights approaches, with emphasis on the principles of equal opportunities, participation, social security and inclusion of people with disabilities, changes their scope of activities from providing social services to struggling with discrimination and increasing public awareness. Furthermore, the cooperation of Russian NGOs with international organizations causes a transfer of 'Western' patterns of organizational structures and modes of action. Management systems, development strategies, and controlling and accounting structures have become increasingly common in Russian NGOs over the course of their funding histories.

But these developments are selective because of specificities of international funding strategies and grant applications. This leads to the division of Russian disability organizations into those that do and do not cooperate internationally. Both groups implement different modes of action and approaches to disability, which means that a 'world polity of disability' can only be established in the Russian context to some extent.

Internationally-funded Russian NGOs have to struggle with a 'refractory' political environment (on both the local and federal levels). This forces them to engage in a 'local decoupling' of language and action[30]: although they use the Western language of human rights in project proposals and final reports when applying and accounting for international grants, Russian NGOs keep their actions and communications towards state officials within the traditional parameters of the state-NGO relationship, which is essentially a social service partnership. The most successful NGOs in the study sample constantly try to strike a balance between realizing human rights projects with international grants while at the same time continuing to provide social services.

---

30 Meyer, John W. / Rowan, Brian: Institutionalized Organizations. Formal Structures as Myth and Ceremony, in: American Journal of Sociology, 1977 (Vol. 83), No. 2, pp. 340–363.

However, international influence on the Russian NGOs' modes of action in terms of advocacy for human rights often opposes the state's positions on that topic and thus faces cultural limits. Past research has shown that successful project implementation partly depends on cooperation between governmental structures and political activists. On the other hand, it is important to appeal to universal and culturally accepted norms (like e.g. physical integrity) and to only later connect them to human rights topics and calls for political change. In Russia, the discussion on human rights does not receive the same response as in Western societies, where the principles of individual rights and liberty are taken more seriously.[31] For disability NGOs, it is thus problematic to employ a human-rights-based approach to disability in a political and cultural context that is so different from their original background.[32] The confrontation between domestic political and international actors has taken Russian NGOs hostage. As a result, both sides risk destroying what they actually want to support – the social integration of people with disabilities. But this aim can only be reached by a coalition of all powers in the field.

---

31   McIntosh Sundstrom, Lisa: Soldier's Rights Groups in Russia, in: Evans, Alfred B. Jr. / Henry, Laura A. / McIntosh Sundstrom, Lisa (eds): Russian Civil Society. A Critical Assessment, Armonk/NY, London: M.E. Sharp, 2006, pp. 179–192: shows that using the example of soldiers' mothers' groups.
32   Thomson, Kate: Disability Organizations in the Regions, in: Evans, Alfred B. Jr. / Henry, Laura A. / McIntosh Sundstrom, Lisa (eds): Russian Civil Society. A Critical Assessment, Armonk/NY, London: M.E. Sharp, 2006, pp. 229–245, here p. 240; see also: Stone, Emma: From the Research Notes of a Foreign Devil. Disability Research in China, in: Barnes, Colin / Mercer, Geof (eds): Doing Disability Research, Leeds: The Disability Press, 1997, pp. 207–226.

Ulla Pape

7. Striving for Social Change. NGOs in the Field of HIV/AIDS, Drug Policy and Human Rights in the Russian Federation

7.1. Introduction

The concept of civil society has been central in the discourse on post-Soviet transition. Western donors have developed a great variety of programmes to assist the formation of civil society in order to promote democratic development in former Communist countries. From today's perspective, however, the outcomes of external democracy assistance can be regarded as meagre, as they have not succeeded in rooting the new ideas in society.

This particularly holds true for Russia, where civic engagement and the development of a participatory political culture can still be regarded as weak. In addition, the state increasingly constrains public space, thereby hampering the development of an active NGO sector. It would, however, be wrong to conclude that there is no civil society in present-day Russia. Many citizens have organized themselves around issues that directly affect them or their family members. In the context of a collapsing social system, they have taken matters into their own hands by creating organizations that respond to concrete needs. In many fields of social policy, e.g. in response to the HIV/AIDS epidemic, Russian NGOs have become key actors and are today more and more accepted as partners of state institutions.

The relationship between NGOs and the Russian state, however, is of a paradoxical nature. On the one hand, state authorities emphasize the role of NGOs in delivering public goods, as they are aware of the fact that civil society actors are much needed to address Russia's pressing social problems. On the other hand, social-sector NGOs have a hard time realizing their respective objectives, because they have limited access to decision-making processes and are increasingly subjected to state control, which is hampering their activity. Russian NGOs that aim to respond to social needs and transform social policy have to find ways to effectively engage with state authorities in order to achieve social policy improvements. In this political process, NGOs thus constantly need to navigate between their objectives and the opportunities provided by the political context.

In studying the complex interplay between NGOs and the state in post-Soviet Russia, this article will apply Sidney Tarrow's concept of political opportunity structures, which can serve as a useful framework to analyse the role of civil society in social policymaking. The article focuses on the examples of three Russian NGOs: (1) the *Union of the Committees of Soldiers' Mothers*, (2) the *Russian Harm Reduction Network* and (3) the *Russian Association of People Living with HIV/AIDS*. All three NGOs were created on the grassroots level in order to respond to concrete social needs. Furthermore, the three organizations are similar in that they all aim to achieve policy changes, be it in the field of human rights protection in the armed forces, drug policy or the response to HIV/AIDS. All three NGOs offer social services to Russian citizens, but also engage in advocacy work. They all deal with topical social problems that have a human rights dimension. The three examples, however, also reveal a number of differences. They vary with respect to the issues they address, the recognition they receive from state institutions, the strategies they apply, and their impact on social policy.

By comparing the political opportunity structures and influence strategies of three Russian NGOs, the article investigates how civil society actors function in the political context of post-Soviet Russia. It addresses the question of why social-sector NGOs have different degrees of success in influencing social policy, and thus aims to contribute to our understanding of social change and civil society development in today's Russia. The outline of the chapter is the following: After elaborating a working definition for civil society and conceptualizing its relation to the state, I will outline the development of civil society in post-Soviet Russia before turning to the key question, which is the interrelation between NGOs and the state. Examining three particular NGOs, I will focus on the strategies they use in order to create opportunities for social change. The information presented here is partly based on interviews with NGO representatives. Finally, I will draw conclusions from the discussed cases of NGO engagement.

7.2. The Complex Interrelation between Civil Society and the State

The first step of the investigation is to elaborate a working definition of civil society and conceptualize its relation to the state. Over the past two decades, the concept of 'civil society' has gained great popularity, both among scholars and policy-makers. According to Gellner, 'civil society' can be defined as 'the space between the state, the market and the family.'[1] As an arena of societal debate and interaction, the term 'civil society' not only refers to organizations, but also encompasses civic principles and values, civic culture and forms of collective action within society. The core of its definition lies in providing an 'arena of uncoerced collective action around shared interests, purposes and values.'[2]

NGOs on their part can be understood as key actors in civil society. Despite their diversity, NGOs share common characteristics. According to the *Johns Hopkins*

---

1 Gellner, Ernest: Conditions of Liberty. Civil Society and its Rivals, London: Hamish Hamilton, 1994.
2 Centre for Civil Society: What is Civil Society?, in: LSE Centre for Civil Society, http://www.lse.ac.uk/collections/CCS/what_is_civil_society.htm, accessed 20 May 2009.

7. Striving for Social Change 91

Comparative Nonprofit Sector Project, NGOs are both non-governmental and non-profit, meaning that they are independent from state structures and do not distribute profits among their members.[3] Moreover, NGOs possess an organizational structure, are self-governing and voluntary in their membership.[4]

The interaction between NGOs and the state is complex and reciprocal. The state shapes the conditions for civil society development by providing legislation and offering modes of societal participation in decision-making processes. State treatment of civil society can range from hostile to benevolent and actively supportive.[5] NGOs in turn have a transformative potential vis-à-vis the state. As service providers they can raise resources for enhancing and reforming public services. Furthermore, they can exert influence on government policies by articulating collective interests and holding political authorities accountable.

A relevant theoretical framework for the analysis of the relationship between the state and civil society can be found in Sidney Tarrow's concept of political opportunity structures, which evolved from the study of social movements.[6] Tarrow's analytical framework can be applied to the given context in order to analyse the conditions and strategies of Russian NGOs vis-à-vis state authorities. In his view, political opportunities and constraints can be defined as 'dimensions of the political environment that provide incentives for collective action by affecting people's expectations for success or failure.'[7] The political context thus shapes the NGOs' conditions. Opportunities for NGOs include expanding access to decision-making processes, shifting alignments in the power structures, taking advantage of the division of elites and seeking out influential allies.[8] Repression, on the other hand, can be understood as a means 'to depress collective action and raise the costs for organising and mobilising opinion.'[9] While direct suppression might be more visible and frightening, Tarrow argues that increasing the costs for organizations can be regarded as an even more effective strategy in the long run.[10] The case of Russian civil society provides a good example. By exerting bureaucratic pressure and creating legal insecurity via ambiguous, often contradictory rules, the government seldom has to officially ban inconvenient organizations; NGOs are indirectly forced out of existence due to a lack of resources. The

---

3   Salamon, Lester M. / Sokolowski, Wojciech / List, Regina: Global Civil Society. An Overview, Baltimore/MD: The Johns Hopkins University, 2003, pp. 7–8.
4   Ibid.
5   Lillehammer, Giske C.: State-NGO Relationships in Transitional Democracies. The case of CPA-ONG – a Government Centre for the Advancement of NGOs in Benin, UNDP, 2003.
6   Tarrow, Sidney: Power in Movement. Social Movements and Contentious Politics, 2nd edn, Cambridge: Cambridge University Press, 1998.
7   Ibid., pp. 76–77.
8   Ibid., pp. 77–80.
9   Ibid., here p. 83.
10 Ibid., here p. 83.

Russian state thus effectively frustrates NGO development and suppresses independent voices from civil society.

Still, political opportunities and constraints are not static, but change over time. Societal actors have a chance, however limited, to employ strategies that allow them to open up opportunities and channel their claims. What does this mean for NGOs in the Russian context? According to Tarrow, the key to opening up political opportunities is expanding access. Regarding the social sector in Russia, the political elite are apparently becoming increasingly aware of social problems. Alarmed by a worrying demographic downturn, Russian politicians are now more willing to put social issues that had previously been treated as low priority on the agenda. In 2006, President Putin officially declared HIV/AIDS to be a national security threat and called for a scaled-up response to the epidemic. Russia's new National Security Strategy, approved in May 2009, also identifies HIV infection and other health problems as factors that increase mortality and thus endanger Russia's national security.[11] Although this new threat perception obviously does not instantly translate into a better social policy or more civil society participation, it nevertheless opens up opportunities for NGOs to formulate interests and advocate for change. The Russian health care system is in dire need of reform. State institutions are therefore inclined to accept NGOs as partners and work toward improving public policy. In this respect, one can argue that relations between the state and society have significantly changed since the end of the Soviet era. Despite a growing tendency to assert control, the political elite cannot fully close its eyes to the nation's alarming social problems. To a certain degree it needs civil society to respond to the problems. This enables NGOs to gain space for themselves and play a role in the formulation and implementation of policy.

What can NGOs do to expand their opportunities? Based on Tarrow's framework, three different strategies can be identified. First, NGOs can gain access to decision-making processes, e.g. by means of lobbying or advocacy work. Second, they can find political allies that are prepared to support their cause. Possible support can come from domestic as well as from international political actors. NGOs can, for example, cooperate with state institutions, which might in turn have a self-interest in working with civil society. Third, they can exert pressure on the authorities by mobilizing support from their constituencies. In their efforts to transform social policy, Russian NGOs achieve different outcomes. I argue that their ability to successfully achieve policy changes both depends on external as well as internal factors. First, the NGOs' transformative potential is shaped by the context of the respective policy issue, its political sensitivity and the government's approach to it. Second, the NGOs' ability to influence policy depends on their capacity to make use of the opportunities provided by the political

---

11 Russian Security Council: Strategy of National Security of the Russian Federation until 2020, 12 May 2009, No. 537, http://www.scrf.gov.ru/documents/99.html

context. This includes the above-mentioned influence strategies of gaining access to decision-making processes, finding political allies and mobilizing public support.

Before turning to the discussion of opportunity structures and influence strategies on the basis of the three examples, I will give a brief overview of civil society development in post-Soviet Russia in order to help the reader to understand the factors that have forged the conditions for NGO action in Russia in general.

7.3. Civil Society Development in Post-Soviet Russia

The concept of civil society has been central in the discourse on post-Soviet transition. After the end of the Soviet Union, Russian civil society went through a process of institutionalization and organizational development. NGOs were granted legal status and received substantial funding from Western donors, which aimed at promoting democracy through civil society support, thereby subscribing to the rationale that a strong civil society is indispensable for democratization. Some scholars, however, argue that external efforts to strengthen civil society produced ambivalent results: Although funding allowed NGOs to develop organizational capacity, they became increasingly detached from their constituencies, engaged in competition among themselves and followed donors' agendas rather than responding to local needs.[12]

Today, the conditions for civil society development in Russia are challenging, with many NGOs facing an unfavourable working environment. In addition to constricting civil liberties, the Russian government has strengthened its control over the non-governmental sector.[13] Negative media reports have associated foreign-funded NGOs with anti-Russian espionage, and, according to Andrey Makarychev, have become a powerful means of de-legitimizing the civil society sector.[14] Moreover, the new NGO law, adopted in 2006, expanded the supervisory powers of the state over foreign and domestic NGOs by tightening the regulations for registration and introducing new reporting requirements.[15] The new regulations have resulted in a decrease in the number of NGOs since 2006, and have hence by some been characterized as an 'effective cleansing' of the civil society sector.[16] The Putin government's restrictive approach towards civil society has earned harsh criticism both within Russia and internationally.

---

12   Henderson, Sarah H.: Selling Civil Society. Western Aid and the Nongovernmental Organisation Sector in Russia, in: Comparative Political Studies, 2002 (Vol. 35), No. 2, pp. 139–166, here pp. 142–143.
13   Fish, Steven M.: Democracy Derailed in Russia. The Failure of Open Politics, Cambridge: Cambridge University Press, 2005, here pp. 67–77.
14   Makarychev, Andrey S.: Politics, the State, and De-Politicization. Putin Project Reassessed, in: Problems of Post-Communism, 2008 (Vol. 55), No. 5, pp. 62–71, here p. 63.
15   The International Center for Not-for-Profit Law: Analysis of Law No. 18-FZ. On Introducing Amendments to Certain Legislative Acts of the Russian Federation, 17 February 2006, www.icnl.org/KNOWLEDGE/news/2006/01-19_Russia_NGO_Law_Analysis.pdf
16   Interview with NGO representative, St Petersburg, 30 September 2008.

However, new developments under Putin's successor, Medvedev, suggest that the Russian authorities are striving to revise their policy towards civil society once again.[17]

In summary, one can conclude that the conditions for civil society development in present-day Russia are difficult. The government displays an ambiguous attitude towards NGOs. By exerting bureaucratic pressure and creating legal insecurity via ambiguous, often contradictory rules, the authorities seldom have to ban inconvenient organizations officially; more often NGOs are indirectly forced out of existence due to a lack of resources. Yet the Russian state does not completely restrict civil society, but selectively leaves space for the development of civil society organizations, particularly in areas where their involvement is regarded to be useful. This means that the opportunities for NGOs are determined by the governments' perception of a given problem and the possible role of NGOs in that area as well as the NGOs' ability to make use of their opportunities by effectively addressing state expectations. Another critical factor is their mobilization potential. In general, Russian NGOs are limited in their capacity to mobilize society, as levels of civic participation generally remain low. However, in the social sector, where problems are tangible for many Russian citizens, NGOs have a chance to rally public support.

7.4. Opportunity Structures and Influence Strategies of Russian NGOs

In the political context, NGOs can use different strategies in order to voice their claims and achieve change. In the analysis of opportunity structures and influence strategies of Russian NGOs, the focus will be on three NGOs that are active in the field of HIV/AIDS, drug policy and human rights protection: (1) the *Union of the Committees of Soldiers' Mothers in Russia*, (2) the *Russian Harm Reduction Network* and (3) the *Russian Association of People Living with HIV*.

Despite their different objectives and fields of activity, the three organizations have a number of common characteristics. First of all, they are network organizations with a strong local basis. They emerged from grass-roots initiatives that were established to represent the interests of particular social groups, such as people living with HIV, drug users and conscripts or soldiers of the Russian military. The abovementioned NGOs, however, do not limit themselves to providing mutual aid, but also strive to defend the rights and interests of their members/clients and participate in political processes to improve policy. In their daily work, the three NGOs combine delivery of

---

[17] In May 2009, the Civil Society Institutions and Human Rights Council under the President of the Russian Federation (CSIHRC) started to elaborate a reform of Russia's NGO legislation with the explicitly formulated objective of correcting the most problematic provision of the 2006 law and creating a more favourable environment for NGOs in Russia. See CSIHRC, http://www.sovetpamfilova.ru, accessed 8 December 2009.

services on a case-by-case basis with advocacy. They thus serve as salient examples of civic engagement on social issues. In the following, I will discuss the three examples in order to provide insight into the factors explaining the NGOs' capability to influence social policy.

7.4.1. The Union of the Committees of Soldiers' Mothers in Russia

The Union of the Committees of Soldiers' Mothers in Russia (UCSMR) is the oldest and most well-known NGO among the three.[18] The first committees were formed in 1989 in protest against the treatment of conscripts. Since then, the movement has developed into one of the strongest voices in Russian civil society.[19] Today, about fifty regional committees of soldiers' mothers exist. Their aim is to defend the rights of conscripts and their families by informing them about their right to refuse military conscription.[20] In addition to providing legal consultations on an individual basis, the NGO is engaged in advocacy work, including campaigning for the protection of human rights in the armed forces and the abolishment of obligatory military service.

The particular strength of these committees is their backing in society and their mobilization potential. The conditions of military service, including the legal situation of conscripts, directly affect many Russian families. The image of mothers as protectors demanding rights for their sons has been highly resonant in Russian society, and this credibility has imbued the NGO with moral authority.[21] To a certain degree, the NGO has also been successful in gaining access to political processes. In 2002, a member of the board, Ida Kuklina, was invited to join the *Russian Presidential Council on Civil Society Institutions and Human Rights*.[22] This high-level forum enabled the soldiers' mothers to articulate their positions. Furthermore, the NGO is a member of the *Public Chamber* in a number of Russian regions.

Access to political decision-making processes, however, has been largely blocked for the soldiers' mothers. The Ministry of Defence has not been amenable to cooperating with the committee, which is hardly surprising given how sensitive the issue of the military organization is and how far-reaching the NGOs demands are, including

---

18　Union of the Committees of Soldiers Mothers of Russia / Soyuz komitetov Soldatskikh Materei Rossii, http://www.ucsmr.ru, accessed 14 May 2009; see also: All-Russian Public Organisation 'Committee of Soldiers' Mothers', http://www.soldiers-mothers-rus.ru, accessed 12 May 2008.
19　Sundstrom, Lisa McIntosh: Soldiers' Rights Groups in Russia. Civil Society through Russian and Western Eyes, in: Evans, Alfred B. / Henry, Laura A. / Sundstrom, Lisa McIntosh (eds): Russian Civil Society. A Critical Assessment, New York: Sharpe, 2006, pp. 178–196, here p. 179.
20　Human Rights Organisations Soldiers' Mothers of St. Petersburg, http://www.soldiersmothers.ru/pages/english/presentation.htm, accessed 10 May 2009.
21　Sundstrom, Lisa McIntosh: Soldiers' Rights Groups in Russia. Civil Society through Russian and Western Eyes, in: Evans, Alfred B. / Henry, Laura A. / Sundstrom, Lisa McIntosh (eds): Russian Civil Society. A Critical Assessment, New York: Sharpe, 2006, pp.178–196, here p. 187.
22　Russian Presidential Council on Civil Society Institutions and Human Rights, http://www.sovet pamfilova.ru, accessed 27 May 2009.

their goal of abolishing conscription. The organization has frequently been criticized by state officials, including the minister of defence.[23] The soldiers' mothers' attempts to form a political party in 2004 were not successful. On the contrary, all signs indicate that state authorities are doing everything in their power to marginalize the influence of the NGO.

7.4.2. The Russian Harm Reduction Network

The Russian Harm Reduction Network (RHRN) is a coalition whose aim is to 'promote harm reduction strategies in order to respond to the HIV/AIDS epidemic and other adverse consequences related to drug use, strengthen public health, and realize the civil rights of drug users and all citizens of Russia.'[24] Harm reduction includes programmes that are focused on mitigating the harm associated with drug use, e.g. needle exchange and substitution therapy. The RHRN can be regarded as an advocacy organization with a specific policy objective. It calls for the introduction of harm reduction programmes as a means to effectively respond to the spread of HIV-infection among injecting drug users. The network was founded in 2003 and consists of twenty-four member organizations and fifteen individual members. With the support of international donors, the RHRN cooperates with local partners to conduct needle exchange projects throughout Russia. In addition to those local projects, the network engages in advocacy work on the regional and federal levels.

The RHRN is able to articulate its positions primarily due to the support it receives from international organizations, such as UNAIDS or the International Harm Reduction Development Programme (IHRD). Moreover, the network receives substantial funding from international donors. Financial support from the Global Fund, for instance, currently amounts to 16 million US dollars.[25] Via the United Nations General Assembly Special Session (UNGASS) reporting mechanism, the network also has access to political processes. In 2008, the RHRN participated in the preparation of the national report about the implementation of the objectives of the *Declaration of Commitment on HIV/AIDS*. The UNGASS reports are to be prepared every two years and include an opportunity for civil society involvement. Beyond international support, the RHRN has also found political partners in Russia; harm reduction strategies have for example found supporters in the health care system. In 2004, the introduction of needle exchange

---

23 Engleman, Eric: Russian Soldiers' Mothers Work Together, 14 January 2003, in: Johnson's Russia List, http://www.cdi.org/russia/johnson/7016-12.cfm
24 Russian Harm Reduction Network, http://harmreduction.ru, accessed 29 April 2009.
25 The Global Fund to fight AIDS, Tuberculosis and Malaria: Russian Federation, Round 5, http://www.theglobalfund.org/programs/grant/?compid=1197&grantid=483&lang=en&CountryId=RUS, accessed 29 May 2009.

projects was recommended by Russia's chief sanitary physician, Gennadiy Onishenko.[26] Its participation in the Country Coordination Mechanism (CCM) of the Global Fund[27] and other high-level commissions allows the RHRN to interact with health care officials and advocate for its positions. Many of the organization's local projects are implemented in cooperation with state institutions, e.g. the local AIDS centres. AIDS centres officials often have a self-interest in this collaboration, as joint projects enable them to develop services.

But the RHRN also faces opposition from many sides. Many Russian politicians and health care specialists remain highly critical of harm reduction programmes. Their wariness likely stems from their reluctance to shift away from the country's traditionally conservative drug policy. Substitution therapy remains legally banned in Russia. Needle exchange projects also lack a clear legislative basis, which creates a risk for local implementers.[28] Many projects fail due to the opposition of the local branches of the *Committee on Drug Control* or societal groups, which often argue that harm reduction promotes drug use and endangers young people. This strong opposition, from state institutions like the *Committee on Drug Control* as well as from society, forms an insuperable barrier for the advocacy of harm reduction in Russia and significantly restricts the RHRN's ability to exert influence on policy-making.

7.4.3. The Russian Association of People Living with HIV

The Russian Association of People Living with HIV is a network representing the rights and interests of HIV-positive people in Russia. On the federal level the association is currently in the process of institutional development.[29] It emerged from different regional organizations, such as the movement 'FrontAIDS'[30] and the NGO 'Community of People Living with HIV'[31]. In many regions, people living with HIV (PLWH) have organized themselves into self-help groups, often based on the local AIDS centres. In May 2009 the Russian Association of PLWH was officially registered as countrywide umbrella organization. It is based on individual membership and provides an internal mailing

---

26 Decree on Measures Directed to the Counteraction of the Spread of HIV-infection in the Russian Federation / Postanovlenie 'Ob aktivizatsii meropriyatii napravlennykh na protivodeistvie rasprostranenyu VICh-infektsii v Rossiiskoi Federatsii', 14 January 2004, in: Federal Service for Supervision in Consumer Rights Protection and Human Welfare, http://www.rospotrebnadzor.ru
27 The Global Fund to fight AIDS, Tuberculosis and Malaria: Country Coordinating Mechanism, http://www.theglobalfund.org/programs/ccm/?CountryId=RUS&lang=en, accessed 25 May 2009.
28 Interview NGO representative, St Petersburg, 6 October 2008.
29 Interview NGO representative, Moscow, 15 February 2008, see also: UNDP: Support to institutional development of the Russian Association of People living with HIV (PLHIV), http://www.undp.ru/index.phtml?iso=RU&lid=1&cmd=programs5, accessed 28 May 2009.
30 FrontADIS, http://www.frontaids.org, accessed 28 May 2009.
31 Community of People Living with HIV, http://www.positivenet.ru/, accessed 30 May 2009.

list, connecting about 200 members throughout the country.[32] In addition to implementing services and providing support for their members, the association strives to engage in advocacy work to defend the rights of PLWH in Russia, particularly in terms of access to antiretroviral therapy and other medical services as well as human rights protection. An important facet of the association is the information exchange it has with local groups, which allows the network to monitor local access to treatment. The organization is thereby able to hold the institutions accountable if promised services are not delivered.

The Russian Association of People Living with HIV has access to political processes due to the support it receives from international organizations. The UNGASS Declaration particularly emphasizes the need to include PLWH in any effective response to HIV/AIDS.[33] This creates opportunities for participation. The impact of the association on decision-making processes, however, is limited, partly due to poorly developed capacities. Still, it has succeeded in establishing contacts with political actors, such as the *Parliamentary Commission on HIV/AIDS*.[34] It is also engaged with state institutions on the local level. AIDS centres have an interest in cooperating with PLWH organizations or initiative groups, because they can help enhance patient outreach and improve treatment adherence on the basis of peer-to-peer counselling. The mobilization potential of the association, on the other hand, is low. HIV-positive people are a marginalized group in Russian society. Moreover, the community itself is divided, resulting in a low level of self-organization. This impedes the development of a strong advocacy association able to improve the legal and social situation of PLWH in Russia.

7.5. Are NGOs Able to Achieve Social Change?

The NGOs presented above aim to improve conditions for particular social groups. All three organizations came into existence when citizens joined forces in order to solve problems they were facing in their daily lives. By providing services for members or clients, the NGOs are responding to concrete social needs. However, they do not restrict themselves to mutual aid and social services. Shortcomings in state services as well as insufficient human rights protection have created a necessity to engage in advocacy. The NGOs are thereby striving to change existing policies in order to improve the social situation of their constituency and defend their rights. Their ability to achieve those changes depends both on the context in which they are operating and the strategies

---

32   International Treatment Preparedness Coalition in Eastern Europe and Central Asia: Report on Civil Society Involvement into the Preparation of the Country Report of the Russian Federation for UNGASS 2008, St Petersburg 2008, here p. 5.
33   United Nations General Assembly Special Session dedicated to HIV/AIDS: Declaration on Commitment on HIV/AIDS, 25–27 June 2001, http://data.unaids.org/publications/irc-pub03/aidsdeclaration_en.pdf
34   Interview NGO representative, Moscow, 15 February 2008.

7. Striving for Social Change

they use to open up opportunities for influence, including gaining access to the policy-making process, finding political allies and mobilizing their constituencies.

The study of the three NGOs' influence strategies reveals a mixed record. Although they are striving to achieve change, their access to political decision-making processes remains limited. The *Committees of Soldiers' Mothers* possess significant mobilizing potential in society, but lack access to state institutions and support from political actors, which hinders their ability to exert influence. The *Russian Harm Reduction Network* and the *Russian Association of People Living with HIV* receive substantial support from international organizations, but have little backing in Russian society. Although they find supporters in state institutions, such as AIDS centres that are interested in cooperation, they also face widespread opposition, which prevents them from successfully voicing their recommendations.

Given the context of the civil society sector in Russia, the limited impact of the NGOs comes as no surprise. In Russia's managed democracy, the state effectively controls independent civic engagement. Growing concern about social problems on the part of the political elite might, however, open opportunities for NGOs in the future.

Part IV. Civil Society after EU Accession

Julia Langbein

8. Differential Empowerment for Institutional Change. The EU's Impact on State and Non-State Actors in Eastern Europe

8.1. Introduction

The European Union constantly seeks to reproduce its regulatory model beyond its borders.[1] For the past twenty years, the most significant target region in this respect has been Eastern Europe. Prior to their accession in 2004 and 2007, the EU helped ten post-Communist countries to comply with the political and economic Copenhagen criteria and to transpose the 80,000-page *acquis communautaire* into their national law. Apart from the Eastern Enlargement, the EU is also actively exporting its rules to developing market economies in many other parts of the world, such as the East European and Mediterranean countries in the European Neighbourhood, Latin America, Asia and Africa.[2]

Recent scholarship suggests that the EU should be conceived as a transnational integration regime (TIR) in its efforts to promote rule transfer. According to Bruszt and McDermott (2009), TIRs

> are more than trade pacts, aid projects or harmonization systems, as they increasingly offer developing countries normative models, resources and integration mechanisms to engage in institutional change. In acting as development programmes, TIRs differ not simply in terms of their incentives and largesse but particularly in terms of their emphasis on institutional capacities, their empowerment of diverse stakeholder groups and their ability to merge monitoring and learning at both the national and supranational level.[3]

This implies that the EU's impact on domestic change does not stop at applying positive or negative conditionality and offering market access. Based on empirical findings from the East European accession countries, Bruszt and McDermott argue that EU activities and programmes tend to encourage European business associations and other NGOs, horizontal networks, and experts to engage in various mechanisms including assistance and monitoring. These efforts have empowered domestic state and non-state

---

1 Bretherton, Charlotte / Vogler, John: The European Union as a global actor, London, New York: Routledge, 1999; Grugel, Jean: New Regionalism and Modes of Governance. Comparing US and EU Strategies in Latin America, in: European Journal of International Relations, 2004 (Vol. 10), No. 4, pp. 603–626.
2 Schimmelfennig, Frank: Europeanisation beyond Europe, in: Living Review on European Governance, 2007 (Vol. 2), No. 1, http://www.livingreviews.org/lreg-2007-1
3 Bruszt, Laszlo / McDermott, Gerald: Transnational Integration Regimes as Development Programmes, in: Bruszt, Laszlo / Holzhacker, Ron (eds): Transnationalization of States, Economies and Civil Societies. New Modes of Governance in Europe, New York: Springer, 2009, p. 24.

actors in EU candidate countries to shape institution-building processes. The conceptualization of the EU as a TIR takes into account that the regulation of market economies is no longer in the hands of state actors alone. In fact, the growing body of literature on regulatory governance emphasizes the significance of non-state actors for facilitating, legitimizing and stabilizing institutional change. While states still supply regulatory functions, private self-regulation is on the rise as a consequence of globalizing markets and increasing competitive pressures.[4] Non-state actors do not only demand new rules or help to steer the economy by providing information about rules compliance on the ground: In various regulatory settings, non-state actors, e.g. private firms, also set their own standards without public interference.[5]

However, the domestic impact of the EU as a TIR differs across target countries. The EU's impact varies not only with respect to the incentives it offers in the form of membership or trade agreements as most scholars suggest,[6] but also in the way it fosters domestic institution-building capacities of government agencies, business associations and firms across the various target regions. Consequently, the EU triggers diverse outcomes in terms of domestic institutional change and convergence with its rules.[7]

The goal of this chapter is to explain the different outcomes regarding the adoption of EU food standards and the respective rules of enforcement in candidate and neighbouring countries. Given the importance of the agricultural sector for many developing market economies, the ability of a country to implement internationally acknowledged food standards in a reliable manner greatly determines its market

---

4 Jordana, Jacint / Levi-Faur, David (eds): The Politics of Regulations. Institutions and Regulatory Reform for the Age of Governance, Cheltenham: Edward Elgar, 2004; Djelic, Marie-Laure / Sahlin-Andersson, Kerstin (eds): Transnational Governance. Institutional Dynamics of Regulation, Cambridge: Cambridge University Press, 2007.
5 Knill, Christoph / Lehmkuhl, Dirk: Private Actors and the State. Internationalization and Changing Patterns of Governance, in: Governance, 2002 (Vol. 5), No. 1, pp. 41–64.
6 Kelley, Judith: New Wine in Old Wineskins. Promoting Political Reforms through the New European Neighbourhood Policy, in: Journal of Common Market Studies, 2006 (Vol. 44), No. 1, pp. 29–55; Schimmelfennig, Frank: Europeanisation beyond Europe, in: Living Review on European Governance, 2007 (Vol. 2), No. 1, http://www.livingreviews.org/lreg-2007-1; Bauer, Michael W. / Knill, Christoph / Pitschel, Diana: Differential Europeanization in Eastern Europe. The Impact of Diverse EU Regulatory Governance Patterns, in: Journal of European Integration, 2007 (Vol. 29), No. 4, pp. 405–424.
7 Bruszt, Laszlo / Holzhacker, Ron: Three Converging Literatures of Transnationalization. Introduction, in: Bruszt, Laszlo / Holzhacker, Rohn (eds): Transnationalization of States, Economies and Civil Societies. New Modes of Governance in Europe, New York: Springer, 2009, pp. 1–21; Langbein, Julia: Transnationalization and Change in Economic Institutions. The Case of Ukraine and Industrial Standards Regulations, in: Bruszt, Laszlo / Holzhacker, Ron (eds): Transnationalization of States, Economies and Civil Societies. New Modes of Governance in Europe, New York: Springer, 2009, pp. 107–133; Wolczuk, Kataryna: Implementation without Coordination. The Impact of EU Conditionality on Ukraine under the European Neighbourhood Policy, in: Europe-Asia-Studies, 2009 (Vol. 61), No. 2, pp. 187–211.

access abroad.[8] More specifically, I scrutinize why EU food safety regulations have been successfully applied by the Czech agricultural sector, while Ukraine has only been able to meet EU food standards in the grain sector. I argue that the various outcomes can be explained by the differential empowerment of Czech and Ukrainian state and non-state actors arising from the various combinations of mechanisms and actors that the EU has employed in the two countries under scrutiny.

8.2. Food Safety Regulation in the Czech Republic and Ukraine

The comparative study is based on a most similar research design. Convergence with EU food safety regulations differs in the Czech Republic and Ukraine despite the fact that the agricultural sectors in the two countries displayed a set of similarities in the early stages of the institution-building process:

First, the two countries experienced immense declines in agricultural output from 1992 to 1994 following the breakup of the Soviet Union.[9] In addition, the competitiveness of Czech and Ukrainian farms was hampered at that time due to technical inefficiencies and higher commodity prices than those on the protected EU market.[10] By the late 1990s, both countries still lacked relevant food safety legislation and had weak capacities for certifying and monitoring food safety in accordance with EU requirements.[11]

Second, following the privatization of land in the first half of the 1990s, the Czech and Ukrainian agricultural industries consisted of privatized large farms and numerous small farms owned by private households and cooperatives.[12] In 2001, 90% of agricul-

---

8 Gatzweiler, Franz W. / Judis, Renate / Hagedorn, Konrad: Sustainable Agriculture in Central and Eastern European Countries, Aachen: Shaker Verlag, 2002; World Bank: Ukraine. Agricultural competitiveness, Washington D. C.: World Bank, 2008.

9 Swinnen, J.: Ten Years of Agricultural Transition in Central and Eastern Europe. Some Lessons for Ukraine, in: von Cramon-Taubadel, S. / Zorya, S. / Striewe, L. (eds): Policies and Agricultural Development in Ukraine, Aachen: Shaker Verlag, 2001, pp. 6–17; OECD: Agricultural Policies in Transition Economies. Trends in Policies and Support, Paris, 2002.

10 Jacoby, Wade: The Enlargement of the European Union and NATO. Ordering from the Menu in Central Europe, Cambridge: Cambridge University Press, 2004; von Cramon-Taubadel, S. / Zorya, S.: (When) will Ukraine be a global player on World Agricultural Markets?, Paper prepared for the Xth EAAE Congress 'Exploring Diversity in the European Agri-Food System', Zaragoza (Spain), 28–31 August 2002, http://ageconsearch.umn.edu/bitstream/24912/1/cp02zo17.pdf

11 European Commission: Agricultural Situation and Prospects in the Central and Eastern European Countries. The Czech Republic, May 1998, http://ec.europa.eu/agriculture/publi/peco/czech/czech_en.pdf; von Cramon-Taubadel, Stephan / Striewe, Ludwig: Die Transformation der Landwirtschaft in der Ukraine. Ein weites Feld, Kiel: Wissenschaftsverlag Vauk Kiel KG, 1999.

12 Gatzweiler, Franz W. / Judis, Renate / Hagedorn, Konrad: Sustainable Agriculture in Central and Eastern European Countries, Aachen: Shaker Verlag, 2002; World Bank: Ukraine. Agricultural competitiveness, Washington D. C.: World Bank, 2008.

tural land in the Czech Republic was cultivated by 13.6% of the farms.[13] As for Ukraine, 10% of the farms cultivated 90% of the country's commercial farmland in 2003.[14] Large farms are expected to face fewer difficulties in upgrading their production to meet EU food standards than small and medium farms. This is because the latter two will not be able to profit from economies of scale.[15] Given the similar composition of the Czech and Ukrainian agricultural sectors in terms of ownership, one would have expected the two countries to have very similar rather than dissimilar outcomes regarding their convergence with EU food safety regulations.

Third, the two countries lacked autonomous business associations at the beginning of the 1990s as a consequence of their socialist legacies. During state-socialism, state technocrats and state-run trade unions worked closely together. While mediation between state and social interests was thus not totally absent, the state held the monopoly over the policy-making process.[16] Therefore, corporatist linkages between the state and economy in the two countries should have prevented agricultural business associations from pressuring their governments to support harmonization with EU food standards and alignment with the EU's rules of enforcement. In addition, the absence of autonomous business associations, which would have defended the interests of small and medium farms, made it less likely that the evolution of EU food safety institutions would be legitimized and monitored by a substantial number of rule targets in the two countries. In sum, both countries lacked supportive and strong domestic demand for EU food safety regulations at the beginning of the 1990s.

Fourth, in both cases policymakers and farmers were unfamiliar with EU food safety regulations and did not possess any knowledge about their content.

Notwithstanding these similarities, the Czech Republic had managed to adopt the major parts of EU food safety regulations and received permission to trade most of its food products within the EU Single Market by May 2004.[17] In contrast, Ukraine has only managed to export grain to the EU but is not allowed to export more sophisticated products (such as dairy or meat products) to the EU. Further, the country lacks

---

13 Yakova, Iglicka: Czech Republic, 'Europe' and its farmers. How is Agricultural Interest Intermediation Affected by Accession to the EU, in: European Political Economy Review, 2005/06 (Vol. 3), No. 2, pp. 112–142.
14 Pleines, Heiko: Der politische Einfluss der Kohlelobbies in Polen, Russland und der Ukraine. Eine vergleichende Politikfeldanalyse, Arbeitspapiere und Materialien der Forschungsstelle Osteuropa, 2006, No. 80, http://www.forschungsstelle.uni-bremen.de/images/stories/pdf/ap/fsoAP80.pdf
15 Dunn, Elizabeth: Trojan pig. Paradoxes of food safety regulation, in: Environment and Planning, 2003 (Vol. 35), No. 8, pp. 1493–1511.
16 Yakova, Iglicka: Czech Republic, 'Europe' and its farmers. How is Agricultural Interest Intermediation Affected by Accession to the EU, in: European Political Economy Review, 2005/06 (Vol. 3), No. 2, pp. 112–142.
17 European Commission: Final Report of a Mission carried out in the Czech Republic from 18 to 22 October, 2004, (DG SANCO) 7179/2004-MR Final, 25 January 2005, http://www.mze.cz/attachments/7179_final_report.pdf

8. Differential Empowerment for Institutional Change

a food safety system that allows private and public bodies to control standards compliance.[18] This is despite the fact that Ukraine should have had a higher incentive to align with EU safety regulations than the Czech Republic given the stronger significance of the agricultural sector for Ukraine's national economy. In the Czech Republic, the agricultural sector accounted for 8% of GDP and 7% of total employment in 1998, while the share of food and agriculture in Czech total exports accounted for only 2%. In contrast, the agricultural sector accounted for 19% of Ukraine's GDP in 1998 and for 23% of total employment in 1999. Food and agriculture accounted for 11% of Ukraine's total exports in 2000.[19]

Why has the Czech Republic managed to align with the EU food safety regulations in terms of standards harmonization and enforcement while Ukraine has only achieved similar results in its grain sector despite the two countries' similar overall agricultural conditions in the early 1990s and the higher economic incentives for Ukraine?

8.3. Is It All about Conditionality and Markets?

Scholars of Europeanization will not hesitate to explain the divergent outcomes in the Czech Republic and Ukraine by referring to different degrees of externally imposed incentives, i.e. membership conditionality.[20] The lack of EU membership prospects in the Ukrainian case supposedly explains why the country lags behind in adopting costly European food standards and why it has not restructured its food control system in accordance with EU requirements. In a similar vein, scholars of development will argue that the varying degrees of market opening have triggered the variations in the extent and speed of institutional change across the two countries.[21] Hence, the

---

18　European Commission: ENP Progress Report Ukraine, Commission Staff Working Document, Accompanying the Communication from the Commission to the Council and the European Parliament, Brussels, 4 December 2006 (COM(2006) 726 final); European Commission: Progress Report Ukraine, Commission Staff Working, Document, Accompanying the Communication from the Commission to the Council and the European Parliament 'Implementation of the European Neighbourhood Policy in 2007', April 2008, http://ec.europa.eu/world/enp/pdf/progress2008/ sec08_402_en.pdf; Garcia, Marian: The Challenge of Conforming to Sanitary and Phytosanitary Measures for WTO Accession and EU Exports. The Case of Ukraine, Rome: Food and Agriculture Organisation of the United Nations, 2006.
19　World Bank: The Agrarian Communities of Central and Eastern Europe and the Commonwealth of Independent States. An update on Status and Progress in 2000, Washington: World Bank, 2001.
20　Schimmelfennig, Frank: Europeanisation beyond Europe, in: Living Reviews in European Governance, 2007 (Vol. 2), No. 1, http://www.livingreviews.org/lreg-2007-1; Michael W. / Knill, Christoph / Pitschel, Dianca: Differential Europeanization in Eastern Europe: The Impact of Diverse EU Regulatory Governance Patterns, in: Journal of European Integration, 2007 (Vol. 29), No. 4, pp. 405–424; Vachudova, Milana: Europe undivided. Democracy, and integration after communism, Oxford, New York: Oxford University Press, 2005.
21　Lederman, D. / Maloney, W. F. / Servén, L.: Lessons from NAFTA for Latin America and the Caribbean, Stanford/CA: Stanford University Press, 2005; Vogel, F

prospect of gaining access to the EU market for agricultural products posed a high incentive for Czech policymakers and owners of large farms to support alignment with EU food standards.[22] In contrast, the EU implements low import quotas on agricultural commodities from third countries, particularly if European farmers and food processors produce the same commodities. This is also the case if third countries meet EU food standards. Even the Deep Free Trade Agreement (FTA+), which the EU and Ukraine started to negotiate in February 2008, only foresees a selective inclusion of the agricultural sector at the time of this writing.[23] However, with respect to grain and some other non-processed foods, the EU market has been quite open for Ukrainian imports. In fact, the EU is the most important export destination for Ukrainian grain, mostly wheat, next to North America, South Korea and the Middle East. Ukraine's share in wheat exports to the EU-27 rose from 2% in 1999 to 50% in 2008.[24] Except for the grain sector, Ukrainian policymakers and food producers thus have weaker market incentives to adopt EU food standards than their Czech counterparts.

In addition to varying degrees of conditionality and market opening, the EU's impact on candidate and neighbouring countries also differs with respect to two other mechanisms through which European and domestic state and non-state actors interact with each other: assistance and monitoring. *Assistance* encompasses the externally sponsored transfer of knowledge, skills and financial resources through seminars, trainings, or exchange of experts and empowers domestic actors to build or change their regulatory institutions.[25] *Monitoring* entails the development of criteria to assess progress which are then used to repeat the monitoring process on a regular basis to reveal leaders and laggards of reform.[26] Donors or experts in charge of specific assist-

---

and Environmental Regulation in Developing Countries, Cambridge: Cambridge University Press, 1995.

22 Jacoby, Wade: The Enlargement of the European Union and NATO. Ordering from the Menu in Central Europe, Cambridge: Cambridge University Press, 2004, pp. 94–115.

23 The grain sector will certainly be included into the FTA+ since Ukraine is already exporting to the EU, while dairy and meat will be excluded from the FTA+ as long as Ukrainian producers do not manage to adopt respective EU food safety standards. But even in case of compliance, tariff concessions in dairy and meat are unlikely at the moment since the EU will protect its farmers.

24 /FAO: Perspectives and Options for EU Grain Trade with Ukraine, Paris/Rome, 2008, http://geastagri.org/publications/pub_docs/Perspectives%20and%20Options%20for%20EU%20Grain%20Trade.pdf

25 Andonova, Liliana: Transnational Politics of the Environment. The EU and Environmental Policy in Central and Eastern Europe, Cambridge/MA: MIT Press, 2003; Jacoby, Wade: Inspiration, Coalition, and Substitution. External Influences on Postcommunist Transformations, in: World Politics (Vol. 58), No. 4, pp. 623–651; Petrov, Roman: Exporting the Acquis Communautaire into the Legal Systems of Third Countries, in: European Foreign Affairs Review, 2008 (Vol. 13), pp. 33 ff.

26 Andonova, Liliana: Transnational Politics of the Environment. The EU and Environmental Policy in Central and Eastern Europe, Cambridge/MA: MIT Press, 2003; Schimmelfennig, Frank / Sedelmaier, Ulrich: The Europeanization of Central and Eastern Europe, Ithaca/NY: Cornell University Press,

8. Differential Empowerment for Institutional Change 109

ance projects monitor the process by publishing regular reports on progress made and the degree of (non-)compliance. They also refer to concrete steps that need to be taken in the future in order to improve the results.

To be sure, students of Europeanization have already underscored the importance of assistance and monitoring during the pre-accession period of East European EU candidates. However, they have not acknowledged the dyadic or multiplex nature of these mechanisms and therefore ignore the root cause of the differential empowerment of domestic state and non-state actors for institution-building.

According to Bruszt and McDermott, interactions between non-domestic and domestic actors can be 'dyadic' and only occur between two actors, such as the target government and an international organization such as the EU.[27] Interactions can also be 'multiplex', however, and involve and empower more public and private actors, like domestic or non-domestic business associations, experts and regulatory bodies. Assistance is particularly effective in fostering domestic change if knowledge is disseminated to both state and non-state actors. External donors, foreign companies and business associations can diversify the range of non-state actors by providing on-site trainings for domestic companies.[28] Further, they can organize meetings for domestic business associations and their foreign counterparts to coordinate and bind interests for lobbying and monitoring activities.[29] Monitoring is particularly effective if external actors can manage to acquire full information about the progress of regulatory changes. Therefore, it is necessary to diversify domestic actors and empower business associations or other NGOs to provide the needed data. This will make it easier for external experts to obtain access to decentralized information.[30]

Thinking in terms of dyadic and multiplex relationships between domestic and non-domestic state and non-state actors overcomes two analytical limitations of the conditionality and market arguments: First, the approach debunks the assumption underlying the application of conditionality and market incentives that external actors

---

2005; Vachudova, Milana: Europe undivided. Democracy, leverage, and integration after communism, Oxford, New York: Oxford University Press, 2005.

27 Bruszt, Laszlo / McDermott, Gerald: Transnational Integration Regimes as Development Programs, in: Bruszt, Laszlo / Holzhacker, Ron: Transnationalization of States, Economies and Civil Societies. New Modes of Governance in Europe, New York: Springer, 2009, pp. 23–59.

28 Gereffi, G. / Wyman, D. L. (eds): Manufacturing Miracles. Paths of industrialization in Latin America and East Asia, Princeton/NJ: Princeton University Press, 1990.

29 Yakova, Iglicka: Czech Republic, 'Europe' and its farmers. How is Agricultural Interest Intermediation Affected by Accession to the EU, in: European Political Economy Review, 2005/06 (Vol. 3), No. 2, pp. 112–142.

30 McDermott, Gerald: The Politics of Institutional Renovation and Economic Upgrading. Recombining the Vines that Bind in Argentina, in: Politics and Society, 2007 (Vol. 35), No. 1, pp. 103–143; Sabel, Charles F. / Zeitlin, Jonathan: Learning from Difference. The New Architecture of Experimentalist Governance in the European Union, in: European Governance Papers (EUROGOV), No. C-07 02, 2007, http://www.mzes.unimannheim.de/projekte/typo3/site/fileadmin/wp/abstract/C-07-02.htm

know ex-ante what the right institutions are. Instead, students of development have shown that external actors must collect information about the kinds of adjustments that need to be made and find out why previous attempts at reform did not work.[31] To do so, external actors need to cooperate with domestic public and private actors to reduce information asymmetries about domestic conditions for change.[32] Second, the notion of 'dyadic' and 'multiplex' relationships challenges the rather exclusive focus on the EU as 'the' external force shaping domestic change in Eastern Europe. Students of transnationalism in Eastern Europe have finally started to go beyond the EU's impact. They have found that many other transnational actors, such as international organizations, NGOs, business associations, experts and horizontal networks, have also shaped institutional change in Eastern Europe.[33] How have the multiplex and dyadic natures of assistance and monitoring shaped the diverse outcomes vis-à-vis Czech and Ukrainian convergence with EU food safety regulations?

8.4. The Czech Case. Strong Domestic Empowerment through Multiplex Interactions

Bruszt and McDermott note that the EU and the Czech government had spent about ninety million euros by the end of 2003 to build up the institutional framework of food safety control and support Czech industries in meeting EU standards.[34] The authors stress, however, that the simple presence of EU resources does not fully explain the change in Czech food safety regulation in convergence with EU rules. They instead attribute the institutional change to the multiplex relationships between European

---

31 Easterly, William: The White Man's Burden. Why the West's Efforts to Aid the Rest Have Done So Much Ill and So Little Good, New York: Penguin Press, 2006.
32 McDermott, Gerald: The Politics of Institutional Renovation and Economic Upgrading. Recombining the Vines that Bind in Argentina, in: Politics and Society, 2007 (Vol. 35), No. 1, pp. 103–143; Bruszt, Laszlo / McDermott, Gerald: Transnational Integration Regimes as Development Programmes, in: Bruszt, Laszlo / Holzhacker, Ron: Transnationalization of States, Economies and Civil Societies. New Modes of Governance in Europe, New York: Springer, 2009, pp. 23–59.
33 Orenstein, Mitchell / Bloom, Stephen / Lindstrom, Nicole (eds): Transnational Actors in Central and East European Transitions, Pittsburgh/PA: Pittsburgh University Press, 2008; Jacoby, Wade: Inspiration, Coalition, and Substitution. External Influences on Postcommunist Transformations, in: World Politics, 2006 (Vol. 58), No. 4, pp. 623–651; Vliegenthart, Arjan: Transnational Actors and Corporate Governance in ECE. The Case of the EU and the Czech Republic, in: Pickles, John (ed.): State and Society in Post-Socialist Economies, Basingstoke: Palgrave, 2008, pp. 47–68; Lavenex, Sandra: A governance perspective on the European neighbourhood policy. Integration beyond conditionality?, in: Journal of European Public Policy, 2008 (Vol. 15), No. 6, pp. 938–955; Langbein, Julia: Transnationalization and Change in Economic Institutions. The Case of Ukraine and Industrial Standards Regulations, in: Bruszt, Laszlo / Holzhacker, Ron (eds): Transnationalization of States, Economies and Civil Societies. New Modes of Governance in Europe, New York: Springer, 2009.
34 Bruszt, Laszlo / McDermott, Gerald: Transnational Integration Regimes as Development Programmes, in: Bruszt, Laszlo / Holzhacker, Ron: Transnationalization of States, Economies and Civil Societies. New Modes of Governance in Europe, New York: Springer, 2009, pp. 23–59.

8. Differential Empowerment for Institutional Change

and domestic state and non-state actors during the transformation of the Czech agricultural sector.

As far as state actors are concerned, the EU had provided resources and funding to establish a food safety control system in the Czech Ministry of Agriculture and Health by 2002.[35] Thanks to the financial support of the SAPARD programme[36], officials from the EU's Agriculture DG and Health and Consumer Protection DG oversaw the establishment of a system of on-site inspections covering everything from individual Czech farms to border inspection posts.[37] While EU inspectors from the European Food and Veterinary Agency conducted the on-site inspections until the early 2000s, this responsibility was handed over to the Czech agencies in 2003. The EU was then able to concentrate on steering and monitoring the Czech food safety control system and the inspection posts.[38] Assistance for and monitoring of institutional change was further provided by a number of EU twinning programmes that were implemented in the Czech agricultural sector. European experts in administration in EU member states not only transferred knowledge to their Czech counterparts but also acted as important sources for the EU progress reports.[39]

With respect to the empowerment of non-state actors, a study by Yakova[40] (on which the following paragraph draws heavily) reveals that PHARE[41] and SAPARD created new non-state actors in the Czech agricultural sector during accession negotiations. In the early 1990s, farm interests were hardly represented in the Czech policymaking arena due to weak professional associations. The Czech Agricultural Association (AA) has been able to heavily influence agricultural policies since 1998, when its former

---

35 Dolezal, Petr / Janackova, Bibiana: Review of Food Law and some experience related to the accession of the Czech Republic to the EU, Institute for European Policy, Prague, 2005, http://www.europeum.org/doc/arch_eur/from_farm_to_fork_Czech_analysis.pdf
36 SAPARD: Special Accession Programme for Agriculture and Rural Development. The EU launched the SAPARD programme in 2000 to increase the competitiveness of the agricultural sector in the ten East European candidate countries and prepare the candidate to take on EU acquis for agriculture and food safety.
37 Bruszt, Laszlo / McDermott, Gerald: Transnational Integration Regimes as Development Programmes, in: Bruszt, Laszlo / Holzhacker, Ron: Transnationalization of States, Economies and Civil Societies. New Modes of Governance in Europe, New York: Springer, 2009, pp. 23–59.
38 Ibid.
39 Bailey, David / De Propris, Lisa: A Bridge Too Phare? EU Pre-accession Aid and Capacity Building in the Candidate Countries, in: Journal of Common Market Studies, 2004 (Vol. 42), No. 1, pp. 77–98.
40 Yakova, Iglicka: Czech Republic, 'Europe' and its farmers. How is Agricultural Interest Intermediation Affected by Accession to the EU, in: European Political Economy Review, 2005/06 (Vol. 3), No. 2, pp. 112–142.
41 PHARE: Poland and Hungarian Aid for Restructuring of the Economies. PHARE was developed in 1989 to assist economic development in Hungary and Poland and has taken the other ten East European EU candidates over time. PHARE projects prepared candidate countries to align with all chapters of the *acquis communautaire* with a special focus on institution-building and investment financing.

chair became Minister of Agriculture.[42] Further, the AA was the main beneficiary of SAPARD and direct aid since it represented mostly large-scale agricultural enterprises, which cultivated 37% of the total agricultural area in the Czech Republic in 2004. The AA was thus able to combine domestic and non-domestic resources to become the most important EU partner and mediator between the adaptational pressures emanating from the Common Agricultural Policy (CAP) and the interests of local farmers, who bore the brunt of the costs of adaptation. While the AA helped to legitimize the adoption of EU food safety regulations in the Czech Republic, it only represented large-scale enterprises, which faced lower adaptational costs than smaller enterprises due to economies of scale.[43]

To gain broad support for the introduction of EU food standards, EU assistance projects targeted big and small agri-food associations alike in the Czech Republic. For example, the case of the Association of Private Farmers (APF) suggests that EU assistance empowered small associations to build up channels to Czech policymakers and to provide services to their members. The APF represented 7% of the total agricultural land in 2003. Although the APF was not eligible to receive SAPARD support because its members did not own enough hectares to qualify for EU assistance, the association profited from other EU programmes. For instance, EU accession instruments financed meetings between European agri-food associations like COPA-COGECA, national associations from EU member states, and big and small Czech associations like the APF. These meetings allowed the European associations to identify Czech partners, disseminate information about food safety regulations in the EU, and transfer technical assistance for institutional reform. European and Czech participants were able to discuss and agree upon lobbying strategies and how to join forces in the future.

8.5. The Ukrainian Case. Shallow Domestic Empowerment through Dyadic Interactions

The overarching goal of the European Neighbourhood Policy (ENP), which the EU launched in 2004, is to 'bring the ENP countries closer to Europe'. In terms of the agricultural sector, the EU seeks to promote 'convergence with EU standards for sanitary and phyto-sanitary controls [because it] will greatly enhance reciprocal trade between the partner countries and the EU'.[44] In reality, however, EU efforts to promote EU food safety regulations in the framework of the ENP have been quite modest if compared

---

42 Bavorová, Miroslava: Interessenkonflikte in der tschechischen Landwirtschaft, in: Osteuropa-Wirtschaft, 2004 (Vol. 49), No. 3, pp. 237–246.
43 Dunn, Elizabeth: Trojan pig. Paradoxes of food safety regulation, in: Environment and Planning, 2003 (Vol. 35), No. 8, pp. 1493–1511.
44 European Commission: European Neighbourhood Policy Strategy Paper, COM(2004) 373 final, 12 May 2004.

to the support given to East European candidate countries prior to enlargement. In fact, the EU has until now mostly engaged in dyadic relationships with neighbouring countries and has put an emphasis on assistance to government actors.[45]

In industries like the meat and dairy sectors, Ukraine has a good chance of becoming a player on world export markets, including the EU, as soon as local meat and dairy producers adopt EU food safety standards.[46] Compliance with EU food standards will also simplify access to emerging markets in South-East Asia, as they will increase Ukraine's competitiveness vis-à-vis South American producers.[47] However, Ukrainian business associations, companies and other non-state actors rarely have received EU assistance in the framework of the ENP. For instance, the biggest European agri-food association, COPA-COGECA, has no contacts whatsoever to Ukrainian agri-food associations. EU assistance programmes did not promote cooperation or channel technical assistance through European associations to Ukraine the way they did to the Czech Republic.[48] Even the Ukraine branch of the European Business Association, which represents the interests of about 700 European companies operating in Ukraine, does not build up alliances with Ukrainian companies or business organizations and does not provide trainings on EU food safety regulations. This is because most European investors, such as e.g. the dairy producers who bought and modernized production plants in Ukraine and had a market share of 8% in 2006, are not interested in exporting from Ukraine to the EU. First, rural households rather than commercial farms produce 80% of Ukraine's raw milk. These families, especially elderly pensioners, produce milk that does not even meet the highest Ukrainian standards for milk.[49] The decentralized structure of Ukraine's raw milk production hence makes it difficult for Western dairy producers to establish supply chains that comply with EU standards. Second, the self-sufficiency level of the European dairy market is at 120%. Therefore, European investors in Ukraine tend to focus on the Ukrainian market or try to increase dairy exports from their Ukrainian production plants to Russia. In fact, European dairy producers

---

45 In contrast to previous trends, the EU launched a major assistance programme for the rural sector that also addresses non-state actors in 2009. In the framework of this project it is planned to familiarize Ukrainian agri-food producers with the EU food safety system and to address agricultural professional organizations. It remains to be seen to what extent private actors will be empowered and how this will shape change in the local institutions of food safety. Information on the project is provided at www.swap-rural.org.ua

46 Hess, Sebastian / Voget, Bernhard / Ryzhkova, Mariya: The EU Dairy Market. Real Opportunities for Ukraine?, Policy Paper Series No. 19, Kyiv: Institute for Economic Research and Policy Consulting, 2008; Hess, Sebastian / Voget, Bernhard / Kuznetsova, Anna: European Markets for Meat. Real Opportunities for Ukraine, Policy Paper Series No. 24, Kyiv: Institute for Economic Research and Policy Consulting, 2009.

47 Ibid.

48 Interview with a representative of COPA-COGECA, October 2007, Brussels.

49 Garcia, Marian: The Challenge of Conforming to Sanitary and Phytosanitary Measures for WTO Accession and EU Exports. The Case of Ukraine, Rome: Food and Agriculture Organisation of the United Nations, 2006.

operating in Ukraine continue to apply *Gosstandards*, old Soviet product standards, which are still mandatory in Ukraine, rather than the more costly EU food standards.[50]

In contrast to EU efforts during enlargement, EU projects in Ukraine strengthen the power position of state agencies within the food safety control system rather than promote 'producer primary responsibility' as stipulated by the General Food Law of the EU (Article 17.3).[51] Instead of including, for instance, the Ukrainian Association of Private Veterinarians in EU projects, one of the European Commission's TACIS projects provided the State Veterinary Agency with new equipment to conduct food quality controls according to European standards.[52] While the project seems to support Ukraine's convergence with EU food safety regulations at first glance, it instead reduces costs for certification and conformity assessment for European food exporters to Ukraine rather than for Ukrainian food exporters to the EU. This is because Ukrainian food exporters are not capable of producing according to EU food standards in the first place and thus cannot benefit from the newly built capacities of the State Veterinary Agency. According to an EU official,

> the European Commission does not support private business in a third country since such a policy would promote market distortion and produce additional competition for the European agri-food business, especially in a sector as vulnerable and highly protected as the European dairy sector. In contrast to candidate countries, which are expected to achieve mandatory compliance with the acquis communautaire and food safety requirements, Ukraine is not obliged to make all its companies compliant. It is Ukraine's choice to fulfil the requirements.[53]

Ukraine's progress is monitored on a roughly annual basis through the publication of ENP progress reports. These reports are kept on a rather general level, however, and rarely specify problems and possible solutions, unlike the EU reports issued during the enlargement process.[54] This is also due to the fact that Ukrainian agri-food associations are not empowered to serve as mediators between the EU and Ukrainian firms.

It is only in Ukraine's grain sector that assistance and monitoring have been more multiplex in nature. It is important to note that the EU has not been the only non-domestic actor to empower domestic firms, state agencies and associations to adopt and enforce EU grain standards. In fact, the Canadian International Development Agency (CIDA) launched two projects, from 2003 to 2005 and from 2006 to 2009,

---

50 Interviews with a representative of a European dairy company operating in Ukraine and a representative of an international donor organization in Ukraine, November 2008, Kyiv.
51 The EU General Food Law (February 2002) can be accessed at http://eur-lex.europa.eu/pri/en/oj/dat/2002/l_031/l_03120020201en00010024.pdf
52 Interviews with European expert and a representative of the Ukrainian Association of Private Veterinaries, November 2008, Kyiv.
53 Interview with EU official, October 2008.
54 Tulmets, Elsa: 'Experimental governance' in the EU's external relations. The cases of enlargement and of the European Neighbourhood Policy, unpublished manuscript, 2008.

which sought to improve Ukraine's grain quality.⁵⁵ Assistance was targeted at farmers and laboratories and involved associations such as the Ukrainian Grain Association (UGA), which represents local and international grain producers and traders operating in Ukraine. UGA developed policy and legislation in support of their membership and assisted CIDA experts in developing and implementing training programmes. From 2003 to 2005, EU TACIS experts provided recommendations to legislators on how to harmonize wheat standards, completed a draft final version of wheat standards and assessed grain-testing methods at Ukrainian laboratories. Another public actor, the Agrarian Universities, was given support to improve the curricula on sustainable crop production in farm management, develop new teaching methods and establish a technical centre to educate students, agronomists and farmers.⁵⁶ Further, TACIS supported the Ukrainian government in building a credit scheme specifically designed for the agricultural sector to provide small and medium enterprises (SMEs) in the rural sector with financial resources to upgrade their production. Special attention was again given to grain production.

Hence, it is not surprising that Ukraine has made considerable progress in its harmonization with European and international safety and quality standards vis-à-vis its grain trade since the EU and other transnational actors increased the capacity of both the supply side and demand side. As a result, grain exports to the EU, North Africa and the Middle East witnessed a sharp increase from 1999 to 2008. Today, these markets constitute the most important export destinations.⁵⁷ Further, it is important to note that in the past, European importers used Ukrainian wheat predominantly for non-food purposes. However, in 2009 the Ukrainian standardization authority introduced a new wheat standard in compliance with the respective EC Directives. As a result, Ukrainian wheat exporters can now demand a higher market price since their wheat can be used for food purposes, including bread production.⁵⁸ The decision of the EU and other transnational actors to promote institutional change in Ukraine's grain sector is driven by economic incentives. As for the EU, its grain market is much more open than its dairy or meat markets, although it applies certain tariffs to restrict imports of

---

55 See the homepage of the current project at http://www.cugp.com.ua/about.html, last access on 5 December 2009.
56 TACIS project report 'Establishment of an agricultural standards certification and control mechanism in line with WTO-SPS requirements' (completed in 2006) at http://www.sps-info.org.ua/en/library/policypaper/, retrieved 18 October 2008.
57 World Bank: Ukraine. Agricultural competitiveness, Washington D. C.: World Bank, 2008, p. 8; EBRD/FAO: Perspectives and Options for EU Grain Trade with Ukraine, Paris, Rome, 2008, http://www.eastagri.org/publications/pub_docs/Perspectives%20and%20Options%20for%20EU%20 Grain%20Trade.pdf
58 Interview with European expert, October 2009, Kyiv; USDA: Grain Report, 9 March 2009, http://gain.fas.usda.gov/Recent%20GAIN%20Publications/Grain%20and%20Feed%20Update_Kiev_Ukraine_9-3-2009.pdf

Ukrainian grain.[59] While the market mechanism is thus an important necessary condition for change, the investigation of multiplex interactions reveals how Ukrainian actors have been enabled to develop capacities for institution-building.

8.6. Conclusion

The previous analysis revealed that various degrees of conditionality and market opening do not sufficiently explain why EU candidate countries have undertaken faster and more encompassing reforms in the area of food safety regulations than the neighbouring countries. Instead, the EU should be perceived as a transnational integration regime that alters domestic capacities and incentives regarding institutional change very differently across candidate and neighbouring countries.

In the Czech Republic, the EU engaged in multiplex interactions with Czech state and non-state actors in the area of food safety regulation. The EU fostered the empowerment of both big and small Czech agri-food associations and established transnational networks between European and Czech agri-food associations during the enlargement process. As a result, Czech agri-food associations were able to pressure their governments, helped to legitimize the reforms and channelled assistance to Czech agricultural producers. Further, the EU helped to build up the administrative capacity of the Czech state with its PHARE and SAPARD programmes.

In contrast, the transnationalization of institutional change in Ukraine's food safety regulations differs across various sub-sectors: In the dairy and meat sectors, Ukrainian government bodies have received less comprehensive support from European regulators and experts, while many Ukrainian agri-food associations have been totally neglected by the EU and their European counterparts. The analysis of Ukraine's grain sector, however, suggests that change in a neighbouring country is likely to happen even when there are no prospects for EU membership. Institutional development in third countries can come about if the EU and other transnational actors combine conditionality and market incentives with multiplex interactions with domestic state and non-state actors.

---

59   Ibid.

Senka Neuman Stanivuković

9. The Introduction of Regional Self-Governance in the Czech Republic and Slovakia. EU Conditionality vis-à-vis Domestic Societal Pressures

9.1. Introduction

The decentralization of power along territorial lines in post-Communist Europe was a complex and highly contested undertaking with ambiguous results. Whereas some countries organized a politically strong subnational level to address territorial and societal diversities, in other countries decentralization collided with nation-building politics and economic restructuring. In pre-1989 Czechoslovakia, where the system hindered the possibility of power dispersion along vertical and horizontal lines, the dissidents promoted regionalism and localism as a bridge toward pluralizing political thought. Accordingly, in the early 1990s, the public and the political elite recognized an imperative need to restructure the over-centralized, over-bureaucratic and unaccountable territorial administration. Although the early stage of transition portrayed localization and regionalization as imminent components of administrative reforms, consequent efforts focused primarily on a less contested local level restructuring. Nevertheless, the reforms at the municipal level spurred an increase in clientelism and non-transparent decision-making. The consequent drop in public support for decentralization fed into governmental reluctance to proceed with the reforms and blocked the institutionalization of regional self-governance for several years. The separation of Czechoslovakia produced an additional impediment. The subsequent debate opened up deep ideological questions about the necessity of regional self-governance and the nature of democracy vis-à-vis public participation. Given that Prague and Bratislava were to lose significant political and economic competences and risk further fragmentation of state structures, regionalization presented a hazardous move. Regional level reforms re-emerged in national discourse only as a part of EU accession conditionality. The temporal correlation of the introduction of regional self-governance in Central and Eastern European countries (CEECs) with the EU accession leaves an impression that reforms were primarily driven by accession conditionality. Based on the external incentives model, the preponderance of the enlargement literature posits decentralization as a technocratic institutionalization of EU conditionality, citing the temporal correlation of the two processes to support the argumentation.[1]

---

1   The position is enhanced by counterfactual methodology, which defines rule adoption as EU-driven if the state would fail to adopt the rule in the absence of an EU factor. Schimmelfenning,

The creation of a politically strong regional level in the context of territorial administration reforms was advocated by the Commission from the time of the Europe Agreements. Accession conditionality gave the Commission considerable leverage over the applicants, and consequently enabled Brussels to stipulate significant administrative and political adjustments in the field of regional policy via the *acquis* and informal negotiations. The conventional understanding of pre-accession Europeanization as a conditionality-driven, technocratic institutionalization of EU rules by the agency finds sound empirical support.[2] The accession context cast applicants into the role of passive norm recipients, where they were expected to modify legislation in conformity with the *acquis* without taking part in its formation. The weak character of the applicants' institutions and the inexistence of regional self-governance prior to accession negotiations lend additional support to the argument of direct causality between EU conditionality and domestic reforms in the field of territorial administration.

Nonetheless, an alternative reading of pre-accession Europeanization sees the EU's role in decentralization as complementary, and consequently challenges the hypothesis of direct, conditionality-led transposition of the *acquis*. The irresolute *acquis*, in addition to the inconsistency of the Commission's approach, which at the later stage of negotiations substituted decentralization rhetoric for centralized accession preparations, diluted the effect of Europeanization.[3] In contrast to areas in which the *acquis* is *thicker*, the absence of a uniform model of territorial organization across EU member states determines the structural weakness of decentralization conditionality.[4] Because the Commission's demand for regional self-governance lacked institutional grounding, conditionality was read loosely to fit the particularities of the applicants' domestic settings. Accordingly, the domestic level is not only a net receiver of external rules but also an intervening variable which modifies Europeanization in accordance with domestic institutional and historic path dependencies. Empirical support for this argument is found in comparative studies that reveal divergence in domestic policy response to conditionality across CEECs.

Frank / Sedelmeier, Ulrich: Introduction. Conceptualizing the Europeanization of Central and Eastern Europe, in: Schimmelfenning, Frank / Sedelmeier, Ulrich (eds): The Europeanization of Central and Eastern Europe, Ithaca/NY: Cornell University Press, 2005, pp. 1–28, here p. 9.

2   Jacoby, Wade / Pavel Černoch: The Pivotal EU Role in the Creation of Czech Regional Policy, in: Linden, Ronald H. (ed.): Norms and Nannies. The Impact of International Organizations on the Central and East European States, Lanham/MD: Rowman & Littlefield, 2002, pp. 317–340, here p. 319.

3   Brusis, Martin: Between EU Requirements, Competitive Politics, and National Traditions. Re-creating Regions in the Accession Countries of Central and Eastern Europe, in: Keating, Michael (ed.): Regions and Regionalism in Europe, Cheltenham: An Elgar Reference Collection, 2004, pp. 612–640, here p. 616.

4   Hughes, James / Sasse, Gwendolyn / Gordon, Claire: Europeanization and Regionalization in the EU's Enlargement to Central and Eastern Europe. The Myth of Conditionality, Houndmills: Palgrave Macmillan, 2004, p. 166–167.

9. The Introduction of Regional Self-Governance

This contribution confronts these two competing hypotheses by deconstructing preference formation on the domestic level and suggests that although the negotiations encouraged institutional reforms, the Europeanization discourse was internalized differently in domestic debates, resulting in varying policy responses across applicants. Consolidation of regional self-governance occurred in proportion to favourable civil engagement. Thus, regionalization is portrayed as an outcome of the dichotomy between societal cleavages on the one hand and the absorption of Europeanization on the other. Whereas the two established theoretical models offer different accounts of causality between accession conditionality and institutionalization of regional self-governance in CEECs, they are both constrained by the structure-centred methodology, which understands the domestic level either as a net receiver of Europeanization or as an intervening variable. Top-down approaches view conditionality as a central mechanism of Europeanization, and consequently fail to fully acknowledge the horizontal and bottom-up processes that coincide with conditionality. Therefore, the presented text puts forward an actor-centred analysis of public administration reforms in CEECs in light of the 2004/7 EU enlargement. Whereas the conventional account places domestic processes in opposition to exogenous pressures for decentralization, the tentative hypothesis of this chapter views Europeanization as endogenous to domestic change. Accordingly, because Europeanization is understood as an internalized discourse, top-down requirements and bottom-up societal pressures become its parallel constitutive variables. The analysis establishes the extent to which the institutional and political empowerment of the meso level was conditioned by the internalization of Europeanization discourse along existing societal cleavages. In a qualitative comparison of events and considerations leading towards the consolidation of a regional self-governance system in the Czech Republic and in Slovakia, this contribution points to the conditionality bias of the enlargement literature, which overwhelmingly fails to account for the agency's role in *Europeanization Eastern-style*.[5]

The analytical choice of the Czech Republic and Slovakia is appropriate because Europeanization penetrated two comparable institutional settings and collided with similar political traditions. With reference to the relative homogeneity of the domestic and external institutional contexts, the comparison of regionalization in these two countries highlights the weight of domestic cleavages. Whereas the absence of an eloquent public discourse determined the technocratic nature of regionalization in the Czech Republic, reforms were more turbulent in heterogeneous Slovakia.

The analysis relies on Europeanization literature, where Europeanization is defined as the process of internalization of EU norms and rules in domestic discourse. Hence,

---

[5] Goetz, Klaus H.: Making Sence of Post-communist Central Administration. Modernization, Europeanization or Lationization?, in: Journal of European Public Policy, 2001 (Vol. 8), No. 6, pp. 1032–1051, here p. 1050.

the contribution positions itself within the *second generation* research, which is moving away from a linear, top-down understanding of Europeanization. Referring to Radaelli and Pasquier, this corpus challenges the external incentives model, where EU pressure is argued to be a primary change generator for its normativism.[6] The enlargement literature treats the agency as a dependent variable rather than a change-facilitating factor, and consequently marginalizes the specificity of the domestic context of reforms. If Europeanization is understood as a cyclical process rather than as a static independent variable, one can more accurately account for the determinants of domestic preference formation. Hence, by deconstructing preference formation on the domestic level, this chapter offers an empirical assessment of how Europeanization interacts with the institutional, political and cultural specificities of the applicants. Since it defines Europeanization as an internalized domestic discourse, it examines a variety of cognitive and rational mechanisms, such as horizontal norm diffusion, policy learning and creative adoption.

In line with the above-stated parameters, the article is organized around the following questions:
1. To what extent and how did EU regionalization conditionality interact with the domestic institutional setting in the Czech Republic and Slovakia during the accession negotiations?
2. To what extent and how was the Europeanization discourse internalized around societal cleavages in the Czech Republic and Slovakia?
3. How do the results of this study resonate with the broader premises of Europeanization literature?

9.2. Accession Negotiations. Europeanization vis-à-vis the Domestic Level

Although territorial decentralization was perceived as a panacea for the embedded legacy of inefficient and unaccountable administrative structures, Communist path dependencies and the negative experience of the Velvet Divorce significantly diluted reform efforts. The Communist ideology of *democratic centrism* denied the existence of heterogeneous interests and consequently rejected any autonomy of the subnational level. Meso-level politics were administrated by bureaucratic bodies in the service of the state. The system of territorial centralism in conjunction with the overall distrust of the state apparatus discredited the arguments of those who advocated the functional necessity of decentralization. Although the Soviet-based system was abolished in 1990, the subsequent delegation of power to subnational units was only concerned

---
6   Radaelli, Claudio M. / Pasquier, Romain: Conceptual Issues, in: Graziano, Paolo / Vink, Maarten P. (eds): Europeanization. New Research Agendas, Houndmills: Palgrave Macmillan, 2008, pp. 35–45.

with localization and failed to address the re-establishment of the regional level. In addition, the split of Czechoslovakia in 1993 accelerated fears of further fragmentation of state structures. In the subsequently unstable political environment, calls for regionalization were not only silenced but also collided with the more salient matter of privatization. Hence, the issue of regional self-governance was placed in an institutional limbo for several years. Although the Constitution of both countries provided for the establishment of the missing meso level, subsequent political interactions paved the way for étatism rather than regionalism. In the Czech Republic, domestic discourse was characterized by the ideological and political split between regionalism and centralism. The centre-right ODS portrayed regionalization as an unnecessary and bureaucratic intervention into natural market flows. The debate in Slovakia centred on socio-economic and politico-ethnic cleavages, with Mečiar positioning decentralization against state-building rhetoric.

Hence, Europeanization did not penetrate a tabula-rasa-like environment. EU norms operated against the centrist tendencies of ruling parties, sectoral policy-making and limited bottom-up support for regionalization. The late 1990s saw a significant increase in EU presence in national debates over decentralization.[7] Whereas the *acquis* puts forward procedural rather than institutional reforms under Chapter 21, regular progress reports reveal the Commission's preference for strong regional self-governance with democratically elected representatives and substantive legal and financial autonomy.[8] Pre-accession negotiations shifted the opportunity structures at the domestic level and consequently encouraged bottom-up regionalization.[9] However, in the absence of a firm constitutional framework, neither the Commission nor the applicants saw the conditions as strict targets and have applied them loosely. Domestic discourse analysis reveals Europeanization as a facilitator of regionalization, while the end reforms in the Czech Republic and Slovakia took diverse forms due to the divergence in how the political actors and the broader public internalized Europeanization along the existing societal cleavages.

---

7 Schepereel, John A.: Governing the Czech Republic and Slovakia. Between State Socialism and the European Union, Boulder/CO: Lynne Rienner Publishers, 2003, p. 6.

8 The final provision of the Chapter asks applicants to have 'an institutional framework in place and adequate administrative capacity to ensure programming, implementation, monitoring and evaluation in a sound and cost-effective manner from the point of view of management and financial control.' European Commission: Chapter 21 – Regional Policy and Co-ordination of Structural Instruments, in: Europa.eu, December 2004, http://ec.europa.eu/enlargement/archives/enlargement_process/future_prospects/negotiations/eu10_bulgaria_romania/chapters/chap_21_en.htm; Regular Report on the Czech Republic's Progress towards Accession SEC (2001) 1746, European Commission, Brussels, 2001, pp. 1–124, here pp. 80–83; Regular Report on the Czech Republic's Progress towards Accession SEC (2002) 1402, European Commission, Brussels, 2002, pp. 1–156, here pp. 101–103.

9 Baun, Michael / Dan Marek: Směrem ke snižování regionálního deficitu?, in: Mezinárodní vztahy, 2006 (Vol. 41), No. 1, pp. 44–57, here p. 50.

Fundamental ideological disagreements combined with a lack of financial resources resulted in a political deadlock in the matter of regional self-governance in the Czech Republic throughout the 1990s. Various calls for regionalization, supported either by the historic specificity of Moravia and Silesia or as a functional mechanism for tackling the growing economic disparity between Moravia and Bohemia, were successfully ignored by Klaus, who saw a strong nation-state as a model for economic prosperity and political unity. Discouraged by the lack of consensus, the opposition turned to international designs to highlight the uniqueness of not having a regional policy in the European context. The EU was used as a legitimizing factor in support of regionalization as a solution to regionally allocated economic disparities. Jacoby and Černoch emphasize the pivotal role of the Commission in breaking the deadlock, although duelling ideologies continued to characterize the domestic political discourse.[10] Forces outside of the governing cabinet supported by civil servants responded positively to the Commission's communication and fostered technical amendments sympathetic to regionalization. However, the *acquis* and the subsequently developed horizontal norm diffusion were unable to circumvent the Union's diminishing commitment to the reforms and centralized ideology of the governing elite, which vetoed pro-regionalization reforms beyond the introduction of a Constitutional Act on the Formation of the Regions and a politically limp Ministry of Regional Development. The government established fourteen regional authorities, but it failed to address the responsibilities of these regional governments and their consequent relationship with Prague. The legislation was only a cosmetic attempt to satisfy the Commission. The debate continued until April 2000, with the institutional and policy framework for regional government being introduced only after the fall of the Klaus government. In accordance with the Regional Development Act, the regions were given legal and financial competences over a substantial number of issues. Post-Klaus Europeanization of the Czech territorial administration was constructed as an integral component of a wider project of bringing the government closer to the citizens.[11] Due to its technocratic nature, the reform encountered minimal societal opposition, resulting in its relatively unobstructed operationalization. Nevertheless, the limited public interest in the process reflected negatively on the weight of the policies, which focused more on maintaining the status quo while appeasing the EU than on bringing about substantial subnational empowerment.

---

10   Jacoby, Wade / Pavel Černoch: The Pivotal EU Role in the Creation of Czech Regional Policy, in: Linden, Ronald H. (ed.): Norms and Nannies. The Impact of International Organizations on the Central and East European States, Lanham/MD: Rowman & Littlefield, 2002, pp. 317–340, here p. 327.
11   Brusis, Martin: Regionalisation in the Czech and Slovak Republics. Comparing the Influence of the European Union, in: Keating, Michael / Hughes, James (eds): The Regional Challenge in Central and Eastern Europe, Territorial Restructuring and European Integration, Paris: Peter Lang, 2003, pp. 89–105, here p. 91.

9. The Introduction of Regional Self-Governance

In contrast to the Czech case, the Slovak path was highly politicized along socio-economic and politico-ethnic cleavages. Slovak mobilized civil society, supported by the subnational levels, promoted decentralization as a democratic answer to the authoritarianism of the Mečiar era.[12] Although subnational territorial borders were drawn under Mečiar, the process took the form of a centrally managed power deconcentration featuring centrally appointed district administrators with zero competences.[13] Moreover, the number and boundaries of the created regions conflicted with ethno-historic traditions and as such enhanced further re-centralization of policymaking. Regional self-governance would provide minorities with an opportunity for political participation and was therefore strongly opposed by pro-nationalistic forces. Although Mečiar's policies were well received among certain segments of society, the introduced territorial power distribution fully disregarded the societal heterogeneity of the state, and for that reason encountered massive opposition. The Mečiar model was contested domestically and internationally since it hindered the development of democratic pluralism and fed into the nationalistic ideology of the ruling elite.[14] Hence, the decentralization discourse in the period from 1993 until 1998 was characterized by broad ethnic, political and economic societal divisions. Reforms introducing regional self-governance vocalized debates concerning nation-building and identity formation in Slovakia. Actors in Slovakia had many diverse visions about how the reforms should be formulated. Consequently, whereas the critique of the existing territorial governance model strongly argued against the ruling party, the subsequent coalition government led by Miloš Dzurinda, brought to power in the 1998 elections, was united only in its opposition against Mečiar. Dzurinda utilized the adherence to EU norms and principles to stop the authoritarianism of his predecessor, and consequently focused his governing agenda on EU accession. His platform encompassed a comprehensive reform of public administration. The reform was to amend the Mečiar model and to consolidate the political and economic powers of the regions. Nonetheless, whereas the threat of exclusion from the EU club contributed to the pro-democratic turn in Slovak politics, Europeanization was unable to overcome the deeply rooted societal divisions reflected in the composition of the coalition government. As different societal and political fractions interpreted Europeanization to benefit their own ideational and political agendas, conditionality was sidelined in the process of determining an overall regional policy. In the post-Mečiar context, the political will for decentralization was never questioned, but the disagreements about its exact nature blocked

---

12   Ibid.
13   NR SR č. 221/1996 Z. z. o územnom a správnom usporiadaní Slovenskej republiky, in: Územné a správne usporiadanie Slovenskej republiky, May 2006, http://www.civil.gov.sk/p11/p11-01.shtm
14   Sloboda, Dušan: Slovensko a regionálne rozdiely. Teórie, regióny, indikátory, metódy, Bratislava: M.R.Stefanik Conservative Institute, 2006.

reforms regardless of the Commission's critique.[15] The question of regionalization caused a governmental split; coalition parties could not formulate a unified position with respect to either the form of territorial division or the extent of regional competences. Hence, the programme, introduced by expert-advisor Nižňanský, proposed far-reaching decentralization of decision-making competences, finances and political power along the tripartite municipality-region-state structure. It was thus responsive to societal heterogeneity but also to EU pressures, but failed when subjected to political scrutiny in the parliament. The subsequent adoption of act 302/2001 was an agonizing process characterized by political bargaining, heated public debate and party politics. The act institutionalized a vertical transfer of competences to the regional level, but the boundaries of the eight self-governing regions remained unchanged. A weakened version of Nižňanský's plan was introduced as a face-saving measure with legislative competences and funding channels that were left largely unspecified. The coexistence of the three levels was to be determined in an ad-hoc manner.

The comparison of Czech and Slovak reforms up to the closure of Chapter 21 reveals that both countries confirmed the centrist territorial legacy, seeing that the meso level remained subordinate to political processes in Prague and Bratislava. Europeanization accompanied domestic ideological cleavages and party politics. Inconsistencies in the *acquis* and soft conditionality produced *decentralized centralization* influenced by domestic path dependencies, with EU norms being absorbed on paper but not carried out. Divergence in the consolidation of regional governance in the Czech Republic and Slovakia is attributable to divergence in societal structures, which are more heterogeneous in Slovakia than in the Czech Republic. In terms of the institutional model, the Czech Republic integrated administrative regional assemblies with the elected regional government, whereas Slovakia opted for a strict institutional separation of the two bodies.[16] The disintegrated structure provides the central government with significant leverage over regional policy-making and can foster duplication of action. In relation to the consolidation of regional decision-making, regions act both autonomously and in line with centrally determined polices. However, by granting regions with a power of regional initiative, the Czech reform allowed for a higher degree of bottom-up mobilization of regional interests in comparison to the Slovak one. In addition, the Czech meso level was given a wider list of independent competences and partial financial autonomy. The Slovak process was more cosmetic than substantial, leaving several significant questions undetermined.

---

15 Agenda 2000 – Commission Opinion on Slovakia's Application for Membership of the European Union DOC/97/20, Brussels: European Commission, 1997, pp. 1–143, here p. 101.
16 Brusis, Martin: Regionalisation in the Czech and Slovak Republics. Comparing the Influence of the European Union, in: Keating, Michael / Hughes, James (eds): The Regional Challenge in Central and Eastern Europe, Territorial Restructuring and European Integration, Paris: Peter Lang, 2003, pp. 89–105, here p. 92.

9.3. Bottom-up Mobilization for Regional Self-Governance

Despite the relative uniformity of EU norms, the assessment of territorial-administration reforms in the Czech Republic and Slovakia indicates variance in both the model of regional governance and the legislative and political strength of the regional level. Whereas in both countries regionalization coincided with an increase in the Commission's pressure on Bratislava and Prague, the domestic context determined significant divergences in the form and extent of decentralization. This chapter proceeds to examine how Europeanization resonated against the presence of societal cleavages or the lack thereof and consequently determined the differences in policy responses in both countries.

The establishment of the regional level in the Czech Republic was a top-down project of the central government aiming to bring territorial administration in conformity with EU conditionality and additional international variables; it was not constructed around particular domestic needs such as the problem of unemployment in the eastern part of the country. Moreover, the voices of Moravia and Silesia, two historically distinct territories, were overpowered by the centrist ideology of the national government, the legacy of the Velvet Divorce, and the nonexistence of region-based identity. Europeanization had a pivotal position, whereas the role of the domestic level is seen as responsive in mediating EU demands. Hence, societal involvement in the process was minor. Consequently, the regionalization of the Czech Republic in the post-Klaus period was relatively unobstructed in bringing about full transposition of the *acquis*. However, this came at the expense of utilizing existing channels of representation at the national and supranational levels. The technocratic character of the accession negotiations marginalized the position of subnational units, which were excluded from the negotiations but were nevertheless expected to absorb and implement externally determined demands. The weak responsiveness of the population and the regional structures toward the EU as well as their resistance to regionalization can be traced back to a regional deficit of the enlargement process.[17] The institutionalization of regionalization conditionality in the Czech Republic confirms the theory of rule adoption in line with the external incentives model, although legal adherence was not followed by cognitive and behavioural internalization of the norm.[18]

However, the Slovak case study calls into question the universal applicability of this theoretical mode. The analysis points to extensive domestic mobilization in favour

---

17 Hughes, James / Sasse, Gwendolyn / Gordon, Claire: The Regional Deficit in Eastward Enlargement of the European Union. Top Down Policies and Bottom Up Reactions, in: ESRC One Europe or Several, Working Paper 29/01, Brighton: Sussex European Institute, 2001, pp. 1–57, here p. 20.
18 Jacoby, Wade: External Incentives and Lesson-Drawing in Regional Policy and Health Care, in: Schimmelfennig, Frank / Sedelmeier, Ulrich (eds): The Europeanization of Central and Eastern Europe, Ithaca/NY: Cornell University Press, 2005, pp. 91–111, here p. 97.

of and against decentralization, where the Europeanization discourse was internalized as a legitimizing factor in the rhetoric of the pro-regionalization fractions. Cognitive and horizontal diffusion of the Europeanization discourse was more decisive for Slovak regionalization than the rational pressure of adopting conditionality. Brusis describes Slovak reforms as a 'political project in its own right', whereby civil society joined experts in an effort to expand democracy and political pluralism in relation to the central state.[19] This provided for a continuation of decentralization reforms even in the absence of the Commission's involvement, which did not occur in the Czech context. Actual consolidation of regional self-governance came about in the second term of Dzurinda's government, after the accession.[20] Bottom-up mobilization arose as an answer to political opportunism of the Mečiar era, in which regional borders, drawn according to political loyalties to maximize the political benefits of the ruling elite, disregarded socio-economic and ethno-historic territorial specificities. The diversity of Slovak society contributed considerably to the cleavage between the centrists and regionalists, and regional, ethnic, social and economic heterogeneity added a political dimension to the regionalization debate. Societal cleavages are traced along the following lines: west to east, mountain to lowland, rural to urban, and along ethnic and religious differences. The legacy of being on the border between West and East and living under different empires and regimes had disrupted national identity formation. What Kundera refers to as a state of 'eternal uncertainty' resulted in a paradoxical situation in which citizens identified with local communities while submissively accepting centrally imposed decisions. As the construction of national identity resumed along the lines of populist rhetoric, regionalization was portrayed as the fragmentation of power, and regionalization efforts vocalized the trajectory between nation-building on the one hand and regional/local and European identity on the other.

Accordingly, the nationalist path found more fertile ground in ethnically heterogeneous Slovakia than in the rather unitary Czech Republic. On the one hand, the negative perception of minorities in Slovakia hampered regionalization, which was portrayed as an attack on the stability of state structures and led to disintegration along ethnic lines. On the other hand, the discriminatory treatment of minorities resulted in the expression of ethnic regionalism and autonomy aspirations, especially at the border regions with a large Hungarian minority. The ambition of the ethnic Hungarian

---

19 Brusis, Martin: Regionalisation in the Czech and Slovak Republics. Comparing the Influence of the European Union, in: Keating, Michael / Hughes, James (eds): The Regional Challenge in Central and Eastern Europe, Territorial Restructuring and European Integration, Paris: Peter Lang, 2003, pp. 89–105, here p. 92.
20 The institutionalization of regional self-governance in Slovakia was finalized in 2005, when the government decentralized the financial system in favour of the regions. Nižňanský, Viktor / Kňažek, Miroslav: Bilancia nekonečného príbehu 1995–2005, in: Nižňanský, Viktor (ed.): Decentralizácia na Slovensku, Bratislava: Úrad vlády Slovenskej republiky. Kancelária splnomocnenca vlády SR pre decentralizáciu verejnej správy, 2005, pp. 1–431, here p. 337.

party SMK to unite Hungarians in one administrative unit by forming a region around Komárno placed the ethnic societal cleavage at the core of the regional self-governance debate. Socio-economic differences and a large divide between the urban and rural populations also contributed to the matter. In particular, the eastern and mountainous territories, which depend heavily on state subsidies, rejected reforms, afraid that decentralization might jeopardize their ties with Bratislava.[21] Years of political marginalization and economic backwardness erased the culture of civil engagement and cemented the citizens' submissive behavioural patterns towards policies and politics once set by Vienna, Budapest or Moscow, and nowadays by Bratislava and Brussels. The conservative environment determined aversive attitudes towards modernization, change and reforms, while sustaining political indifference, egalitarianism, and collectivism.[22] This proved to be fertile ground for post-1989 ethnocentrism and populism. In contrast, due to a direct correlation between economic growth and pro-democratic attitudes on the one hand, and regional and local identification on the other, the economically more developed southern and western regions tend to be critical of paternalism and étatism.[23]

Hence, the decentralization of Slovak administrative structures highlighted societal cleavages dispersed along regional territorial borders. As the Europeanization discourse was internalized differently by different societal groups, EU conditionality did not play a major role in resolving the troublesome consolidation of regional self-governance. A palette of different societal groups ranging from trade unions, academics, minority representatives, and regional associations mobilized their diverse ideas about the form, number, and competences of regional territorial units, while many of them referred to EU conditionality to legitimize their particular version of reforms. In the end, the deeply rooted path dependencies of the previous regimes entrenched in the political culture collided with the unwillingness of Bratislava to renounce power and consequently marginalized pro-regionalization supporters. Controversial questions about the purpose of district offices and the design of regional borders were left unanswered. This provoked criticism and disappointment among NGOs and regional associations. Moreover, it discredited the government and further destabilized an already weak coalition. Further steps towards financial and political decentralization were made in response to an increase in public support for regionalization and regional identity shaping. Despite its troublesome and lengthy nature, consolidation

---

21 Buček, Milan: Regional Disparities in Transition in the Slovak Republic, in: European Urban and Regional Studies, 1999 (Vol. 6), No. 4, pp. 360–364, here p. 362.
22 Danglová, Olga: Populism in Local Politics and Issues, in: Slovak Foreign Policy Affairs, 2005, No. 1, pp. 85–92, here p. 86.
23 Bitušíková, Alexandra: The Global vs. the Local – European vs. National. Paradoxes of New Identities, in: Skalník, Peter (ed.): Sociocultural Anthropology at the Turn of the Century. Voices from the Periphery, Prague: Set Out, 2000, pp. 51–61, here p. 52.

of regional self-governance has proven to be more meaningful in Slovakia than in the Czech Republic. In the context of limited bottom-up pressures for decentralization, Czech regional interests remain either unaddressed or are promoted by the central government. This contrasts to the Slovak case, where the presence of domestic advocates of regional self-governance has determined reforms beyond the *acquis*. Slovak regional offices enjoy a higher degree of legitimacy and are more accountable with respect to the electorate's interests.

9.4. Conclusion. Societal Bottom-up Mobilization in Light of the Broader Europeanization Literature

This chapter aligns with the shift toward Europeanization in EU studies while aiming to disprove the EU-centricity of enlargement theorizing. Rather than defining Europeanization as a static independent variable, the applied theoretical framework describes it as a cyclical process endogenous to domestic change. Although one should not disregard the external incentives model when assessing pre-accession Europeanization, the horizontal and cognitive dispersion of Europeanization played a stronger role in the legislative and behavioural adoption of decentralization than conditionality. The lack of major bottom-up mobilization determined the technocracy of rule adoption vis-à-vis conditionality in the Czech Republic. However, the Slovak case points to the defining role of societal cleavages in bringing about and/or opposing decentralization. The Europeanization discourse was internalized in the rhetoric of different social groups, making the process of domestic preference formation more receptive of the EU as a norm facilitator than of the *acquis*. Hence, the comparative study of regionalization in the Czech Republic and Slovakia suggests that the interpretation of Europeanization as a cyclical development internalized into domestic discourse is more pertinent to horizontal norm diffusion and the presence of bottom-up mobilization than the conventional top-down external incentives model, even in the context of enlargement.

Lars Breuer

10. German and Polish 'Memory from Below'

10.1. Introduction

European memory is currently a prominent topic in the social sciences and beyond. The idea of a common European memory (as part of a common European set of values) is often presented as a normative category, described as a necessary complement to the already existing political and economic integration into the European Union and its top-down bias. However, this so-called scientific 'search for the European' sometimes has a top-down bias itself. This especially applies to studies on European memory, where even empirical research is mostly focused on official or at least publicly available records of memory (like mass media, parliamentary debates, etc.). Yet it seems to be necessary to include other domains of memory as well. For example, recent empirical studies on family memory in different European countries[1] have shown significant disparities between public memory and family memory, both in terms of content and structure. I would like to suggest a differentiation between the three domains of *official*, *public* and *vernacular memory*. This division is of course purely analytical and has to be understood as a working definition, not as an elaborated theoretical concept. The *public memory* means recollections of past events distributed by and available through mass media (TV, newspapers, books, movies, etc.). In terms of spreading memory narratives, the public memory is the 'default'. *Official memory* describes the institutionalization of those narratives in official practices of commemoration (memorials, commemoration days, speeches by state representatives and the like). *Vernacular memory* then stands for the appropriation and reproduction of public memory narratives by 'ordinary people' in everyday communication, etc.

In analysing forty group discussions with members of different social groups in Germany and Poland (see data and methods), I have focused on the vernacular memory, which I also refer to as 'memory from below'. This category concerns memories that are casually passed on in daily face-to-face communications within small memory communities (families, peer groups, etc.). Of course, these memories are deeply informed by public memory narratives, but my interest lies in examining how they are appropriated, modified, and reassembled by individuals.

---

[1] Welzer, Harald / Moller, Sabine / Tschuggnall, Karoline: 'Opa war kein Nazi'. Nationalsozialismus und Holocaust im Familiengedächtnis, Frankfurt/Main: Fischer, 2002; Welzer, Harald (ed.): Der Krieg der Erinnerung. Holocaust, Kollaboration und Widerstand im europäischen Gedächtnis. Frankfurt/Main: Fischer, 2007.

It should be mentioned that in sociological memory studies, *memory* is used in a very broad sense, not necessarily referring to individual experiences. Following the approach of Halbwachs,[2] remembering is seen as an active and constructive process, in which the past is not just reproduced, but rather remade in the present for present purposes.[3] Thus, memory is strongly connected to the (re-)construction of collective identities. Memory is always collective, since it is social frameworks and patterns (which are not reducible to individual psychological processes) that provide the cues for certain individual images of the past. Nevertheless, every individual remembers differently, or, as sociologist Jeffrey Olick puts it: 'Social networks shape what individuals remember, but it is only individuals who do the remembering'.[4] As I do not view memories as 'authentic' representations of the past, I am neither interested in finding out what 'really' happened, nor in validating how 'correct' certain memories are. Rather, I want to explore how people conceive of certain past events and what meaning they attribute to them for the present.

The key question of my Ph.D. is how self-images and images of 'the other' (nation and/or memory community) are shaped in everyday communication about memory by different social groups. This leads to the following research questions:

- Which memory narratives are articulated in the respondents' vernacular memories, i.e. memories of members of different social groups in Germany and Poland?
- How are narratives from official and public memory appropriated and reflected? How do these collective memories relate to various forms of collective self-understanding?
- What kinds of attributions are being made to one's own in-group and to members of other groups?
- Are there any significant patterns in the attribution of roles (like perpetrator or victim)?

10.2. Data and Methodology

My empirical basis consists of forty stimulated group discussions in Germany and Poland conducted between 2006 and 2008. Group discussions were chosen as a method that offers a suitable analysis of the social construction of opinions and atti-

---

2   Halbwachs, Maurice: On collective memory, Chicago: University of Chicago Press, 1992. For an overview on current studies see Erll, Astrid / Nünning, Ansgar: Cultural memory studies. An international and interdisciplinary handbook, Berlin: de Gruyter, 2008.
3   Olick, Jeffrey K. / Robbins, Joyce: Social memory studies. From 'collective memory' to the historical sociology of mnemonic practices, in: Annual Review of Sociology, 1998, (Vol. 24), pp. 105–140.
4   Olick, Jeffrey K.: Collective Memory. The Two Cultures, in: Sociological Theory, 1999 (Vol. 17), No. 3, pp. 333–348.

tudes.[5] The interaction between participants, which in the ideal case resembles a casual conversation, not only shows what the participants consider to be relevant in a certain context, but also allows insights into the appropriation and negotiation of what I call 'memory from below'.

Presupposing that National Socialism, World War II and its consequences are still crucial points of reference for both the respondents' collective memory and their collective self-understanding, Germany and Poland were chosen because of their extremely different wartime experiences. On the one hand, Germany represents a 'perpetrator nation' (occupying force, responsible for severe war crimes and the Holocaust), while Poland is considered a 'victim nation' (a multiply occupied country suffering big losses with millions of Jewish and non-Jewish Poles being killed in WWII). On the other hand, the two nations deal with this past in strikingly divergent ways (see background).

In order to explore the junction between public and vernacular memory, group discussions with members of various groups were conducted, ranging from age cohorts (pupils, students, pensioners) to people who in one way or another deal with memories in their everyday lives (history teachers, politicians, journalists, staff of memorial sites). The groups, consisting of 3–8 individuals each, were recruited in a combination of matched random, cluster, and convenience sampling.

After a short introduction about the aims of the project, the respondents were presented with a stimulus of five photographs showing different war and post-war scenes. The pictures were meant to trigger connotations, comments and even conversation among the respondents. After forty-five minutes of open discussion, a sixth picture symbolizing the European Union was presented, accompanied by some questions about the possibility, necessity, and potential pillars of a (common) European memory.

The group discussions were analysed using a well-tested set of methods based on the assumptions of grounded theory and qualitative content analysis.[6] The entire body of material was coded with the help of MAXqda software.[7] After the coding, several particular sequences were analysed in depth.

---

5   Bohnsack, Ralf / Przyborski, Aglaja / Schäffer, Burkhard (eds): Das Gruppendiskussionsverfahren in der Forschungspraxis, Opladen: Budrich, 2006; Lamnek, Siegfried: Gruppendiskussion. Theorie und Praxis, Basel: Beltz, 2005.
6   For the general assumptions see Glaser, Barney G. / Strauss, Anselm L.: The Discovery of Grounded Theory. Strategies for Qualitative Research, Chicago: Aldine, 1967; Mayring, Philipp: Qualitative Inhaltsanalyse. Grundlagen und Techniken, Weinheim et al.: Beltz, 2008; For the particular methods applied see Jensen, Olaf: Induktive Kategorienbildung als Basis Qualitativer Inhaltsanalyse, in: Mayring, Philipp / Gläser-Zikuda, Michaela (eds): Die Praxis der qualitativen Inhaltsanalyse, Weinheim et al.: Beltz, 2005, pp. 255–275.
7   Kuckartz, Udo (ed.): Einführung in die computergestützte Analyse qualitativer Daten, Wiesbaden: VS Verlag für Sozialwissenschaften, 2007; Kuckartz, Udo / Grunenberg, Heiko / Dresing, Thorsten: Qualitative Datenanalyse. Computergestützt. Methodische Hintergründe und Beispiele aus der Forschungspraxis, Wiesbaden: VS Verlag für Sozialwissenschaften, 2007.

10.3. Background. Public and Official Memory

As a basis for the comparison of the vernacular memory in Germany and Poland, I will first briefly sketch the prevailing public memory in the two countries:

10.3.1. Germany

Before 1989, two states with distinctive memory cultures existed in Germany: In East Germany (GDR), the state ideology of anti-fascism served to avoid any further inquiry into questions of guilt or responsibility with respect to Germany's role in World War II. In West Germany (FRG), from the 1960s onwards there was a fierce debate between two opposing political camps about the commemoration of World War II. While advocates of *'Vergangenheitsbewältigung'* ('coming to terms with the past') demanded an admission of German guilt and a critical investigation of the National Socialist past, supporters of a *'Schlussstrich'* ('bottom line') criticized the reduction of German history to National Socialism and demanded a 'normalization' of German nationalism. Both in the GDR and in the FRG, there was a major difference between the official and the vernacular memory. In the latter, the fate and suffering of non-Jewish German soldiers and civilians was ubiquitous, while any actual acknowledgment of Nazi Germany's guilt or empathy for its victims was very limited.

After 1990, unified Germany had to redefine its political and cultural identity, including its relationship to its 'dark past'. The 1990s were characterized by vigorous public memory debates not only about the guilt of 'ordinary Germans',[8] but also about the importance of the remembrance of National Socialism for today's Germany – including the question of how much money should be spent on commemorative efforts.[9] The debates of the 1990s were no longer about conflicting interpretations of the past, but rather about different ways of dealing with it. At least on the level of official and public memory, the discourse of *'Vergangenheitsbewältigung'* eventually prevailed and a sort of 'memory consensus' emerged. At this juncture, the main question was whether the ubiquitous sceptical view of national history should be considered a hindrance

---

8   For the debate about Goldhagen see Goldhagen, Daniel J.: Hitler's willing executioners. Ordinary Germans and the Holocaust, London: Little, Brown and Company, 1996; Schoeps, Julius H. / Augstein, Rudolf (ed.): Ein Volk von Mördern? Die Dokumentation zur Goldhagen-Kontroverse um die Rolle der Deutschen im Holocaust, Hamburg: Hoffmann und Campe, 1996; About the so-called Wehrmacht exhibition see Hamburger Institut für Sozialforschung (ed.): Vernichtungskrieg. Verbrechen der Wehrmacht 1941 bis 1944. Ausstellungskatalog, Hamburg: Hamburger Edition, 1995.

9   About the compensation for former Nazi slave-labourers see Gruppe offene Rechnungen (ed.): The Final Insult. Das Diktat gegen die Überlebenden. Deutsche Erinnerungsabwehr und Nichtentschädigung der NS-Sklavenarbeit, Münster: Unrast-Verlag, 2003; about the construction of the Berlin Holocaust Memorial see Leggewie, Claus / Meyer, Erik: 'Ein Ort, an den man gerne geht'. Das Holocaust-Mahnmal und die deutsche Geschichtspolitik nach 1989, München: Carl Hanser Verlag, 2005.

to German national identity or perhaps as the basis of it. The discourse of 'normalization' was adapted by the red-green coalition government. In 1998, Chancellor Gerhard Schröder stressed German responsibility for World War II and the Holocaust, but emphasized that Germany, which is now a 'self-confident' nation, no longer feels stigmatized by references to its past. Subsequently, relying on this confidence, public memory has increasingly focused on Germans as victims (of Allied bombings, expulsions or as 'war children'). *Trauma* has become a universal shorthand for wartime memory. Hence, this discourse is characterized by its emotionality: While the commemoration of Nazi crimes and their victims has always been somewhat pedagogical and superficial (i.e. coming from the head rather than from the heart), many Germans express much more empathy when speaking about their own suffering.

In addition, the distancing from the National Socialist past has become a decisive part of German national identity. Being German today means the absolute opposite of what it did during the 'Third Reich': Many Germans now consider themselves devoted Europeans and identify with universal values. Germany has even made moral capital out of being the 'inventor and world champion of *Vergangenheitsbewältigung*'.[10] On the international level, Germany's way of critically dealing with the past has become a benchmark. Germans even occasionally tend to exhibit a moral arrogance when criticizing other nations' alleged insufficiency in confronting their 'dark pasts'.

10.3.2. Poland

Up to now, Polish national identity has been strongly influenced by the historical experience of fragile statehood and the fear of powerful neighbours Germany (Prussia) and Russia (USSR). The dual occupation of Poland by Germans and Soviets in 1939 still resonates as a national trauma. The People's Republic of Poland (1952–89) was characterized by a huge gap between the vernacular memory and the state-controlled official/public memory (most visible in the conflicts about the commemoration of the Home Army (AK) and the Warsaw Rising).[11] According to official memory, Poland was an ally of the victorious Soviet Union, which had liberated it from Fascism. In vernacular memory, however, the Soviets were considered an occupational force that had committed atrocities against Poles (such as the 1940 *Katyń* massacre), let down the Polish resistance [e.g. by not supporting the 1944 *Warsaw Rising*, and even persecuting its members (arresting Home Army fighters after 1944)]. The only point upon which all domains of memory agreed was on the enmity with Germany.

---

10   Frei, Norbert: 1945 und wir. Das Dritte Reich im Bewußtsein der Deutschen, München: C.H. Beck, 2005, p. 7.
11   According to Davies, the Soviets basically watched the German crackdown of the rising from close distance, see Davies, Norman: Rising '44. The Battle for Warsaw, New York: Viking, 2004.

After 1989, many issues unexplored by Communist memory politics (the so-called 'white stains') had to be examined. This sometimes led to highly controversial debates, some of which seriously challenged the historical self-image of the Poles as a nation of victims (especially the debates about Polish anti-Semitism and the *Jedwabne* massacre).[12] Memory conflicts centred on a number of relationships (Polish-Russian, Polish-German, Polish-Jewish and Polish-Ukrainian). Unlike in Germany, the notion of a 'century of two totalitarian regimes' has become common wisdom in Poland. One topic that was first openly discussed after 1989 was the forced migration of Poles from the former Polish eastern territories (Kresy), but also the forced migration of Germans and the Polonization of the so-called 'regained territories'.[13] In picturing forced migration as a common fate, many Poles actually developed empathy with the Germans who were forced to leave the former German territories after World War II.

After Poland's 'return to Europe' in 2004 (i.e. by joining the EU and NATO), a real memory boom ensued, with questions of identity becoming increasingly important. Many Poles felt a need to catch up with the self-confident and somewhat nationalist memory discourses taking place in other European countries (namely Germany and Russia). The politics of memory gathered steam in Polish politics. The right-wing party *Law and Justice* (*PiS*) in particular fanned fear about the alleged 'falsification of history' from abroad and demanded the defence of the 'historical truth', thus reviving images of Polish martyrdom.[14] This view was fiercely criticized by more liberal Poles, who demanded a more multi-perspective, dialogue-based approach to memory.[15] These two views actually exist in official, public and vernacular memory (as will be shown). In other words, a memory consensus has not yet been achieved.

In addition to the above-mentioned issues, a debate about the political changes ushered in by the *Solidarity* trade union in 1989 has recently burgeoned. The transformational elites (including the symbolic figure Lech Wałęsa) now stand accused of having cooperated with the Communist regime. This debate has polarized advocates and critics alike of the events that took place after 1989.

---

12 See Gross, Jan T.: Neighbors. The Destruction of the Jewish Community in Jedwabne, Princeton/NJ: Princeton University Press, 2001.
13 As an example for a vernacular approach see: Wylegała, Anna: Memory, Memories and Rootedness. A New Polish Community in a Formerly German Town, in: Fischer, Sabine / Pleines, Heiko (eds.): The EU and Central & Eastern Europe. Successes and Failures of Europeanization in Politics and Society, Stuttgart: ibidem, 2009, pp. 111–120.
14 The Warsaw Rising Museum, opened in 2004, can be seen in this light. See the museum's website at http://www.1944.pl, accessed 11 December 2009.
15 This view is reflected in the concept for the planned Museum of the Second World War in Gdańsk. See the museum's website at http://www.muzeum1939.pl, accessed 11 December 2009.

10.4. 'Memory from Below' in Germany and Poland

Having given an account of the public memory in Germany and Poland, I will now present some findings about the vernacular memory in the two countries. But before I do, some preliminary remarks about the material are in order: Due to the open design of the group discussions, the material is extremely heterogeneous. There are huge differences not only in terms of *what* people speak about, but also *how* they speak about things. While some groups more or less focused on describing the photographs, others told stories from their own personal experiences, and yet others largely commented on their country's memory culture or current political affairs. The data cannot therefore claim representativity in any sense. The study is rather an exploration of different patterns of vernacular memory. Since there is unfortunately not enough space to describe the various patterns in detail, I will restrict myself to presenting some important trends.

One significant result is that no clearly distinct memory communities emerged with respect to specific variables like age, gender, educational background, etc. Furthermore, there was a great deal of variety and disparity within the group discussions (as mentioned above). Thus, homogenous national memory cultures were not found to exist in the sample, with heterogeneous discourses and memory narratives clearly prevailing instead. In addition, the largest differences did not occur between groups within one country, but between German and Polish groups. This is why I will mainly be juxtaposing the two countries in the subsequent discussion.

When looking at the *historical events* mentioned by the respondents, three topics dominate: in accordance with the photographs presented, respondents in both countries referred most frequently to World War II, the Holocaust and to forced migration. *World War II*, for example, was mentioned roughly equally often in both countries, but in a markedly different way. In the German groups, many references were somewhat abstract and referred to the war as such. Almost half of the war events cited were bombings, mostly (at least implicitly) the Allied bombings of German cities. In the Polish groups, only a small fraction of statements dealt with bombings at all. However, the 1945 bombing of *Dresden* seems to be a well-known *lieu de mémoire*[16] in Poland as well.

Understandably, the Polish respondents mostly referred to war events in their own country, including atrocities and mass killings. Additionally, three central *lieux de mémoire* in Polish public memory were frequently mentioned in the Polish group discussions as well: *Jedwabne,* representing the issue of Polish collaboration in the Holocaust, *Katyń,* standing for the mass killings of Poles by Soviet forces, and the 1944

---

16 The term derivates from Pierre Nora's concept of *Lieux de mémoire* (realms of memory). See Nora, Pierre: Realms of Memory. Rethinking the French Past, 2 Vol., New York: Columbia University Press, 1996.

Warsaw Uprising as a symbol of the Polish nation fighting for its self-determination. In the German group discussions, these three key events of Polish wartime memory hardly played a role. The last of these was only referred to three times, while the other two were not mentioned a single time.

Overall, there was a striking imbalance between Poles talking about Germans as compared to Germans talking about Poles. In all of the Polish groups, the relationship to Germans and Russians was by far the most vividly discussed topic, while the German respondents barely spoke about Poles at all. However, this disparity is by no means unique to this material; it clearly supports corresponding findings in studies dealing with public memory.

The imbalance was even more striking when the topic of forced migration, a subject which is framed very differently in the two countries and continues to be a highly controversial issue in German-Polish politics, came up. In Germany, forced migration is commonly referred to as the *Vertreibung* (expulsion), a term which at least tacitly is usually limited to the fate of ethnic Germans. In Poland, *wysiedlenie* (resettlement) is a very important, but also very controversial, issue linked to the question of national identity. Hence, it is not very surprising that the Polish respondents mentioned the topic twice as often as their German counterparts. What is amazing is that even the expulsion of ethnic Germans was actually referred to more frequently by the Poles than by the Germans in the study. This clearly refutes a common notion in the German political debate, namely that there has never been any acknowledgement of German suffering in Poland. Conversely, there are only six mentions of the forced migration of Poles in the entire German material. Actually, only a few German respondents, most of them proficient in history, mentioned groups of expellees other than ethnic Germans at all.

10.5. (Role) Attributions

Memory narratives and collective forms of self-understanding are mainly linked by attributions, i.e. ascriptions of certain roles, images and sometimes stereotypes to specified groups (or individuals). I wanted to analyse how collective these attributions are, i.e. to what extent they refer to individuals, certain groups, whole nations, or if they even go beyond the national level. In the analysis, I found the attributions to have four dimensions:

First, there are *explicit and implicit attributions*. An attribution is defined as implicit if an explicit or literal reference is missing, but can be reconstructed from the context. For example, if a respondent speaks about expellees without mentioning any nationality, but the historical background refers only to people of a specific ethnic group. Second, there was a clear dominance of *national attributions* in the group discussions, which means that roles were attributed to people as members of a particular nation. This applies to about 60% of the identified attributions in the material.

Third, with regard to the content, three main types of role ascriptions were present – within the national attributions as well as beyond: In *perpetratorship*, guilt or responsibility for wrongdoings is attributed. In *victimhood*, individual or collective suffering is acknowledged. The most interesting and also the most complex type of attributions are *ambivalent attributions*, in which perpetratorship or victimhood is attributed, but at the same time strongly individualized, legitimized or relativized by other arguments. Fourth, it is analytically quite revealing to differentiate between *self-attributions*, which are assigned to one's own in-group, and *hetero-attributions*, which target other groups.

In the following, I would like to take a closer look at the national attributions regarding Germans and Poles (by numbers the most important ones in the material). Among the *self-attributions*, victimhood was by far the most dominant type, tallying over 40% in the Polish and over 70% in the German group discussions. More generally, victimhood was by far the most frequently attributed role. The *victim* has seemingly become the new hero of history, whereas *heroes*, the protagonists of traditional historiography, were virtually absent in the group discussions. Perhaps the role of the victim is so appealing because it is associated with a high moral status. More interesting, however, are the self-attributions of perpetratorship. They were about equally numerous in the Polish and German groups, which is quite remarkable considering the historical background. Only 16% of German self-attributions depicted Germans as perpetrators, which is in clear contrast to German public or official memory, in which German perpetratorship receives far more emphasis. More than twice as many attributions were ambivalent ones. In many cases, Hitler alone was held accountable for all of the evil that was wrought. The perpetrators were often referred to as *Nazis* (them), whereas the victims were depicted as *Germans* (we).

When comparing self- to hetero-attributions, the aforementioned imbalance becomes evident: Polish respondents actually made more attributions referring to Germans than to their own nation, whereas the Germans predominantly talked about themselves. Only 7% of their national attributions referred to Poles. The small number of 26 cases does not leave much space for further interpretation. Yet considering the historical facts, it is worth noting that the German respondents attributed perpetratorship to Poles just as often as they ascribed victimhood to Poles.

Of course, all of these figures and percentages refer to certain groups of statements, not to the respondents themselves. Moreover, the different attributions are by no means mutually exclusive. The same respondent might depict Germans as aggressors, and at the same time acknowledge the suffering of German civilians. I would like to illustrate this with some larger trends.

In many group discussions, events were portrayed in such abstract and vague terms that the question of perpetratorship or responsibility did not even arise – people simply became victims of 'the times' or 'the war'. Thus, there is kind of a 'missing link' – events do have clearly nameable victims, but no clear cause(r). This especially applies to the accounts given in the German group discussions, where any ascription of perpetratorship would have been self-incriminating. Hetero-attributions of German perpetratorship in the Polish group discussions were much more clear-cut, which is understandable, since they are less morally charged in that context. Polish respondents referred to actual historical events and to culpable individuals far more often than their German counterparts did. Many times, the issue of (false) generalizations was raised, i.e. whether group-wise role-ascriptions are fair or if one ought to differentiate on an individual level. Especially among the Polish respondents, there were several vigorous debates about German suffering. While some argued that this suffering was deserved because the Germans started the war, others claimed that sufferers should not be placed in a hierarchy (e.g. along national lines), since suffering is always experienced by single individuals and thus has to be acknowledged on an individual level. In accordance with the struggle in the realm of Polish public memory (see above), this can be interpreted as a dispute over national attributions vs. individual and universal ones. In Germany, this dispute is largely lacking. The German respondents in the study tended to universalize both victimhood (which they decoupled from actual responsibility) and perpetratorship (by referring to crimes committed by other nations, or, as one German respondent put it: 'Every country has its Holocaust').

10.6. Conclusion

In conclusion, the discussion material prompts a few general observations. The use of abstract and blurry terms, which promotes the generalization of both perpetratorship and victimhood, was a common pattern among the German respondents, and even more prevalent among the younger and well-educated Germans. A possible explanation for this practice might be the immediate function for their self-understanding: The desire to be a victim just like anyone else and the relativization of one's own (alleged) perpetratorship serve as an escape from what many German respondents described as the 'burden of the past'. Although this kind of 'escapist' discourse also exists in German public and even official memory, it seems to be more prevalent and less subtle in vernacular memory. In Poland, similar generalizations occur as well, but are much more contested or challenged by references to disparate, conflicting historical experiences and perspectives. Generally, there was more open dissent between the Polish respondents, also within groups, than was the case among their German counterparts. It seems that the ongoing conflicts in Polish public and official memory are well reflected in vernacular memory as well. In contrast to the German case, a broad Universalist view is not necessarily beneficial in terms of forging a national identity, and thus this perspective was far more subject to (vivid) discussion among respondents.

Part V. Political Participation and Lobbying

David Cadier

11. Can Civil Society Play a Role in Foreign Policy? Societal Groups in the Czech Republic

11.1. Introduction

The anti-Communist movements in Central and Eastern Europe are generally acknowledged as having sparked the renaissance of the civil society concept. However, while their actions before and during the collapse of the Communist regimes have been largely analysed, their role in national post-transition policy-making processes has received far less scrutiny. One reason for this is that many of the societal groups embedded in those dissident movements have since withered away as organizations.[1] For instance, in the Czech Republic, while the legacy of Vaclav Havel and the Charter 77 endures as an ideological compass, it ultimately failed to concretize into a permanent political institution. On the other hand, however, the peculiar climate of the post-Communist transition saw the emergence of different kinds of non-state actors, including think tanks. The need for innovative solutions to both complex and novel problems in the economic and political spheres fuelled the constant demand for policy analysis and recommendations.[2] In other words, these problems created a 'market' for think tank 'goods'. And this was especially the case in the realm of foreign policy, where by definition the state faces eminently intricate issues, and also because the process had somehow become congealed during Czechoslovakia's feudalization to the Soviet Union. This chapter purports to analyse the implication of think tanks and other non-state actors in the contemporary foreign policy making process of the Czech Republic. The overarching objective is to contribute to a general discussion on the putative role of civil society in foreign policy.

Civil society is a contested concept; it has been successively framed by thinkers from divergent schools of thought who neither agree on the nature of civil society

---

[1] Hence, the following question has been mobilizing the literature on civil society: 'how a civil society strong enough to precipitate the collapse of a communist regime could now become weak?' Bernhard, Michael: Civil Society after the first transition, in: Communist and Post-Communist Studies, 1996 (Vol. 29), No. 3, pp. 309–330, here p. 310. For his part, John Glenn conceptualizes dissident civil society in Poland and Czechoslovakia as a 'master frame' in which mobilizing power was taking roots solely in opposition to communism, and hence unable to sustain democratic governance for a new political system beyond the overthrowing of communist regimes. Glenn, John K.: Framing Democracy. Civil Society and Civic Movements in Eastern Europe, Stanford/CA: Stanford University Press, 2001.

[2] Kimball, Jonathan: From Dependency to the Market. The Uncertain future for think tanks in Central and Eastern Europe, in: McGann, John / Weaver, Kent (eds): Think Tank & Civil Societies. Catalyst for Ideas and Action, New Brunswick/NJ: Transaction Publishers, 2000, pp. 251–272.

itself nor on the functions it is supposed to perform. Historically, the term was coined by political theorists of the Enlightenment – above all by Alexis de Tocqueville – and further conceptualized by Gramsci, Arendt and Habermas.[3] The definitions of civil society are as motley as its intellectual roots. While most scholars are congruent in defining civil society in opposition to government, their interpretations of its interplay with the state are rather diverse: civil society is alternatively perceived as legitimizing or resisting governments, developing partnerships with them or compensating for their deficiencies. In an endeavour to approach the concept of civil society in both a comprehensive and rigorous manner, this study will rely on the analytical frame developed by Michael Edwards. He identifies three models – *associational life*, *good society* and *public sphere* – which correspond to the three ideal-types of civil society.[4] The first ideal-type, *associational life*, refers to civil society as a 'noun', i.e. to the space between the family and the state where associations and networks have the purpose of advancing interests and facilitate common action. While in the first model civil society is characterized by the absence of any common political agenda, in the *good society* ideal-type civil society is defined in normative terms and understood as an 'adjective'. It is essentially a metaphor for the institutionalization of civility and, in the words of Vaclav Havel, the 'social order towards which all modern democratic societies are gradually working'.[5] Finally, the last category conceptualizes civil society as the public sphere, i.e. as an arena for the exercise of active citizenship and democratic deliberation, explicitly drawing on the theories of Jürgen Habermas. While the categories are not mutually exclusive and the divisions are not quite so clear-cut in reality, this framework will prove useful in analysing the role of the societal groups involved in the foreign policy making process. It will be argued that they clearly fall into the first model, sometimes exhibiting features of the second but hardly ever those of the third. Furthermore, in attempting to gauge the extent to which those non-state actors can be considered as an emanation of civil society in foreign policy making, their involvement in the process will be analysed in light of the classic functions of civil society. According to Rosenblum and Post, civil society performs three functions crucial to democracy: it provides a centre for political resistance against capricious governments, organizes people for democratic participation; and socializing them with the political values necessary for self-government (e.g. sociability or trust).[6] To be sure, the nature and roles

---

3   For a compilation of classic texts on civil society see Hodgkinson, Virginia / Foley, Michael (eds): The civil society reader, Hanover/NH: University Press of New England, 2003.
4   Edwards, Michael: Civil society, Malden/MA: Polity Press, 2004.
5   Quoted in Edwards, Michael: Civil society, Malden/MA: Polity Press, 2004, p. 38. It is this 'neo-Tocquevillian' use of the concept that was mobilized and incarnated by the Czech dissidents.
6   Rosenblum, Nancy / Post, Robert: Introduction, in: Rosenblum, Nancy / Post, Robert (eds): Civil Society and Government, Princeton/NJ: Princeton University Press, 2002, pp. 1–25.

of societal groups varies depending on the policy realm as well as the given historical and national contexts.

Foreign policy is a peculiar type of public policy, and the non-state actors involved in the process tend to be particular, too. The emphasis will be placed here on those organizations that could broadly be labelled 'think tanks'. The literature generally does so, defining these organizations as having 'policy research functions and policy advisory practices' and retaining 'significant autonomy from government and from societal interests such as firms, interest groups, and political parties'.[7] These general definitions prove unsatisfactory, however, when one attempts to analyse the various groups revolving around the foreign policy making process. Thus, to differentiate them and categorize the concrete examples taken from the Czech case, we shall rely on a classification system consisting of three categories: *research centres* (or 'universities without students'), *'contract tanks'* and *'advocacy tanks'*.[8] *Research centres* have a clear academic proclivity that is reflected in their productions. *Contract tanks* also engage in research but often answer to government commissions and tend to concentrate on policy. Finally, *advocacy tanks* focus on the promotion of a particular idea rather than on comprehensive or practical policy recommendations. These categories will be exemplified by specific groups active in the Czech Republic. Think tanks are unique not only by virtue of their organizational structures, but also due to the nature of their input to the foreign policy process. They will be analysed here as 'policy entrepreneurs' who promote ideas and push them forward onto the public agenda. By channelling expertise to inform – and thus facilitate – decision-making, they act as knowledge networks or 'epistemic communities'.[9] It should be noted, though, that these sorts of networks have been said to 'undermine political accountability by excluding the public'.[10] Therefore, it will be argued – in opposition to the view generally held in the literature – that think tanks can hardly be considered as emanations of civil society, notably because they do not meet all of the criteria described above. Instead, they

---

7   Stone, Diane: Introduction. Think tanks, policy advice and governance, in: Stone, Diane / Denham, Andrew (eds): Think Tank Traditions. Policy research and the politics of ideas, Manchester: Manchester University Press, 2004, pp. 1–16, here p. 4; McGann, John / Weaver, Kent: Introduction, in: McGann, John / Weaver, Kent (eds): Think Tank & Civil Societies. Catalyst for Ideas and Action, New Brunswick/NJ: Transaction Publishers, 2000, pp. 1–35, here p. 5.
8   This classification is mainly built upon the framework offered by McGann, John / Weaver, Kent: Introduction, in: McGann, John / Weaver, Kent (eds): Think Tank & Civil Societies. Catalyst for Ideas and Action, New Brunswick/NJ: Transaction Publishers, 2000, pp. 1–35.
9   Haas, Peter: Epistemic Communities and International Policy Coordination, in: International Organization, 1992 (Vol. 46), No. 1, pp. 1–35.
10 Stone, Diane: Introduction. Think tanks, policy advice and governance, in: Stone, Diane / Denham, Andrew (eds): Think Tank Traditions. Policy research and the politics of ideas, Manchester: Manchester University Press, 2004, pp. 1–16, here p. 13.

are better understood as 'parastate organizations' serving the functions of the state through a form of intellectual corporatism (i.e. embracing the 'state spirit'). [11]

The Czech Republic constitutes a particularly interesting case in this regard. First, as a post-Communist state, it is expected to have a relatively weak civil society due to generally low organizational membership.[12] Second, the philosophy inherited from the dissident movement has shaped Czech foreign policy thinking considerably, steering it toward democracy and human rights promotion – so much so that some refer to the country's foreign policy as a 'civic foreign policy'. Third, the Foreign Ministry external action agenda overlaps (e.g. in the Eastern European Neighbourhood) with that of several well-established societal groups, and the two sets of actors actually appear to be interconnected in numerous ways. Fourth, many major recent foreign policy decisions have been largely unpopular. From those four basic assumptions, two paradoxes clearly emerge. On one hand, Czech foreign policy bears a resilient 'civic' component even though the civil society is particularly weak. On the other hand, foreign policy decisions are chronically unpopular despite the fact that several societal groups are closely interconnected with the Ministry of Foreign Affairs.

These paradoxes are largely rooted in the peculiar nature of the non-state actors involved in the Czech foreign policy process. Thus, in order to further address this puzzle and more generally to scrutinize the putative role of civil society in foreign policy, the study will be guided by two research questions: What kinds of societal groups participate in the Czech foreign policy making process? What is the nature of their input and what kinds of functions are they performing?

The first part will briefly analyse the structure of Czech foreign policy, both in terms of the decision-making system and of the normative traditions underpinning the content of the policy. As will be shown, the limited numbers of key actors as well as the emphasis on democracy promotion paves the way for societal groups' involvement. The second part, the core of the study, will consist of a discussion on the nature and role of the non-state actors involved in the foreign policy making process. Think tanks are particularly active in the Czech Republic, promoting policy recommendations both upstream and downstream in the process. Subsequently, to better gauge their impact, two foreign policy issues will be utilized as case studies: the Eastern Partnership (launched under the Czech EU Presidency) and participation in the American Ballistic Missile Defence (BMD) system. Because they more or less stand at the opposite ends of the foreign policy spectrum in terms of the likelihood of civil society involvement, those two cases will permit us to draw some general conclusions about the role of civil society in foreign policy making. Indeed, the former case involves an extensive policy

---

11   Parmar, Inderjeet: Think tanks and power in foreign policy, New York: Palgrave Macmillan, 2004.
12   Howard, Marc Morjé: The weakness of postcommunist civil society, in: Journal of Democracy, 2002 (Vol. 13), No. 1, pp. 157–169.

encompassing legal, economic and political aspects (including some, e.g. democracy promotion, which are 'civil society prone'), uploaded at the European level and to be implemented conjointly by diverse actors. In contrast, the latter case concerns a technical issue pertaining to national security and was negotiated bilaterally (and for many years, in secrecy) with the United States.

11.2. A 'Civic Foreign Policy'?

Traditionally, Foreign Policy Analysis (FPA) distinguishes between *structures* (domestic or international) and *actors* (internal or external); both will be analysed (in that order). External factors create constraints and opportunities, but the choice of response ultimately depends upon domestic factors, which will be our focus here. Deborah Gerner identifies three types of domestic factors in foreign policy: societal sources, bureaucratic structures and ideational aspects of decision-making.[13] A closer look at the structure of decision-making (the organizational model, constitutional arrangements, etc.) and the core elements of foreign policy thinking (political culture, beliefs, world vision, etc.) will help to delineate societal groups' room for manoeuvre.

11.2.1. Structure of Decision-Making

According to the Czech constitution, the government is responsible for conducting foreign policy. In addition, however, article 63 stipulates that the president shall 'represent the State with respect to other countries'.[14] President Vaclav Klaus has consistently cultivated this ambiguity, indulging in multiple acts of defiance against EU integration and defending an interpretation of the 2008 Georgian crisis that contradicted the government's stance.[15] It is worth noting that the president and prime minister holding office during the crisis belonged – at the time – to the same political party (ODS).[16]

In a classical FPA approach, this dissonance could be structurally explicated through the *Bureaucratic Politics Model*, where foreign policy is the result of a bargaining game between actors with different priorities according to their institutional positioning.[17] However, the Czech foreign policy system is of a far lesser complexity than the system

---

13 Gerner, Deborah J.: The Evolution of Foreign Policy Analysis, in: Neack, Laura / Hay, Jeanne / Haney, Patrick (eds): Foreign Policy Analysis. Continuity and Change in its Second Generation, Englewood Cliffs/NJ: Prentice-Hall, 1995, pp. 17–32.
14 http://www.hrad.cz/en/czech-republic/constitution-of-the-cr.shtml
15 On the role of Vaclav Klaus during the Czech EU Presidency see: Král, David / Bartovic, Vladimír / Řiháčková, Věra (eds): The 2009 Czech EU Presidency, Stockholm: Swedish Institute for European Policy Studies, 2009, pp. 18–23. On the dissonance of view on the Georgian crisis see Cadier, David: CFSP and central European strategic culture. The Visegrad countries and the Georgian crisis, paper presented at the 2009 EU-Consent PhD Market, Brussels, February 2009.
16 Interviews in the Ministry of Foreign Affairs, Prague, May 2009.
17 Allison, Graham: Conceptual models and the Cuban Missile Crisis, in: American Political Science Review, 1969 (Vol. 63), No 3, pp. 689–718.

for which this analytical frame was developed (i.e. the American system). Moreover, as we shall see, the two successive Czech presidents adopted rather antagonistic postures on several issues during their terms. This suggests that where you sit does *not* necessarily determine where you stand. Rather, it is the personalities and world visions of individual policy-makers that seem to chart the course, especially since the number of people who actually set the foreign policy agenda is limited.[18] In other words, the decision-making structure itself has a relatively minor impact on the outcome of the Czech foreign policy making process.

Based on this characterization of the Czech decision-making configuration, what is the potential window of opportunity for societal groups? On the one hand, the limited complexity (i.e. stretching) of the decision-making structure offers few opportunities to 'break into' the process. On the other hand, however, the limited number of decisive actors and centres of power facilitate lobbying. As Ivan Krastev emphasized in his study on Central and Eastern Europe, governments seldom rely on memos, and so influence thus depends upon the personal access that idea entrepreneurs have to decision-makers.[19] Secondly, this configuration serves to confer great importance upon the decision-makers' world visions and, more generally, upon the ideas themselves.

11.2.2. Democracy Promotion and the Havel Legacy

Several scholars have underscored the importance of the beliefs, ideas and values underpinning policy-makers' world visions.[20] In terms of enduring ideational compass, the most prominent figure is undeniably Vaclav Havel, whose legacy continues to influence Czech foreign policy.[21] As president of Czechoslovakia – and then of the Czech Republic – from 1989 to 2003, Havel considerably shaped Czech foreign policy thinking through both his actions and his aura, setting what Rick Fawn labels an 'ideology of foreign policy'. By applying dissident philosophy to international relations, Havel framed a 'civic foreign policy' inspired by humanist principles as well as moral imperatives and aimed at promoting democratic values.[22] His foreign policy can also

---

18 For instance, the aforementioned discordance of views between the prime minister and the president on the topic of the Georgian crisis had more to do with their personalities than their functions.
19 Krastev, Ivan: The Liberal Estate. Reflections on the politics of Think Thanks in Central and Eastern Europe, in: McGann, John / Weaver, Kent (eds): Think Thank & Civil Societies: Catalyst for Ideas and Action, New Brunswick/NJ: Transaction Publishers, 2000, pp. 273–291
20 Goldstein, Judith / Keohane, Robert: Ideas and Foreign Policy. Beliefs, Institutions, and Political Change, Ithaca/NY: Cornell University Press, 1993; See also Adler, Emmanuel: Constructivism and International Relations, in: Carlneas, Walter / Simmons, Beth / Risse, Thomas (eds): Handbook of International Relations, London: Sage Publications, 2002, pp. 95–118.
21 On the legacy of the Czech dissidence see Rupnik, Jacques: Charte 77, origines et héritages, in: La Nouvelle Alternative, 2007 (Vol. 22), Nos. 72–73.
22 Fawn, Rick: Reconstituting a national identity. Ideologies in Czech foreign policy after the split, in: Journal of Communist Studies and Transition Politics, 2003 (Vol. 19), No. 3, pp. 204–228.

be labelled as 'civic' in the sense that most of the key policy-makers in his administration came from a civil society organization (Charter 77). On the other hand, Vaclav Klaus framed the 'competing ideology', which he – unlike Havel – managed to anchor in a political party (namely the ODS). Klaus' foreign policy vision was steeped in the tradition of exceptionalism, advocating a historical role for the Czech Republic in reviving democracy and the market economy in the post-Cold War world. In other words, 'universal values have characterized both the content and the aims of Czech foreign policy. This was brought to the fore by both Havel and Klaus.'[23]

Democracy promotion has thus been a major and resilient feature of Czech foreign policy. But in addition to simply generating policy statements and white papers,[24] it has also resulted in concrete policies and official stances. Prague's unwavering dedication to democratization has sometimes led to its isolation in the EU with respect to the question of human rights promotion.[25] Indeed, Czech foreign policy has devoted significant attention to three countries (namely Cuba, Belarus and Burma), a focus that can hardly be explained in terms of geopolitical interests. Beyond bilateral relations, this particular insistence on human rights and democracy promotion more generally inspires a programmatic approach, most notably towards the Eastern European Neighbourhood initiative (as will be discussed further down). Because 'values-oriented diplomacy is supported by all the mainstream Czech parliamentary political parties, democracy assistance has become one of the Czech Republic's top foreign policy priorities.'[26]

The 'civic legacy' in foreign policy inherited from the dissident movement and from Vaclav Havel in particular, although more or less salient depending on the government, has symbolically paved the way for civil society organizations. Similarly, democracy promotion constitutes a domain particularly prone to societal group involvement. Hence, both from a structural and an ideological point of view, there seems to be ample room for societal groups in the Czech foreign policy making process. However, their actual involvement or importance as well as the functions they perform depend on the nature of the organization and the issue at stake.

---

23 Ibid., here p. 224.
24 Ministry of Foreign Affairs: Transition Program Concept, 2005, http://www.mzv.cz/jnp/en/foreign_relations/neverejne/archives_2002_2005/transition_promotion_program_concept.html
25 The legacy of Vaclav Havel's dissident spirit, in: The Economist, 30 August 2007.
26 Bartovic, Vladimír: Limited Resources, Global Ambitions. The Czech Republic's Democracy Assistance Policies and Priorities, in: Kucharczyk, Jacek / Lovitt, Jeff: Democracy's New Champions, Prague: PASOS, 2008, pp. 29–49, here p. 29.

11.3. Societal Groups in Foreign Policy

11.3.1. Nature of the Actors Involved

The term 'societal groups' refers in this chapter to non-governmental associations of individuals pursuing non-profit goals; it was chosen because it appears more encompassing and less connotative than the term 'NGO'.[27] In the Czech Republic, the groups dealing with external relations issues are not uniform, but very few can actually be described as NGOs in the aforementioned sense. In fact, to varying degrees, all of them perform the traditional roles associated with think tanks: they research and advise on immediate policy concerns; evaluate government programmes; facilitate issue networking and the exchange of ideas; supply and train personnel; and interpret policies and current events for the media.[28] These groups can therefore be classified according to the typology of think tanks given above.

Academic research centres represent the first category of think tanks. The most prominent example is the *Institute of International Relations*,[29] which has a clear academic orientation and produces a steady stream of scholarly journals, analytical papers and conferences. Its academic emphasis enables it to strive for independence, but the Institute nonetheless remains linked to the Ministry of Foreign Affairs, which is involved in its funding.[30] The second category, 'contract tanks', provide analysis in the form of reports that are often directly commissioned by government agencies. Thus, in comparison to academic research centres, these entities have less latitude in setting their agenda. Rather than engaging in academic debates, they instead tend to focus on a specific set of policy issues, promoting (i.e. lobbying) them and producing policy recommendations (i.e. expertise). The two most important actors in this category are the *Prague Security Studies Institute* (PSSI), which has a clear Atlanticist proclivity, and the *Institute for European Policy* (EUROPEUM), which focuses more on the EU.[31] Largely utilized by government agencies, they tend to concentrate on the three areas (trans-Atlantic relations, the Eastern European Neighbourhood, and energy security) that consti-

---

27 The latter tends to refer to organizations focusing on humanitarian aspects, as confirmed by the definition given by the World Bank, according to which NGOs are groups that have 'primarily humanitarian or co-operative objectives'. Quoted in Warleigh, Alex: 'Europeanizing' Civil Society. NGOs as Agents of Political Socialization, in: Journal of Common Market Studies, 2001 (Vol. 39), No. 4, pp. 619–639, here p. 622.
28 McGann, John / Weaver, Kent: Introduction, in: McGann, John / Weaver, Kent (eds): Think Tank & Civil Societies. Catalyst for Ideas and Action, New Brunswick/NJ: Transaction Publishers, 2000, pp. 1–35, especially pp. 5–6.
29 http://www.iir.cz
30 For instance, the former director of the institute now holds a high-level position at NATO's headquarters.
31 http://www.pssi.cz; http://www.europeum.org

11. Can Civil Society Play a Role in Foreign Policy?

tute the Czech Republic's priorities in terms of external relations.[32] The third group, 'advocacy tanks', tend to have a more ideological bent and therefore focus less on policy recommendation than on the advancement of ideas. For instance, the *Association of International Affairs* (AMO) provides a general forum on international politics but also cultivated a specificity in democracy promotion in Eastern Europe, e.g. developing education programmes for Belarus and Ukraine.[33] Other advocacy tanks, *Ano Pro Evropu* and *Evropské Hodnoty*, concentrate on promoting European integration.[34] Finally, beyond think tanks, some NGOs with a humanitarian agenda are also concerned with international affairs or at least conduct transnational activities. The most powerful example of these in all of Central Europe is undeniably the Czech organization *People in Need* (PIN), whose agenda centres on development and democracy assistance.[35] Even though its focus is narrower than the contract tanks' and its approach is less neutral than the academic research centres', PIN is also funded by the MFA.[36] Furthermore, the former director currently holds the position of deputy foreign minister.

A closer look at the various 'internationalist' societal groups in the Czech Republic revealed some personal ties with the Ministry of Foreign Affairs, but most importantly also uncovered some common ground in terms of issues and priorities. This convergence of focus between diplomacy and societal groups (and think tanks especially) inspires further study of the putative functions they perform in the foreign policy making process. Does this overlap somehow 'prove' that those societal groups are actually significantly involved in foreign policy? And if so, are they playing the role of domestic sources (i.e. generating inputs) or instruments (i.e. delivering outputs) of diplomacy?

11.3.2. Functions Performed by Societal Groups in the Foreign Policy Making Process

The study of the government-societal group interface – in other words, the configuration of their interactions – offers some indications regarding their possible functions. Cooper and Hocking advanced a typology in which they identified three forms of government-NGO synergy.[37] In the first configuration, societal groups perform the function of a *kick-starter*, engaging in proactive behaviour and thereby contributing to the framing of the government agenda on issues relating to their own activities. In

---

32 It is worth noting that Alexandr Vondra, the former Minister for EU affairs and one of the leading figures in current Czech foreign policy thinking, has worked at PSSI.
33 http://www.amo.cz
34 http://www.anoproevropu.cz; http://www.evropskehodnoty.cz
35 http://www.clovekvtisni.cz/
36 As for EUROPEUM, IIR or AMO, some PIN projects were funded by the Ministry. For a list of projects financed in 2008 see: http://www.mzv.eu/wwwo/mzv/default.asp?id=56095&ido=21027&idj=1&amb=1, accessed 20 January 2009.
37 Cooper Andrew F. / Hocking Brian: Governments, Non-governmental Organisations and the Re-calibration of Diplomacy, in: Global Society, 2000 (Vol. 14), No. 3, pp. 370–374.

the second configuration, societal groups serve as an *agent*, taking on a facilitative – and sometimes subcontracted – role that supports the activities of the government. In the third type, the groups assume the role of a *joint manager*, working with the government in institution-building activities. This last configuration constitutes the most substantial form of societal group involvement in foreign policy; in this constellation, a kind of 'strategic alliance, partnership, or multi-party co-operative venture through which know-how is shared and some mode of formal or informal division of labour is established' between the two types of actors.[38]

In order to elucidate the functions performed by societal groups in the Czech foreign policy making process, the above typology will be employed in the two case studies below. Furthermore, it is hoped that the analysis of their activities will reveal the extent to which the groups can be said to perform the classic functions of civil society.

11.4. Foreign Policy Issues and the Impact of Societal Groups

11.4.1. The Eastern Partnership

EU policy towards its Eastern Neighbourhood figured prominently in the Czech EU Presidency programme and more generally constitutes one of the cardinal priorities of the Visegrad countries in the framework of the Common and Foreign Security Policy (CFSP).[39] However, the levels of support and activism varied among the four countries, and the Czech Republic in particular passed through distinct stages.

In the absence of a border with this region and because the 'Return to Europe' rhetoric implied a distancing from the East, Prague largely ignored the Eastern Neighbourhood at first, focusing instead on the Balkans.[40] However, the Czech Republic gradually invested in policies pertaining to the Eastern Neighbourhood, creating a dedicated department within the Foreign Ministry in 2004 and presenting a non-paper during its presidency of the Visegrad Group. This evolution was concretized in the launching of the Eastern Partnership at the 7 May 2009 Prague Summit.

---

38   Ibid., here p. 373.
39   On the content of the Eastern Partnership and on the role of the Visegrad Countries in its coming into being see Cadier, David / Parmentier, Florent: UE Partneriat Oriental. Quelles Perspectives, 12 December 2009, http://www.diploweb.com/UE-Partenariat-Oriental-quelles.html. For an academic analysis of the ENP dynamic see Rupnik, Jacques (ed.): Les Banlieues de l'Europe, Paris: Presses de Sciences Po, 2007.
40   Kratochvíl, Petr / Tulmets, Elsa: La Politique Orientale de la République Tchèque et la Politique Européenne de Voisinage, in: Revue d'études comparatives Est-Ouest, 2009 (Vol. 40), No 1, pp. 72–98.

11. Can Civil Society Play a Role in Foreign Policy?

Undeniably, this new attention to the East was prompted by external events, such as the prospective EU presidency and the conflict in Georgia in August 2008.[41] But at the domestic level, it was the implication and activism of societal groups that proved instrumental in inscribing the Eastern Neighbourhood on the government agenda. Indeed, they organized a plethora of conferences on the matter, consistently advocating greater Czech involvement in the region, thus playing the role of the *kick-starter*. Czech societal groups also fulfilled the *agent* function, notably in uploading this focus to the EU level.[42] The most salient example in this regard was PSSI, which contracted a project – bankrolled by the Visegrad Fund – purporting to 'increase and sustain the role of the Visegrad Countries in shaping the political agenda of EU institutions.'[43] Finally, through their educational training programmes (e.g. AMO) and civil society capacity-building activities (e.g. EUROPEUM), Czech societal groups have also acted as *joint managers* in cooperation with the government.

As a matter of fact, the role of NGOs in civil society-building in the Eastern Neighbourhood has been increasingly advocated by both policy-makers and scholars.[44] However, the NGOs' actual ability to 'Europeanize' civil society has been called into question. Alex Warleigh, for instance, has argued that NGOs are unsuited to this task due to their inability to foster political socialization among their supporters and to their own insufficiently democratic governance procedure.[45] This criticism, or at least the first point, is somewhat applicable to the societal groups studied here: they do not necessarily encourage Czech citizens to engage politically in the Eastern Neighbourhood issue. Instead, they interact with the government and nascent civil society organizations of the Eastern Neighbourhood countries, aiming to reinforce the latter with the help of the former.

---

41 Tulmets, Elsa: Preparing the EU Presidency. The Czech Contribution to the Project of 'Eastern Partnership', in: Polish Quarterly of International Affairs, 2008, No. 4, pp. 79–98.
42 Beyond the question of the Eastern Neighbourhood, the role of think tanks in communicating the new member states' preferences at the EU level is interestingly exemplified by the European Policies Initiatives (EPI), which aims at enhancing the new member states' capacity to impact the framing of a common European policy. See http://eupi.osi.bg
43 Schneider, Jiří: Central European Contribution to the Eastern Policy of the EU, Project Summary, Prague Security Studies Institute, December 2008, http://www.pssi.cz/files/documents/pass/factsheet_prosinec2008_final.pdf
44 Thiers, Robin / Rommens, Thijs: Strengthening the ENP through Regional Civil Society Cooperation, in: CEU Political Science Journal, 2009 (Vol. 4), No 1, pp. 26–47; European Commission: Non-Paper. Strengthening the Civil Society Dimension of the ENP, http://ec.europa.eu/world/enp/pdf/non-paper_civil-society-dimension_en.pdf, accessed 29 May 2009.
45 Warleigh, Alex: 'Europeanizing' Civil Society. NGOs as Agents of Political Socialization, in: Journal of Common Market Studies, 2001 (Vol. 39), No. 4, pp. 619–639.

11.4.2. The Ballistic Missile Defence Shield

As noted earlier, several of the Czech Republic's major foreign policy decisions have lacked popular support. This can be interpreted as civil society's inability to impact the foreign policy making process and explained by looking at the potential limitations of the three different actors involved. One possible explanation would be the state's imperviousness to civil society inputs. While it is true to some extent that external relations constitutes some kind of governmental *domaine reservé*, the Czech Republic has a parliamentary system and political parties do influence foreign policy; witness the political battles in Parliament over the Lisbon Treaty and the BMD system. Secondly, the citizens' lack of influence on the foreign policy making process could stem from the societal groups' inability or unwillingness to act as a transmission belt articulating and conveying public opinion or concerns. As was observed in the case of democracy assistance in the Eastern Neighbourhood, societal groups are playing the role of agent or joint manager in relation to the government. Finally, a third potential explanation, and perhaps the most compelling, concerns the citizens and their lack of interest in foreign policy issues when it comes to voting. While they might have opinions on matters pertaining to external relations, they do not tend to vote according to these particular issues, and hence policy-makers do not have to worry about making unpopular foreign policy decisions. The ODS party is a striking example in this regard: although its MPs tend to adopt rather Euro-sceptical stances, its voters number among the most Europhile (along with those of the Green party) in the Czech electorate. In fact, very few of the aforementioned unpopular foreign policy issues have actually been politicized. The question of installing a 'radar' for the US Ballistic Missile Defence (BMD) system was an exception.

The Czech Republic's involvement in the US Ballistic Missile Defence (BMD) system began in 2002 and was to consist of installing a tracking radar base in Brdy (southwest of Prague).[46] The original plan has since been scrapped by the Obama Administration, but the strategic investment of Czech decision-makers in this project as well as the popular opposition to it nonetheless makes it a didactic foreign policy issue.[47] President Obama renounced the BMD project as conceived by his predecessor due to technical uncertainties, but also in an effort to engage with Russia, especially regarding the Iranian dossier. The Treaty was also in jeopardy in the Czech Parliament, where the main opposition party clearly denounced it. The Social Democrats (CSSD) indeed cap-

---

46 For an overview on the BMD system see Hynek, Nikola: Protiraketová obrana v současném strategickém a politickém kontextu. Vztah k odstrašování a dopad třetího pilíře na dynamiku mezi relevantními aktéry, in: Mezinárodní vztahy, 2008 (Vol. 4), pp. 5–31.
47 Cadier, David: Bouclier Antimissile. Réactions centre-européennes, in: telos-eu.com, 30 September 2009, http://www.telos-eu.com/fr/article/bouclier_antimissile_reactions_centre_europeenne

italized on popular disapproval of the radar by making it one of the major features of their foreign policy platform.

The societal opposition to the radar was articulated by the *No Base Initiative* group (NBI), which regularly sets up information points, organizes public demonstrations and channels the issue to the media.[48] The annoyed reaction of security experts and policy-makers to NBI's activities hints at their perceptions on the putative role played by civil society in foreign policy making: '[T]hey oppose this project in the same manner they oppose the construction of an airport near a village.'[49] However, such 'securitization' endeavours are legion in foreign policy, and to be fair, the arguments advanced by the No Base Initiative are quite broad, ranging from strategic to sanitary considerations.[50] But because the group challenges the scope of the state in foreign policy and aims at facilitating citizens' engagement on this issue, NBI does fulfil the functions of a civil society group to some extent. Nevertheless, it should be noted that this mobilization was not so much a spontaneous upload by the citizens, but rather a top-down initiative launched by one person, none other than the shadow foreign minister (i.e. main foreign policy expert) of the Social Democratic party.

11.5. Conclusion

With respect to its structure and most importantly to its content (with particular emphasis on democracy promotion), Czech foreign policy theoretically allows room for civil society involvement. And several societal groups do in fact interact with the Foreign Ministry, partaking in the formulation and implementation of policies to some extent. This is especially salient in the field of democracy promotion in the Eastern European Neighbourhood, where several think tanks have acted as kick-starters, agents or joint managers in relation to the government. However, although these entities perform the functions of policy entrepreneurs in the foreign policy making process, they do not seem to embody the classic role of civil society. Think tanks clearly belong to Michael Edwards' first model of civil society as 'associational life' and sometimes act in accordance with the 'good society' (i.e. normative) model when it comes to democracy promotion, but fail to fulfil the function of the 'public sphere'. It therefore seems more accurate to label them as 'parastate organizations'. Interestingly, however, while they fall short of limiting the scope of the state and rallying the solidarity and engagement of national citizens at home, they perform those functions abroad.

---

48 www.nezakladnam.cz
49 Experts Conference, Prague 2009.
50 Securitization is the discursive process by which policy-makers frame a political question in terms of a security problem in an endeavour to remove it from the realm of debate. Wæver, Ole: Securitization and Desecuritization, in: Lipschutz, Ronnie (ed.): On Security, New York: Columbia University Press, 1995, pp. 46–86.

This state of play is not confined to the Czech context, however; it is borne of an essentially difficult state-civil society synergy with respect to foreign policy. Due to limited resources, the Czech government has been willing to involve societal groups in certain foreign policy areas. However, involvement should not be equated with empowerment; as emphasized by Susan Strange, this redistribution of tasks does not reflect a transfer of authority from the government to societal groups, but demonstrates its willingness to let them fill a certain vacuum vis-à-vis responsibilities.[51] Those societal groups can thus hardly be expected to fulfil the classic civil society function of limiting state power; they instead complement it, especially in the realm of foreign policy, which remains based on interstate relations. This is not their objective in any case, and nor are they explicitly trying to channel public participation, another classic function of civil society. In this regard, a major impediment to the involvement of civil society in foreign policy is the citizens' relative lack of interest in many foreign policy issues. For instance, the theme of democracy promotion, one of the pillars of Czech foreign policy, has been depicted by some as an 'elite project often rebuffed by much of the population'[52].

It thus appears complicated for civil society organizations to actually play a role in the foreign policy making process, even in one that has a 'civic' tradition. However, while the think tanks studied here hardly fulfil the functions of civil society at the domestic (vertical) level, they might be able to perform them at the transnational (horizontal) level in the future. Indeed, by engaging abroad in societal capacity-building (and thus facilitating political involvement), they might be contributing to the gradual emergence of transnational civil society networks.

---

51   Strange, Susan: The Retreat of the State. The Diffusion of Power in the World Economy, Cambridge: Cambridge University Press, 1996, p. 14.
52   Fawn, Rick: Reconstituting a national identity. Ideologies in Czech foreign policy after the split, in: Journal of Communist Studies and Transition Politics, 2003 (Vol. 19), No. 3, pp. 204–228, p. 205.

Olena Fimyar

12. The (Un)Importance of Public Opinion in Educational Policy-Making in Post-Communist Ukraine. Education Policy 'Elites' on the Role of Civil Society in Policy Formation

12.1. Introduction

Mainstream political sciences and post-Communist studies have produced voluminous research documenting the regime change in the countries of the former Soviet Union, including Ukraine. In the majority of these studies Ukraine is visualized as a borderline nation whose independence was cut short by the centuries and decades of foreign domination (by the Austro-Hungarian, Russian and Soviet empires), as a result of which Ukraine inherited a highly fragmented polity and society.[1] Apart from explaining and critiquing historical and Soviet continuities, these studies attempt to theorize recent post-independence political developments, which are presented as an eclectic mixture of the legacies of the previous regime and encroaching Western influences and discourses.[2]

In particular, knowledge claims proposed by post-Communist studies are often constructed as elaborate critiques of the state's inability to modernize and adhere to Western/European/liberal democratic norms. This critique is meticulously and consistently supported by argumentation, graphs, tables, statistics and other *visibilities*,

---

[1] Cf. Kuzio, T.: Ukraine. State and Nation Building, London, New York: Routledge, 1998; Motyl, A. J.: The Non-Russian States, in: Freedom Review, 1997 (Vol. 28), No. 1, pp. 56–60, Way, L.: 'Pluralism by Default and the Sources of Political Liberalization in Weak States', presented at the conference 'Dynamics of Electoral Authoritarianism', Mexico City, 1–4 April 2004, Princeton University, 23 October 2003, Yale University Leitner Lecture Series, 25 March 2003; Wilson, A.: The Ukrainians. Unexpected Nation, New Haven/CT, London: Yale University Press, 2000.

[2] Dryzek, J. / Holmes, L.: Post-Communist Democratization. Political discourses across thirteen countries, Cambridge: Cambridge University Press, 2002; Krawchenko, B.: Administrative Reform in Ukraine. Setting the Agenda, Discussion Paper, No. 3, Open Society Institute, Budapest: Local Government and Public Service Reform Initiative, 1997; Kuzio, T. / D'Anieri, P. (eds): Dilemmas of State-Led Nation Building in Ukraine, Westport: Praeger Publishers, 2002; Riabchuk, M.: Ambivalence or Ambiguity? Why Ukraine is Trapped between East and West, in: Velychenko, S. (ed.): Ukraine, the EU and Russia. History, culture and international relations, New York: Palgrave Macmillan, 2007; Sundakov, A.: Public Sector Reforms in Ukraine. On the path of transformation, Discussion Papers, No. 18, Open Society Institute, Budapest: Local Government and Public Service Reform Initiative, 2001; Way, L.: 'Pluralism by Default and the Sources of Political Liberalization in Weak States', presented at the conference 'Dynamics of Electoral Authoritarianism', Mexico City, 1–4 April 2004, Princeton University, 23 October 2003, Yale University Leitner Lecture Series, 25 March 2003; Wilson, A.: Virtual Politics. Faking democracy in the post-Soviet world, London: Yale University Press, 2005.

which assist in categorizing, visualizing and *knowing* the change.[3] The examples of state monopoly, persistent Soviet legacies in political and institutional arrangements, policy-making practices and societal attitudes are often criticized as obstacles to pro-market reforms and democratic transformations.[4] Furthermore, these knowledge claims are utilized as benchmarks against the grid of Western 'normality' and are usually coated in liberal notions of democracy, civil society, human rights and market economy.[5] Vocabularies offered by these studies are used as 'normalization', needs identification and problematization techniques for the governments in the respective countries to refocus their 'governmental gaze' with the promise of quick and calculable improvements.[6]

The developments in Ukrainian education did not attract the same level of academic interest as Ukrainian politics. Despite this difference, education research follows a similar line of criticism mounted against the state monopoly in educational policy-making and against the instances of reversion to authoritarianism in university and classroom settings.[7] The studies maintain that the shifts in discourses have not (yet) brought change to the existing Soviet-type institutional cultures and decision-making practices. As a result, the governance of present-day Ukrainian education is exercised through a rigid centralized bureaucracy, while pedagogy presents a complex mixture of the old and new systems, with teachers trained in individualized methods reverting to authoritarian teaching as a tried method for raising students' performance. The studies emphasize the widening gaps between policy discourses and classroom practices, growing dissatisfaction with the reform strategy on the part of the

---

3   Cf. Gordon, C.: Governmental rationality. An introduction, in: Burchell, G. / Gordon, C. / Miller, P. (eds): The Foucault Effect. Studies in Governmentality, Hemel Hempstead: Harvester Wheatsheaf, 1991; Miller, P. / Rose, N.: Governing the Present. Administering social, economic and personal life, Cambridge: Polity Press, 2008.
4   Kuzio, T.: Ukraine. State and Nation Building, London, New York: Routledge, 1998; Riabchuk, M.: Vid Malorosii do Ukrainy. Paradoksy zapiznilogo natsiestvorennya, Kyiv: Krytyka, 2000; Riabchuk, M.: Ambivalence or Ambiguity? Why Ukraine is Trapped between East and West, in: Velychenko, S. (ed.): Ukraine, the EU and Russia. History, culture and international relations, New York: Palgrave Macmillan, 2007; Way, L.: 'Pluralism by Default and the Sources of Political Liberalization in Weak States', presented at the conference 'Dynamics of Electoral Authoritarianism', Mexico City, 1–4 April 2004, Princeton University, 23 October 2003, Yale University Leitner Lecture Series, 25 March 2003.
5   Cf. Ryavec, K.: Russian bureaucracy. Power and pathology, Lanham/MD: Rowman & Littlefield, 2005.
6   Cf. Miller, P. / Rose, N.: Governing the Present. Administering social, economic and personal life, Cambridge: Polity Press, 2008.
7   Sundakov, A.: Public Sector Reforms in Ukraine. On the path of transformation, Discussion Papers, No. 18, Open Society Institute, Budapest: Local Government and Public Service Reform Initiative, 2001; Krawchenko, B.: Administrative Reform in Ukraine. Setting the Agenda, Discussion Paper, No. 3, Open Society Institute, Budapest: Local Government and Public Service Reform Initiative, 1997; Koshmanova, T. / Ravchyna, T.: Teacher preparation in a post-totalitarian society. An interpretation of Ukrainian teacher educators' stereotypes, in: International Journal of Qualitative Studies in Education, 2008 (Vol. 21), No. 2, March–April, pp. 137–158.

12. Public Opinion in Educational Policy-Making in Post-Communist Ukraine

practitioners and strong nation-building and market-oriented rhetoric on the part of the official policy-makers.[8] These studies analyse educational reformation as a state-led governmental endeavour aimed at moulding new generations of Ukrainian citizens – bearers of national and European democratic ideals and values – and explore societal reactions to these newly imposed subjectivities.[9]

Prior to proceeding with the argument, it is important to outline the sets of issues this chapter does *not* cover. First, this contribution does not offer an account of educational reforms initiated in the past seventeen years in Ukraine. Second, the analysis of societal attitudes towards these policies is also beyond the scope of this chapter. The works by other commentators[10] have addressed these questions in some depth However, to give a reader a general overview of the field of education policy in Ukraine, Table A, entitled Genealogy of educational reform in post-Communist Ukraine,[11] was included in Appendix 1. Two major points advanced in Table A need to be mentioned here. During the seventeen years of policy-making, there was a significant shift in the objectives of educational reformation. The strong nation- and state-building rhetoric of the first decade of the country's independence gradually lost its prominence in the policy arena and by now has been replaced with (what I call) 'catching-up' Europeanization policies, i.e. sets of reforms aimed at aligning the standards of Ukrainian education with

---

8   Sundakov, A.: Public Sector Reforms in Ukraine. On the path of transformation, Discussion Papers, No. 18, Open Society Institute, Budapest: Local Government and Public Service Reform Initiative, 2001; Fimyar, O.: Educational Policy-Making in Post-Communist Ukraine as an Example of Emerging Governmentality. Discourse analysis of selected curriculum choice and assessment policy documents (1999–2004), in: Journal of Education Policy, 2008, (Vol. 23), No. 6, pp. 571–593; Koshmanova, T. / Ravchyna, T.: Teacher preparation in a post-totalitarian society. An interpretation of Ukrainian teacher educators' stereotypes, in: International Journal of Qualitative Studies in Education, 2008 (Vol. 21), No. 2, March–April, pp. 137–158.

9   Cf. Janmaat, J. G.: Nation-Building in Post-Soviet Ukraine. Educational Policy and the Response of the Russian-speaking Population, Utrecht, Amsterdam: Royal Dutch Geographical Society, Faculty of Social and Behavioral Sciences, Universiteit van Amsterdam, 2000; Janmaat, J. G.: Nation Building, Democratization and Globalization as Competing Priorities in Ukraine's education System, in: Nationalities Papers, 2008 (Vol. 36), No. 1, pp. 1–23; Wanner, C.: Burden of Dreams. History and Identity in Post-Soviet Ukraine, University Park/PA: Pennsylvania State University Press, 1998.

10 See Fimyar, O.: Educational Policy-Making in Post-Communist Ukraine as an Example of Emerging Governmentality. Discourse analysis of selected curriculum choice and assessment policy documents (1999–2004), in: Journal of Education Policy, 2008, (Vol. 23), No. 6, pp. 571–593; Janmaat, J. G.: Nation-Building in Post-Soviet Ukraine. Educational Policy and the Response of the Russian-speaking Population, Utrecht, Amsterdam: Royal Dutch Geographical Society, Faculty of Social and Behavioral Sciences, Universiteit van Amsterdam, 2000; Janmaat, J. G. Nation Building, Democratization and Globalization as Competing Priorities in Ukraine's education System, in: Nationalities Papers, 2008 (Vol. 36), No. 1, pp. 1–23; Wanner, C.: Burden of Dreams. History and Identity in Post-Soviet Ukraine, University Park/PA: Pennsylvania State University Press, 1998.

11 Adapted from: Fimyar, O.: Educational Policy-Making in Post-Communist Ukraine as an Example of Emerging Governmentality. Discourse analysis of selected curriculum choice and assessment policy documents (1999–2004), in: Journal of Education Policy, 2008, (Vol. 23), No. 6, pp. 577–578.

those in Europe. The second decade of independence has witnessed another crucial development in the field of education policy, that is, the growing influence of international policy actors, for example the IRF (International Renaissance Foundation), UNDP, the World Bank and others on the formulation of national policies. The section of the table highlighted in grey contains assessments of policy reforms which are the focus of analysis of a larger study of which this contribution is a part.

12.2. Locating this Study

This chapter is a part of an ongoing Ph.D. research project, which from a governmentality studies perspective analyses discourses, the balance of power and ownership of two reforms of educational assessment. Drawing on documentary analysis and elite interviews with the national and international policy-makers involved in the formulation of these reforms (see Appendix 2), the study examines rationalities, power and the new subjectivities of actors these policies seek to construct. The main methods employed in the study are deconstruction and discourse analysis.[12]

The goals of the studies undertaken from a governmentality perspective are quite different from the mainstream political sciences and post-Communist studies outlined above. In particular, this research does not seek to provide a critique of existing governmental and policy-making rationalities (and practices) nor does it advocate the models and avenues for further reform strategies. Instead the analysis attempts to problematize the 'naturalness' and 'taken-for-grantedness' of the recent pro-European reorientation in post-Communist political and educational discourses. And it does so through deconstructing one of these discourses in particular: the (non)involvement of civil society in educational policy-making in post-Communist Ukraine, as articulated in the interviews of six research participants (see Appendix 2).

The theoretical underpinnings of governmentality studies, or 'analytics of government', have been presented elsewhere.[13] It is important to reiterate here that governmentality studies view government as a continuum which extends from the forms

---

12 On the questions of method see MacLure, M.: Discourse in Educational and Social Research, Buckingham: Open University Press, 2003; Philips, L. / Jorgensen, M. W.: Discourse analysis as Theory and Method, Sage: London 2002; Tonkiss, F.: Analysing Discourse, in: Seale, C. (ed.): Researching Society and Culture, London: Thousand Oaks; New Delhi: Sage, 1998; Wetherell, M. / Taylor, S. / Yates, S. J.: Discourse as Data. A Guide for Analysis, London: Sage in association with The Open University, 2001.
13 Fimyar, O.: Using Governmentality as a Conceptual Tool in Education Policy Research, in: Educate. The Journal of Doctoral Research in Education, www.educatejournal.org, 2008, pp. 3–18; Gordon, C.: Governmental rationality. An introduction, in: Burchell, G. / Gordon, C. / Miller, P. (eds): The Foucault Effect. Studies in Governmentality, Hemel Hempstead: Harvester Wheatsheaf, 1991; Rose, N.: Powers of Freedom. Reframing Political Thought, Cambridge: Cambridge University Press, 1999; Miller, P. / Rose, N.: Governing the Present. Administering social, economic and personal life, Cambridge: Polity Press, 2008.

12. Public Opinion in Educational Policy-Making in Post-Communist Ukraine

of political government, or 'government of others', to the forms of self-regulation as 'government of self'.[14] Understanding government in such broad terms allows one to trace the emergence of particular 'regimes of truth' about the governing of self and others and the ways in which these 'truths' are enacted at a particular point in time in particular societies or contexts. The role of these studies, as Rose puts it,[15] is that of the 'diagnosis' of the 'truths' (about the state, society and individual), which themselves are the products of 'fabrication', whose discursive nature of production is often concealed behind the appeals to rationality and (political) sciences. Thus, to use governmentality as a conceptual tool is to problematize the normatively accepted 'policy narratives' or 'regimes of truth' of European integration, new forms of governance, quality assurance, etc., which, apart from their benign goals of democratization and public involvement in the policy process, instil neoliberal rationalities in post-Communist education. In other words, governmentality studies seek to deconstruct various inconsistent practices and components involved in the production of such truth 'regimes'.

Viewed from a governmentality studies perspective, the policy-making process is understood as a governmental activity (yet not always state-dominated) aimed at reshaping the 'conduct of conduct' of post-Communist countries and their citizens. With its focus on assessment reforms, this study interprets the changes in discourses of educational assessment within the wider context of the shifting rationalities of decision-making in post-Communist education. One such newly introduced policy, the external testing of school graduates reform (standardized testing), is particularly important, because apart from its benign goals of eliminating corruption and providing equal access to higher education, it advances *auditing as an instrument of government* in education, which is part of (neo)liberal mentalities of government. The new rationalities and technologies of auditing work to create measurable and comparable units of information to be used by policy-makers in the agenda-setting and decision-making processes. The introduction of audit cultures in Ukrainian education symbolizes the adoption of Western-type managerial practices of self-auditing and performativity. This marks a departure from Soviet-type *'hard forms'* of power (based on fear of authority) to *'soft'*, self-regulating, but still hierarchical forms of power (based on measurement and performance indicators).

---

14   Cf. Lemke, T.: Foucault, governmentality and critique, Paper presented at the Rethinking Marxism Conference, University of Amherst MA, 21–24 September 2000, p. 12, www.thomaslemkeweb.de/publikationen/Foucault,%20Governmentality,%20and%20Critique%20IV-2.pdf
15   Rose, N.: Powers of Freedom. Reframing Political Thought, Cambridge: Cambridge University Press, 1999, p. 19.

12.3. Continuities and Departures from the Soviet Past. Post-Communist and (Neo)Liberal Policy Initiation Technologies

The discussion presented in the remainder of the chapter revolves around the questions of how policy initiatives emerge in Ukrainian education and how (if at all) public opinion affects the process of educational reformation. The analysis of the interviewees' responses to these questions delineates two distinct and to some extent contrasting ways of initiating and legitimating policy in Ukraine. These contrasting methods of policy initiation will be referred to here as *post-Communist* and *(neo)liberal* policy technologies. The language used by the research interviewees plays an important role in constructing and contrasting these two policy technologies. While the description of *(neo)liberal policy* technology abounds with policy sociology terms such as 'policy model', 'direct pressure', 'indirect pressure', 'expert groups', 'negotiations', 'technical assistance', etc., the use of these terms in *post-Communist* policy technology is minimal. Instead, *post-Communist* policy technology is described by non-specialist and at times emotionally coloured language – 'Tormenting from Below' is one such example. Other examples of non-specialist vocabulary include 'how things are done here', 'how we do it here', 'the chaos that we have here' and 'what they have there'.

Two things are important in these non-specialist descriptions. First, these explanations are based on a pronounced 'here'/'there' dichotomy, a powerful category of thought that can be traced back to the Soviet and Cold War eras. However, the 'here'/'there' dichotomy remains strong in the post-Communist period as well. Moreover, it has now been intensified by the growing inferiority complex of national vs. Western political, social, economic, technological, etc. standards.[16] Despite the attempts to avoid conventional categorizations in this analysis, the naming of policy formation technologies as *post-Communist* and *(neo)liberal* may appear to mimic the above here/there dichotomy. However, this is not the case, because what one sees in the policy-making arena in Ukraine is not a here/there divide, but rather the effects of the 'there', i.e. Western rationalities and technologies, being translated and embedded into the 'here', i.e. the national educational context. Or, in other words, one witnesses the 'there' being merged with the 'here' with all the accompanying uneven consequences and effects. Second, the evident lack of policy terms in the accounts of the internal interviewees does not comply with the straightforward but insufficient explanation that policy sociology as an evolving body of knowledge has not yet become a part of the political, bureaucratic or practitioner discourses. As follow-up interviews and further communication with research participants suggest, for many, the choice of non-specialist language is dictated by the fact that the Western 'academic' concepts fail to

---

16 Cf. Pilkington, H.: Russia's youth and its culture. A nation's constructors and constructed, London, New York: Routledge, 1994, p. 199.

12. Public Opinion in Educational Policy-Making in Post-Communist Ukraine

adequately describe Ukrainian political, social, economic and policy-making 'realities', which are so 'different', 'deviant' or even 'pathological' compared to what is expected to be a national norm or international practice.[17]

Let us now consider Table 12-1, which presents two contrasting policy technologies – *post-Communist*, illustrated through the *'Reformation from Above'* and *'Tormenting from Below'* policy cases, and *(neo)liberal*, illustrated through the *'Direct External Pressure'* and *'Indirect External Pressure'* policy models. Table 12-1 maps out the field of educational policy formation, whereby the elements of both the traditional and new approaches to policy formation coexist, interact and compete for primacy. The traditional top-down approach is described as outdated and in need of modernization, while the neo-liberal approaches are shown in a more favourable light and considered better alternatives; it is expected that they will eventually replace the traditional top-down model. It is also important to note that although Table 12-1 represents the views of only two research participants, neither of whom is a high-ranking ministerial official, these individuals nevertheless worked in the Ministry and their quotes aptly summarize the ways in which policy initiatives take shape in Ukrainian education.

Table 12-1: Post-Communist and (Neo)Liberal Policy Initiation Technologies

I. Post-Communist Policy Initiation Technologies	II. (Neo)Liberal Policy Initiation Technologies
1.1 'Reformation from Above'	2.1 'Direct External Pressure'
'One model is when someone from the Ministry [initiates policy], and usually, it is **the Minister**, because in our system the **initiative is still punishable**, [and therefore] none of the lower-ranking officials will ever propose anything. So if **something strikes the Minister's fancy**, he will start doing it. The best example is when the former Minister went to Berlin in 2003 and at the Ministers' meeting he suddenly learned that Russia had joined the Bologna Declaration. He was terribly annoyed by this fact, because **he knew nothing** about the Bologna process. He came back, called an **urgent** ministerial meeting, and **'pumped up' his subordinates**. By December 2003 the programme for Ukraine to join the Bologna process, including **the dates, quarters and executives**, etc. had been set up. And they even launched it: the credit system, **ten** universities joined, **twenty** universities joined, **100** universities joined, etc. So this is one [example of a model] from above. (Interviewee B, male, *International Renaissance Foundation*, Kyiv)	Another example is the **Renaissance Foundation**, which has some funding to organize people who want some changes in education. Then we **organize expert groups**, bring in **foreign experts** who can tell us how it is done in other countries and who can help **analyse** our legislature. We **study an issue** and come up with an initiative. For example, **testing:** this initiative came from the Renaissance Foundation and for some time the **Ministry was against** it, but when the Minister found out that Russia had the 'Unified State Exam', Lithuania had it, that is all the countries that want to move forward had it, he **became a 'promoter'** of this initiative. That is one example [of direct pressure] from external sources. (Interviewee B, male, *International Renaissance Foundation*, Kyiv)

continued overleaf

---

17 Cf. Ryavec, K.: Russian bureaucracy. Power and pathology, Lanham/MD: Rowman & Littlefield, 2005.

I. Post-Communist Policy Initiation Technologies	II. (Neo)Liberal Policy Initiation Technologies
1.2 'Tormenting from Below' I started the gymnasium from the **grass-roots** initiative. We formed a **Public Committee** which **tormented** the local government from below until it finally passed a **necessary decision**. It is possible to say that **sometimes** in **some localities** grass-roots level initiatives have worked, for example, the teaching community on the regional level organized this or that educational establishment. (Research Interviewee I, male, *Directorate of Educational Projects, Ukrainian Ministry of Education and Science*, Kyiv).	**2.2 'Indirect External Pressure'** There are also indirect pressures, for example the **World Bank** project. I witnessed the negotiations which started in 2001, so **five years of negotiations**, preparations, etc. Then there was a grant from the government of Japan – seven hundred thousand – for technical assistance. This is a World Bank project now, but they always emphasize – **we do not interfere** – **we give money**, the government asks – we give money. But it is still a form of pressure and the World Bank is interested in **changing the system** and this is very good, but at the same time the Bank is interested in **being a creditor**. And now that not a lot of countries want to borrow from the World Bank, there is this sort of compromise, and this is the indirect pressure. (Interviewee B, male, *International Renaissance Foundation*, Kyiv)

The above table raises many discourses, including Soviet-style (post-Communist) and Western (neo-liberal) managerial and administrative practices, rigidity and authoritarian tendencies in the Ministry, the importance of research-based policy decisions advocated by international organizations, the steering effect of World Bank loans on educational policy-making, the revolutionary image of local activists and the difficulties they face in reaching out to the local authorities.

12.4. Post-Communist Policy Technology and the (Un)Importance of Public Opinion

Let us now examine each of the policy technologies in greater detail and consider how the (un)importance of public opinion is articulated in each of these technologies. In the above table *post-Communist* policy initiation technology is presented as having direct continuity with the Soviet past. The quotation describing the *'Reformation from Above'* model reflects a strong subordination discourse and power hierarchy, which underpin decision-making procedures at the ministerial level. There is a strict institutional hierarchy: initiatives coming from lower officialdom are suppressed and 'punishable', the mode of governance is coercive (the Minister was said to have '"pumped up" his subordinates'), reform initiation is non-transparent and spontaneous ('if something strikes the Minister's fancy'), awareness about global educational developments and debates around them is minimal ('he knew nothing about the Bologna process'), the impetus for reform initiation is that 'all the countries that want to move forward

12. Public Opinion in Educational Policy-Making in Post-Communist Ukraine

had it' and not necessarily because it is relevant to Ukrainian circumstances. The attitude of the Ministry towards external advice changes from negative to highly positive – to the extent that the Minister becomes a 'promoter' of the external initiative. The main underpinnings behind this change are political, which in education took the form of a new orthodoxy strategy – *voluntary Europeanization*. However, despite the discursive reorientation towards European agendas, policy-making practices cling to their Soviet roots. It is evident in the description of a 'forced' implementation of the Bologna reform, which is similar to the 'show-off' cases of industrial acceleration during Soviet times:

> By December 2003 the programme for Ukraine to join the Bologna process, including the dates, quarters and executives, etc. had been set up. And they even launched it: the credit system, ten universities joined, twenty universities joined, 100 universities joined. *(Interviewee B, male, International Renaissance Foundation, Kyiv)*

However, the demand for subordination by the power hierarchy as a traditional 'hard' form of power is not limited to post-Communist policy technology; it can also be traced in the tension between the authoritative 'I' and 'we' in the *'Tormenting from Below'* model.

The majority of the respondents described the policy-making arena as a social and institutional field, which up until now has preserved many Soviet (authoritarian) principles. The persistence of the 'command-administrative system', which is based on coercion rather than rationalization, is criticized along with the underdevelopment of 'civil society' and the passivity of the practitioners in their unquestioning acceptance of top-down reforms.

> The command-administrative system continues to function. Unfortunately, society has not yet developed its civil institutions, civil awareness. The absolute majority of the educators are waiting for these reforms [and] implement the ones which are 'dumped' from above. When the reforms are being prepared on the top, they [top policy-makers] do not feel any need to study public opinion towards implementation of this or that reform because this is how our tradition is. As they say, if you sit high enough you can see far and wide and you can do everything. Therefore, to my deepest regret, these reforms are coming from above and not from the grass-roots level and that is why we have all these complications. *(Interviewee G, male, Kharkiv National University, Editor-in-chief of the 'Testing and Monitoring in Education' Journal, Kharkiv)*

The non-transparent and closed nature of the policy-making process on the ministerial level is presented as another instance of continuity with the Soviet past. Policy decisions passed behind the closed doors of ministerial cabinets, without prior public consultations (which the respondent labelled the 'cabinet character' of policy-making), are seen as major obstacles to educational development because:

> All these reforms had 'a cabinet character' ... [In Ukraine] there is no mechanism in place to listen to the representatives of the public and afterwards come to a certain policy decision. *(Interviewee J, male, Ukrainian Centre for Assessing Education Quality, Kyiv)*

The tendency to compare policy-making in Ukraine with policy processes in Western countries was the 'common-sense' logic employed in many of the interviewees' accounts. In this comparison, the Ukrainian model is revealed to be inefficient, outdated and in need of long-term strategy and modernization.

Table 12-2: For example, in the United States ... and in Ukraine ...

For example, in the **United States**, if you have a good suggestion, you usually create a proposal, you send it somewhere, it may get revised or it may not be accepted at all, but basically that's the way you work with it. You know you have something concrete that you want to do, you have a project and you know that this is gonna help, you put together pieces of paper and you send them in. (Interviewee A, female, *American Council for International Education*, Kyiv)	Here in **Ukraine**, it's a little bit different. And it does not matter how many pieces of paper [you submit]. Actually, the more pieces of paper you send the worse it is, because nobody's gonna read it, because they just don't have the people, they don't have a structure that can actually handle that. So sometimes what you do is you make a suggestion when you are speaking with someone, and maybe three years down the road they will actually come back to you and say: 'Remember when we talked about this or that...?'. Or you continue to make small suggestions, small comments and they might actually become incorporated in the end into something that the Ministry is doing. (Interviewee A, female, *American Council for International Education*, Kyiv)

Another set of opinions suggests that the relationship between the centralized bureaucracy and civil society is gradually changing. The following quote outlines how the Ministry has come to notice the problem of 'public opinion'.

> The problem is that in the beginning they [the state organs] did not want and did not know that it is possible to hear the public. Even if we say 'the public', some sort of public opinion still exists. So in the beginning they knew: 'We are the Ministry, the organs of the Educational Administration [semantically close to Control]'. Even the word 'to administer' speaks for itself. And this is not only on the level of the Ministry. The same picture is at the lower level of educational administration, when educational authorities want 'to administer' education. So in the beginning there was no mention of civil society. But, in the end, even with great difficulties, civil society in Ukraine is evolving, so then obviously they [the Ministry] had to take public opinion into account. *(Interviewee B, male, International Renaissance Foundation, Kyiv)*

However, as the interviewee maintains, being 'noticed' does not mean being 'heard'. Public opinion has become a buzzword appropriated and adapted by the centralized bureaucracy for pragmatic survival purposes. The metaphor of imitation embedded in the following quote captures the relationship between the centralized bureaucracy and liberal discourses, one of which is 'civil society':

> Ukrainian bureaucracy has learned how to imitate [democracy], that is, it catches the discourse and then on the level of rhetoric and slogans proclaims its progressive intentions.[18]

---

18 Cf. Wilson, A.: Virtual Politics. Faking democracy in the post-Soviet world, London: Yale University Press, 2005.

Yet the system still remains hierarchical, and therefore the more different challenges to the system emerge the more the system strives to constrain them and the more it fails, the more it skids. And the Ministry every so often is preoccupied with constraining what cannot be constrained any further and that's where this 'bureaucratic syndrome' comes from. *(Interviewee B, male, International Renaissance Foundation, Kyiv)*

Ministerial officials respond to the above criticisms by suggesting that in post-Communist Ukraine 'public opinion' is constantly in the making and therefore cannot be the basis for long-term planning and reforms:

> You cannot govern education in such a big country on the basis of public opinion. You have to take public opinion into account, but you cannot base your decisions on it. If we decide on the strategy, for example, student-centred learning, we have to implement this strategy. Maybe we make a step which is not 100% successful, but let's say 80%, we will still be able to correct it. But if we wait until the public opinion is formed, which will eventually push us toward implementing the change, then we will lag behind more and more. That is, we have to form the segment of public opinion in support of this or that innovation, no doubt here, it will make it easier to implement the change. But if we wait until all public opinion is in support of the initiative – it means being a shepherd and not a leader in this sphere. *(Interviewee H, male, Academy of Pedagogical Sciences, Former Top Rank Official, Ukrainian Ministry of Education and Science, Kyiv)*

In the above quote the Ministry perceives itself as the vanguard of society and public opinion is viewed as contingent and malleable, something to be 'formed' and 'shaped', something deemed largely unimportant in the policy-making process.

12.5. (Neo)Liberal Policy Technology and the Uses of Public Opinion

(Neo)liberal policy technology is constructed as the antithesis and critique of the above-discussed *post-Communist* policy technology. The *'Direct External Pressure'* and *'Indirect External Pressure'* models presented in Table 1 reveal how external policy actors such as the International Renaissance Foundation (IRF), World Bank, United Nations Development Programme (UNDP), American Council, British Council, Cambridge Education and others use 'soft' forms of power to initiate and legitimize policy initiatives. Although the external actors differ in their agendas and degrees of involvement in national policy-making, there is one major commonality between them. This commonality is the language and logic of (neo)liberalism that guides these agencies. The language articulated by these agencies is the language of expertise, networking, negotiation, debating, diagnosing, calculation and normalization, and their administrative and managerial discourses are usually coated in technical and apolitical terms. This is despite their open political stance as promoters of democracy, an open society and a market economy. For example, in non-political terms, the external agencies define their role in policy-making as 'fairly administrative' (Interviewee A, female, *American Council for International Education*, Kyiv). The administration of policy

initiatives, i.e. the governmental programmes aimed at shaping the conduct of others, proceeds according to the following scenario. First, the agencies organize 'people who want some changes' into expert groups; second, they invite foreign specialists, who provide expertise on the national legislation; third, they finance selected initiatives suggested by these 'communities of experts'. Through networking and training, local experts are socialized into the common (Western) language of reform, common (neo-liberal) modes of perception, and common approaches to problem formulation and solution-finding. Through these assemblages of terms, techniques, experts and knowledge claims, reality is constructed as something amenable to diagnosis and cure, research and solution, modification and progress.[19] In education, the external testing of school graduates reform (standardized examination) is constructed as one such 'cure'.

Another important difference between the technologies is the locus of policy initiation. While the top-down reforms are the initiatives of the Minister alone, reforms initiated by the external agencies have an apolitical character and are presented as outcomes of the analytical work of local 'communities of experts' and informed discussions of 'organized public campaigns':

> For example, the Bologna process. The Ministry decided through their top-down directive – everything starts from the top, practitioners do not understand much and everything is done very mechanically. We tried to organize a public campaign and explain what the Bologna process is. *(Interviewee B, male, International Renaissance Foundation, Kyiv)*

By organizing public campaigns, external policy actors, and in particular the International Renaissance Foundation (IRF), invest in making the voice of the local 'communities of experts' heard, or, to use the language of the IRF, 'enhancing the internal capacity for reformation'. Yet although externally influenced policy initiatives are presented as 'the voices' of different 'communities of experts', the 'reform packages' advocated by the external agencies – standardized testing, decentralization, marketization, etc. – do not vary much across post-Communist countries. Hence, the voices of the 'communities of experts' and the 'public opinion' at large are often used to legitimize the 'one-model-fits-all' policy initiatives of the external agencies.

It is significant that despite the pronounced differences between the *post-Communist* and *(neo)liberal* policy technologies, the ways these technologies make use of public opinion appear to be rather similar. For example, although the driving force behind the external testing of school graduates reform was the IRF, one of the research interviewees involved in this reform raised doubts that the negative attitudes of the general public towards the reform would affect the implementation of the reform:

> I am involved in the external testing reform and I know its many problems. But even up to now we do not know the public's opinion about this reform. I can only guess: it is as if

---

19 Cf. Miller, P. / Rose, N.: Governing the Present. Administering social, economic and personal life, Cambridge: Polity Press, 2008, pp. 64–65.

I know it under my skin that the societal attitude towards this reform is negative, but no one cares much about it, no one is interested in public opinion. And on the local level they will continue to implement the reform and on the top they know if the orders are written, they will be implemented. This is all totally wrong. *(Interviewee G, male, Kharkiv National University, Editor-in-chief of the 'Testing and Monitoring in Education' Journal, Kharkiv)*

12.6. Concluding Remarks

To sum up, inspired by Foucault's discussion of government as the 'conduct of conduct',[20] this chapter offered an alternative to the mainstream political sciences and post-Communist studies analysis. The chapter questioned the dominant approach of interpreting the post-1990s developments in post-Communist countries as a crisis of legitimacy of the Communist regimes, which contend with the internal and external pressures of democratization. Viewed from the governmentality perspective, these developments are not conceptualized in liberal-democratic terms as political moves towards greater liberalism and democracy (and hence lesser state interference). On the contrary, the paternalistic role of the national government in a state-led reformation remains strong and tends to intensify in the aftermath of independence, which is reminiscent of the *'shepherd-flock'* articulation of pastoral power in Foucauldian terms.[21]

In that case, how can we interpret the post-1990s developments from a governmentality studies perspective? Moving beyond the speculations about the unitary direction of regime change from Communism towards either *liberalism*, *'pluralism by default'*[22], *'feudalism'*[23] or *'competitive authoritarianism'*[24], governmentality studies focus on the heterogeneous and multifaceted present-day practices and rationalities of government. These practices are not seen as representing steps to successive types of society (more liberal – more advanced), but as inevitably (intentionally or unintentionally) encompassing both authoritarian and liberal tendencies and thus are likely to manifest various states of domination and prospects for 'freedom' as defined within the existing power relations.[25] Viewed from this perspective, the 1990s signalled a crisis of Communist governmental rationalities – i.e. the mentality of government, but not governmental practices (the actions of government). Authoritarian practices of gov-

---

20 Foucault, M.: Governmentality, in: Burchell, G. / Gordon, C. / Miller, P. (eds): The Foucault Effect. Studies in Governmentality, Hemel Hempstead: Harvester Wheatsheaf, 1991, pp. 87–104.
21 Ibid.
22 Way, L.: Pluralism by Default and the Sources of Political Liberalization in Weak States, presented at the conference 'Dynamics of Electoral Authoritarianism', Mexico City, 1–4 April 2004, 2003, Princeton University, 23 October 2003, Yale University Leitner Lecture Series, 25 March 2003.
23 Verdery, K.: What Was Socialism, and What Comes Next?, Princeton/NJ: Princeton University Press, 1996.
24 Levitsky, S. / Way, L.: The Rise of Competitive Authoritarianism, in: Journal of Democracy, 2002 (Vol. 13), No. 2, pp. 51–65.
25 Cf. Dean, M.: Governmentality. Power and Rule in Modern Society, London: Sage Publications, 1999.

ernment as the 'conduct of conduct' have managed to endure the changing line of reasoning about how the government should be exercised. The discourse of the (un) importance of public opinion provides an example of this argument.

Viewed from the perspective of governmentality studies, educational policy-making was conceptualized as a governmental activity (yet not always state-dominated) aimed at reshaping the 'conduct of conduct' of post-Communist countries and their citizens. The analysis revealed two distinct approaches to initiating policy in Ukraine, namely the *post-Communist* and *(neo)liberal* policy technologies, which in their own ways deem public opinion largely insignificant in the process of policy formation and implementation. The discussion presented here offered insight into the changing relationship between the centralized educational bureaucracy and civil society. The argument maintained that the ongoing engagement of this 'unexpected nation'[26] with neo-liberal models of capitalism and democracy has triggered the emergence of new, often externally influenced, political and educational discourses. However, the shifts in discourses have not (yet) brought change to existing Soviet-type institutional cultures and decision-making practices. As a result, the governance of present-day Ukrainian education is exercised through a rigid centralized bureaucracy, while discourses of democratization, decentralization and public involvement in policy formation are nevertheless also becoming prominent.

---

26 Wilson, A.: Virtual Politics. Faking democracy in the post-Soviet world, London: Yale University Press, 2005.

12.7. Appendix 1: Genealogy of Educational Reform in Post-Communist Ukraine[27]

Stages of reform in CIS[28] (adapted from Crighton 2002[29])	Genealogy of educational reforms: the case of Ukraine
The first stage: • Is characterized by 'the initial euphoria about new-found freedoms' • Policies are aimed at re-establishing educational traditions and structures that existed before the imposition of external Communist domination • Partial devolution of financial responsibilities to local government resulting in immense cuts of funding for the educational sector *The second stage:* • Is targeted at gaining national leadership of educational reform and achieving coherence among multiple initiatives • The involvement of external advice tends to be the greatest during this stage • The dominant focus is on the top-down implementation rather than on practical changes at the classroom and school levels	**Nation- and State-Building Policies of the First Decade of Reformation** *1991–1993 reforms – 'creating new subjects and actors':* • Creating new structural units of national 'expertise' (e.g. National Academy of Pedagogical Sciences) • Providing legislative framework for establishing private educational institutions *1993–1995 reforms – '"unmaking" Soviet education':* • Restructuring the curriculum of the humanities, depoliticising the system of education and ridding it of 'Soviet' ideology • Introducing the official post-independent history narrative into the curriculum • Changing from mainly Russian to Ukrainian as the primary language of instruction *1995–1999 reforms – 'reacting to hyperinflation: shifting financial responsibility to local budgets':* • A period of 'stagnation' caused by the four-fold reduction in the education budget • The reforms initiated the transferral of budget burdens from national to local levels **'Catching-up' Europeanization Policies of the Second Decade of Reformation** *1999–2001 reforms – 'ratifying the programmes of government':* • The Parliament adopted The Law on General Secondary Education (LGSE) in 1999. Together with The Law on Education (LE) and The National Doctrine of Education (NDE), it envisages significant changes in the structure, duration, curriculum and assessment policies in general secondary education • Ukraine joined Bologna process, which is aimed at the creation of the common European Higher Education Area

continued overleaf

---

27 Adapted from: Fimyar, O.: Educational Policy-Making in Post-Communist Ukraine as an Example of Emerging Governmentality. Discourse analysis of selected curriculum choice and assessment policy documents (1999–2004), in: Journal of Education Policy, 2008 (Vol. 23), No. 6, pp. 577–78.
28 Commonwealth of Independent States
29 Crighton, J.: The hazards of transplanting education reform: A view from the classrooms of post-communist schools, 2002, http://www.worldbank.org/html/prddr/trans/julaugsep02/pgs51-54.htm

Stages of reform in CIS (adapted from Crighton 2002)	Genealogy of educational reforms: the case of Ukraine
The third stage: • At the governmental level, discourses about quality education are at the centre of the reform • At the level of schools, there is a 'reform fatigue' resulting from a chronic lack of resources	**2001 – present reform: Assessment policy reforms aimed at 'introducing competence-based assessment and audit cultures in education'.** • 12-Point Grading Scale Reform initiated by the UMES was aimed at institutionalizing discourses of competence-based assessment and widening the former Soviet 5-point grading scale to 12-points • External testing of school graduates (standardized examinations) reform initiated and piloted regionally by the IRF (International Renaissance Foundation/Soros Foundation Ukraine). In 2009, ownership over the reform was transferred to the Ministry and the reform was implemented at the national level.

12.8. Appendix 2: Research Participants[30]

Interviewee's Designation	Interviewee's Gender	Interviewee's Affiliation
International Organizations		
Interviewee A	female	American Council for International Education, Kyiv
Interviewee B	male	International Renaissance Foundation, Kyiv
Interviewee C	male	Cambridge Education, Cambridge, UK
Interviewee D	female	American Institutes for Research, Washington DC, USA
Academia		
Interviewee E	female	Testing Technologies Centre at the Ministry of Health, National Medical University of O.O. Bohomolets, Kyiv
Interviewee F	male	Kyiv Mohyla Academy, Kyiv
Interviewee G	male	Kharkiv National University, Editor-in-chief of the 'Testing and Monitoring in Education' Journal, Kharkiv
Ministry of Education and Sciences		
Interviewee H	male	Academy of Pedagogical Sciences, former top-ranking official, Ministry of Education and Sciences of Ukraine, Kyiv
Interviewee I	male	Directorate of Educational Projects, Ministry of Education and Sciences of Ukraine, Kyiv
Centre of Educational Quality Assessment		
Interviewee J	male	Ukrainian Centre for Assessing Education Quality, Kyiv
Interviewee K	female	Regional Centre for Assessing Education Quality, Lviv

---

30 This contribution is based on the interviews with the six research participants, Interviewees A, B, G, H, I and J, who were directly involved in the formulation and introduction of the external testing of the school graduates reform. Other interviewees were included in the sample for triangulation purposes.

Interviewee's Designation	Interviewee's Gender	Interviewee's Affiliation
Unions, Associations, NGOs and Professional Media		
Interviewee L	male	National Teachers Union, Kyiv
Interviewee M	female	Ukrainian Association of School Heads, Head of a Specialized School, Kyiv
Interviewee N	female	Professional Newspaper for School Administrators, Kyiv
In-Service Teacher Training Institutes, Local Educational Authorities and Teachers		
Interviewee O	female	In-Service Teacher Training Institute, Lviv
Interviewee P	female	District Educational Authority, Tsyurupynsk, Kherson region
Interviewee Q	female	General Secondary School of I–III levels, Tsyurupynsk, Kherson region
Parliamentary Committee on Science and Education		
Interviewee R	male	Parliamentary Committee on Science and Education, Kyiv

Websites:

www.education.gov.ua – *The Ukrainian Ministry of Education and Science*

www.rada.gov.ua – *Official website of the Ukrainian Parliament*

www.testportal.com.ua – *Ukrainian Centre for Assessing Education Quality*

About the Authors

Franziska Blomberg holds an MA degree in cultural studies from the European-University Viadrina, Frankfurt (Oder)/Germany. Currently she is writing her Ph.D. and is enrolled in the doctoral research programme 'Civil society and external democratization in post-socialist Europe' (a cooperative effort between Viadrina and ETH Zürich/Switzerland).

Bojan Bilić is a doctoral student at the UCL School of Slavonic and Eastern European Studies. He holds a B.Sc. in Psychology from the University of Sheffield, an MA in Sociology and Comparative Politics from Jacobs University Bremen and an MRes in the Social Sciences from the European University Institute, Florence. His doctoral thesis explores Yugoslav civic initiatives immediately prior to and throughout the 1990s conflicts.

Lars Breuer is a Ph.D. fellow at the Institute of Advanced Study in the Humanities (Kulturwissenschaftliches Institut) in Essen, Germany. Since 2007 he has been working on his dissertation with the working title 'Auto- and hetero-stereotypes in the context of European memory cultures'. He holds an MA in Cultural Science from Humboldt University (Berlin).

David Cadier is a third-year Ph.D. candidate at Sciences Po (CERI) in Paris. His dissertation deals with the Czech Republic's foreign and security policies in the EU context (CFSP/ESDP). For the 2008/9 academic year, he was a research fellow at the CEFRES in Prague.

Olena Fimyar is a Ph.D. candidate at the University of Cambridge, Faculty of Education. Her Ph.D. research project analyses discourses, the balance of power and ownership of assessment policy reforms in post-Communist Ukraine from a governmentality studies perspective.

Christian Fröhlich obtained an MA in sociology and cultural sciences at Leipzig University in 2006. He has been a Ph.D. candidate at the Institute for Cultural Sciences (Leipzig University) since 2008.

Julia Langbein is a Ph.D. candidate at the European University Institute in Florence. She is working on a dissertation that analyses how mechanisms of transnationalization shape change in regulatory institutions in the EU's Eastern Neighbourhood. She holds a diploma in political science from the Free University of Berlin and an MA in Russian studies from the European University at St Petersburg.

About the Authors

Ulla Pape is a Ph.D. candidate in the Department of International Relations and International Organization at the University of Groningen, The Netherlands. Prior to starting her Ph.D. research in 2006, she obtained a master's degree in Slavonic languages, Eastern European history and political science from the University of Münster, Germany, and in humanitarian action from the University of Groningen. Her dissertation deals with the role of non-governmental organizations in response to the HIV/AIDS epidemic in the Russian Federation.

Senka Neuman Stanivuković is a Ph.D. candidate at The Groningen Research Institute for the Study of Culture – ICOG, Groningen, the Netherlands. She holds an MA in international relations and an LLM in international law. Her thesis examines the process of Europeanization of territorial governance in the context of Enlargement.

Kacper Szulecki is a Ph.D. researcher at the University of Konstanz, Germany, in the Centre of Excellence 'Cultural Foundations of Integration', 'Idioms of Social Analysis' research group (2008–2011). He holds an M.Sc. in political science from the Vrije Universiteit Amsterdam (2008), and previously he was a student in international relations and sociology at the Universities of Warsaw and Oslo (2003–2007).

Tonči Valentić graduated with a bachelor's degree in philosophy and literature at Zagreb University and a master's degree in sociology and social anthropology at Central European University in Budapest. Currently he is a Ph.D. student in the sociology department at the Faculty of Social Sciences, Ljubljana University.

Patryk Wasiak received an MA degree in sociology from the Institute for Applied Social Sciences as well as an MA degree in art history from the Institute of Art History at Warsaw University. He wrote his dissertation on transnational informal contacts between visual artists in the Soviet Bloc, at the Faculty for Culture and Communication at the Warsaw School of Social Sciences and Humanities.

Series Subscription

Please enter my subscription to the series *Changing Europe*, ISSN 1863-8716, as follows:

starting with
- ❐ volume # 1
- ❐ volume # ___
  - ❐ please also include the following volumes: #___, ___, ___, ___, ___, ___,

- ❐ the next volume being published
  - ❐ please also include the following volumes: #___, ___, ___, ___, ___, ___,

- ❐ 1 copy per volume   OR   ❐ ___ copies per volume

Subscription within Germany:

You will receive every volume at 1st publication at the regular bookseller's price – incl. s & h and VAT.
Payment:
❐ Please bill me for every volume.
❐ Lastschriftverfahren: Ich/wir ermächtige(n) Sie hiermit widerruflich, den Rechnungsbetrag je Band von meinem/unserem folgendem Konto einzuziehen.

Kontoinhaber: _____ Kreditinstitut: _____
Kontonummer: _____ Bankleitzahl: _____

International Subscription:

Payment (incl. s & h and VAT) in advance for
- ❐ 10 volumes/copies (€ 319.80)   ❐ 20 volumes/copies (€ 599.80)
- ❐ 40 volumes/copies (€ 1,099.80)

Please send my books to:

NAME _____ DEPARTMENT _____
ADDRESS _____
POST/ZIP CODE _____ COUNTRY _____
TELEPHONE _____ EMAIL _____

date/signature _____

A hint for librarians in the former Soviet Union: Your academic library might be eligible to receive free-of-cost scholarly literature from Germany via the German Research Foundation. For Russian-language information on this program, see
http://www.dfg.de/forschungsfoerderung/formulare/download/12_54.pdf.

Please fax to: **0511 / 262 2201 (+49 511 262 2201)**
or mail to: *ibidem*-Verlag, Julius-Leber-Weg 11, D-30457 Hannover, Germany
or send an e-mail: ibidem@ibidem-verlag.de

ibidem-Verlag

Melchiorstr. 15

D-70439 Stuttgart

info@ibidem-verlag.de

www.ibidem-verlag.de
www.ibidem.eu
www.edition-noema.de
www.autorenbetreuung.de